A WELSH LEARNER'S HILL AND EISTEDDFOD RAMBLE IN LLŶN

A Celebration of a Place and its People

First Published: 2024

© Text: Jean Brandwood

All rights reserved.
No part of this publication may be reproduced,
stored in a retrieval system,or transmitted in any form, or by any means,
electronic, electrostatic, magnetic tape, mechanical, photocopying,
recording, or otherwise, without prior
permission of the author of the works herein.

ISBN: 978-1-84527-958-5

Published with the financial support of the Books Council of Wales.

Cover design: Eirian Evans

Published by Gwasg Carreg Gwalch 2024
12 Iard yr Orsaf, Llanrwst, Wales LL26 0EH
☎ 01492 642031
books@carreg-gwalch.cymru
website: www.carreg-gwalch.cymru

Published and printed in Wales

Jean Brandwood lives in Greater Manchester and is married with two grown up children. She is an Occupational Therapist currently working for an NHS adult autism service as an assessor and diagnostician. She is passionate about all things Welsh, fell in love with Llŷn in 1991 and began learning the language in 2012.

A Welsh Learner's Hill and Eisteddfod Ramble in Llŷn

A Celebration of a Place and its People

Jean Brandwood

Thank you to:
Jim for sharing the ups and downs of the hills and eisteddfodau, and Tom and Simon for the wonderful memories and for joining us on The Big One.

Des Marshall for your directions for the hill walks.

Diolch i:
bobl sydd wedi helpu efo cyngor a gwybodaeth gan gynnwys: Myrddin ap Dafydd, Eirian Evans a phawb yng Ngwasg Carreg Gwalch

Amanda Lloyd
Ann Williams
Edwin Humphreys
Gerwyn Williams
Lynda Cox
Martyn Croydon
Meinir Pierce Jones
Peter Evans
Rose Williams

Aran a Catrin Jones a phawb yn SSIW am y iaith hardd 'ma ac i bobl Llŷn am eich croeso Cymreig pob tro.

All photographs taken by Jean and Jim Brandwood apart from those taken by Tom Brandwood (thank you):

Interlude – night sky photos
Eisteddfod Ramble 16 – night sky photos
Walk 17 and cover - Views of the Hills and Bays

In memory of Mum and Dad,
Sylvia and John Tonge
I did it!

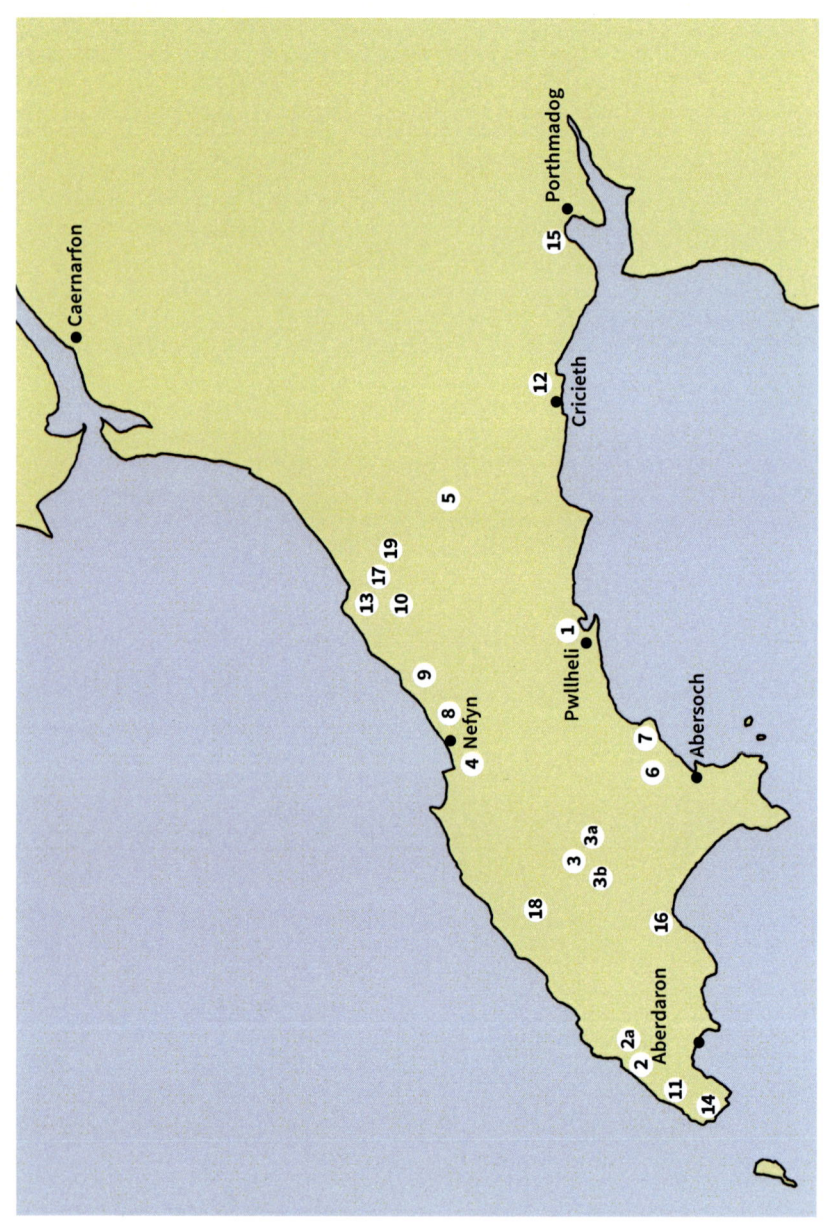

Contents

Introduction	10
So, What Exactly is an Eisteddfod?	14
Walk 1: Pen y Garn, Pwllheli – 1st October 2021	
First Steps	21
Walk 2: Mynydd Carreg, near Porthor – 28th April 2022	
Red Café	25
Eisteddfod Ramble 1 – 28th April 2022	
A Special Visitor at the Caravan	30
Eisteddfod Ramble 2 – 13th May 2022	
Wales Has Got Talent	33
Walk 3: Garn Fadryn, Garn Bach and Moel Caerau, Garnfadryn Village – 28th May 2022	
A Steep Bare Faced Ramble	35
Eisteddfod Ramble 3 – 10th June 2022	
Shanties on the Beach	46
Walk 4: Garn Boduan, near Nefyn – 12th June 2022	
Spitting Frogs	48
Walk 5: Garn Bentyrch, Llangybi – 25th June 2022	
A Miraculous Cornish Saint	53
Eisteddfod Ramble 4 – 25th June 2022	
An Important Proclamation	58
Eisteddfod Ramble 5 – 14th July 2022	
A Poet and War Hero	66
Walk 6: Foel Fawr and a glimpse of Foel Gron and Comin Mynytho, Mynytho village – 16th July 2022	
Putting the Fiddle in the Roof	70
Eisteddfod Ramble 6 – 19th July 2022	
Fallen Oak Trees and a Special Chair	75
Walk 7: Mynydd Tirycwmwd, Llanbedrog – 21st July 2022	
Prickles, Mini Beasts and Heroes	78
Eiateddfod Ramble 7 – 21st July 2022	
A Cultural Evening Stroll	84

Walk 8: Mynydd Nefyn and a wave to Carreglefain, Nefyn
22nd July 2022
    A Back to Front Walk — 88

Eisteddfod Ramble 8 – 23rd July 2022
    A Hall of Fame — 93

Eisteddfod Ramble 9 – 30th July to 4th August 2022
    A Steddfod Part 1 — 96

Walk 9: Moel Tŷ-gwyn, Pistyll – 5th August 2022
    Almost a Hill Walk — 105

Eisteddfod Ramble 10 – 5th to 6th August 2022
    A Steddfod Part 2 — 107

Walk 10: Mynydd Carnguwch, near Llithfaen – 7th August 2022
    Wobbly and Weary on Booby Hill — 112

Walk 11: Mynydd Anelog, Uwchmynydd and a Glimpse of Mynydd Ystum – 20th August 2022
    Confidence Renewed — 118

Eisteddfod Ramble 11 – 21st August 2022
    A talented young musician and a whole village of talent — 125

Walk 12: Moel Ednyfed, Cricieth – 23rd August 2022
    Cow Pats and Roses — 128

Walk 13: Garn Fôr, Yr Eifl, Llithfaen – 25th August 2022
    127 Steps — 133

Eisteddfod Ramble 12 – 8th to 12th September 2022
    The Queen and the National Poet of Wales — 138

Interlude September to November 2022 — 144

Walk 14: Mynydd y Gwyddel, Uwchmynydd and a wave to Mynydd Mawr – 13th November 2022
    The Hills at the End of the World — 146

Eisteddfod Ramble 13 – December 2022 and January 2023
    Welsh Goings on in Manchester — 149

Eisteddfod Ramble 14 – January 2023
    Creative Cricieth — 153

Eisteddfod Ramble 15 – February and March 2023
    Do the Little Things — 163

Walk 15: Moel y Gest, Porthmadog – 3rd March 2023
    Sneezing All the Way   173
Eisteddfod Ramble 16 – March – April 2023
    Soap and a Devil   178
Walk 16: Mynydd Rhiw and Clip y Gylfinir, Rhiw – 9th April 2023
    A Lone Rider and a Chocolate Treat   186
Eisteddfod Ramble 17 – 19 April 2023
    A Chapel Eisteddfod   189
Walk 17: Garn Ganol, Yr Eifl, Llithfaen – 29th April 2023
    The Big One   198
Eisteddfod Ramble 18 – April to May 2023
    Losing the Plot   204
Walk 18: Mynydd Cefnamwlch – Eastern Summit, Penllech 13th May 2023
    A Hare and a Tyre   209
Eisteddfod Ramble 19 – May 2023
    Ironing? What's That?   213
Walk 19: Tre'r Ceiri, Yr Eifl, Llithfaen – 28th May 2023
    A Walk and a Half   219
Eisteddfod Ramble 20 – June and July 2023
    Preparations   225
Eisteddfod Ramble 21 – Saturday 5th August to Saturday 11th August 2023
    Llŷn and Eifionydd Eisteddfod   242
P.S. One Final Eisteddfod and Hill Ramble   277
The Hills are Alive with The Sound of Music   279
Epilogue   280
Glossary   281

Introduction

Between May 2018 and August 2021, I completed an on and off walk along the whole of the Llŷn coastal path with my husband Jim. Having a static caravan in the area, gave us the opportunity to do this at our own leisurely pace and to take in the scenery and natural history of this beautiful peninsula that we have now been visiting for more than thirty years. We completed the coastal path in 42 shortish return journeys. Jim and I have both had cancer, which we are happy and thankful to say was treated successfully, but we both have some residual restrictions due to side effects of the treatment needed, which can slow us down at times. My cancer treatment also caused osteoporosis, which means I'm more at risk of breaking a bone if I fall, so I bear this in mind on our journeys and take a little extra care.

Even taking this into account, we hadn't expected the coastal walk to take us quite as long as it did, but there was good reason – or bad. We were interrupted in 2020 by the Covid – 19 pandemic and ensuing enforced lockdowns. During the first main lockdown, I used the time I would normally have been meeting with friends and family or going to the caravan to start writing about our walks. I enjoyed putting pen to paper (or fingers to the keyboard) to describe our slow-paced adventure and I included our memories of regular family holidays in Llŷn since 1991, my experiences of learning to speak Welsh, and about discoveries that I have made about this special area. Learning Welsh (using an amazing online course called Say Something in Welsh that I can't recommend highly enough) has enhanced my appreciation of Llŷn and opened many unexpected doors to me as a regular visitor. I rambled on about these experiences in my writings that I was later thrilled to have accepted by Gwasg Carreg Gwalch. They combined them with photographs taken by Jim and myself and published them in my book *A Welsh Learner's Ramble on the Llŷn Coastal Path*, in October 2022.

Jim retired soon after we began the walk which meant we were able to get to the caravan for regular long weekends as I only work three days a week. Jim worked as a sheet metal worker and has a Welsh connection that the whole family are proud of. He, along with his brother John and nephew Lee, made the large, metal boxes for Conwy tunnel, which contain emergency phones and other electrical components. Our sons, Tom and Simon (now young adults) got used to my announcement on every journey as we drove through the tunnel on the way from our home close to Manchester to holidays in Llŷn when they were children. This announcement gradually evolved over time from 'Your dad made these metal boxes', to 'We're going through Dad's Tunnel'. Where was I? Be warned... this is yet another ramble in more than one sense of the word.

On completing our coastal walk, we wondered what our next snail-paced adventure could be. Llŷn's two outstanding features are the sea and its peaks, so it didn't take long for us to decide to head for the hills next. Our idea was encouraged further by Des Marshall's excellent book *Walking the Llŷn Hills*, which catalogues the hills of Llŷn in size order and gives a detailed description of walks around, and to the summits of, many of them. We referred to his book often whilst planning these walks. We had walked quite a lot of the hills already in the past with Tom and Simon, but we both liked the idea of revisiting them, and of attempting some new ones if our legs could manage them. And by now I was addicted to writing so I just kept going.

Jim's handywork in Conwy Tunnel

As in my previous book, you will find a QR code for the start of each walk and some description of the routes we took but I recommend Des' book for more reliable directions, especially if you're intent on reaching the summits. We often diverted from his suggested routes to avoid cows or tricky terrain, and for various reasons sometimes didn't reach the summit at all. We didn't feel we had to 'bag' every hill on the peninsula. Where there were a group of hills close together, we were sometimes satisfied to climb one of them and just give a nod or a wave to the others which would have shared similar views from the summit. I intend giving many place names or geographical features their Welsh names throughout the book and there is a glossary at the back where you can find translations. It's interesting to note that there are many different names used for hills in Welsh and these usually identify something about the nature of the hill, for example a **moel** is a bare hill and **mynydd** means mountain and is often also used to describe a larger hill. As in my previous book, I will spell Cricieth with one 'c' in the middle and not two as you will sometimes see it. Double 'c' is never used in the Welsh language. Campaigns continue, to protect Welsh place names and in 2021, a motion was brought by a Gwynedd County councilor, calling for Mount Snowdon and Snowdonia to only be referred to by their Welsh names **Yr Wyddfa** and **Yr Eryri**. I like the response that Tudur Owen, the Welsh comedian, gave in an interview to the idea of it being too difficult for non-Welsh speaking people to pronounce many Welsh place names. He said that he also had difficulties with English place names such as 'Worcestershire or Sluff (or is it Slough?)' As he suggested just have a go at them, look them up and find out how they are pronounced and even more interestingly what they mean as there is often a story behind them.

    At the time of our hill walking there was a lot of excitement for the people of the peninsula as preparations were finally underway for them to host the The National Eisteddfod in 2023. It had been postponed from 2021 due to the pandemic. So, in this book, as well as regularly rambling off the hills to share with you my memories and discoveries related to our walks, I'll also describe any eisteddfod related experiences or revelations that I make. Chapters will alternate between our hill walk tales and those sharing eisteddfod related gossip and I hope to end this book with a report of my experiences at the 2023 Llŷn and Eifionydd National Eisteddfod. Apologies in advance for the number of times I wander away from the hill or eisteddfod paths to ramble about my favourite topics – music, literature, art... oh yes and cafés. But there are so many amazing examples of all of these in Llŷn!

Llŷn is usually the name used to refer to the whole of the peninsula, but there is a division that isn't often mentioned. The southeastern part, between Abererch and Porthmadog is known as Eifionydd and according to locals it is the river Erch that provides the boundary between Llŷn and Eifionydd. So, the 2023 National Eisteddfod is called the 'Llŷn and Eifionydd National Eisteddfod'. However, throughout this book, for ease, I will usually refer to the whole of the peninsula as Llŷn.

So, What Exactly is an Eisteddfod?

The word **eisteddfod** is a combination of the words **eistedd** (meaning 'sit') and **fod** which is mutated from the word **bod** (meaning 'be' or 'place'). The earliest record of the word eisteddfod being used was in the 14th century when it then meant dwelling place. It has also been suggested that the word came from the tradition of awarding a hand-carved chair to the best poet in the ceremony. According to Hywel Teifi Edwards, academic historian and Welsh nationalist, it means sitting together – sounds good to me. The plural of eisteddfod is **eisteddfodau** and I will use this throughout the book instead of eisteddfods which looks and sounds wrong. There are various types of eisteddfodau, which will be explained, and many first language Welsh speakers, when referring to the National Eisteddfod shorten it to '**Steddfod**', and that is what I'll do from now on to save ink.

From experience, I have found that when an eisteddfod is mentioned, the majority of non-Welsh people say 'Oh yes that's the big festival at Llangollen'. What they are referring to is the International Musical Eisteddfod and until I started to learn Welsh, I also thought that this was the only eisteddfod that took place. I have never been to an international one, but since my teens have visited Llangollen a few times and remember seeing posters that mostly featured people dancing in brightly coloured costumes. So, my perception of any eisteddfod for a long time was that it was an annual festival of traditional dance always held at Llangollen. In more recent years, I noticed the posters showed singers and most often Bryn Terfel, the famous opera singer, so I began to realise it was also about singing. Before learning to speak Welsh, what I didn't realise was that this wasn't the only eisteddfod held in Wales and most certainly not the oldest one or indeed the one that is of most importance to Welsh speakers. The International Musical Eisteddfod is a relative baby, with the first one having been held in 1947. It was the idea of Harold Tudor of Coedpoeth, who was a member of the British Council. He wanted to create a festival that promoted education and international peace and goodwill through the medium of music especially. It is now a six-day event held each July, at the Royal International Pavilion in Llangollen, with musicians and dancers from about 50 countries performing and competing in front of audiences of over 50,000. People are invited to compete in the various instrumental, song or dance competitions but as with all eisteddfodau, it isn't just about competing. There are many other activities to be enjoyed on the field and outdoor stages, such as listening to concerts, taking part in workshops and browsing the hundreds of stalls offering produce of every kind. In 2022, a young baritone from North Wales, Emyr Lloyd Jones, was dubbed 'the new Bryn Terfel' when he won the title of the 'Pendine International Voice of the Future', at the International Eisteddfod. Emyr studied at the Royal Northern College of Music in Manchester. Since 2012, I have been organising a social group in Manchester, where learners can meet up for an informal Welsh chat in a café once a month. During the Covid lockdown, we managed to continue meeting, but virtually, using Zoom video conferencing, and since the end of lockdown, these sessions have been kept going even after the reintroduction of the café meet ups. The venue for the face-to-face meetings is currently the spacious city art gallery café, but pre lockdown, when people felt comfortable sitting cosily in a smaller environment, we met in a great little café, called Siop Shop, run by Welsh speaker Iwan from Dolgellau. Occasionally Emyr and his now fiancée Rhiannon Ashley, would be in Siop Shop and would have a chat in Welsh with members of our group. A friendlier couple you couldn't hope to meet. Rhiannon is a soprano and talented singer and conductor, and in 2019, while they were both still studying in Manchester, I was lucky to be able to see them both perform for the Manchester Welsh Society with the Manchester **Aelwyd** Choir in the Welsh chapel in Didsbury. Rhiannon was directing and Emyr was a member of the choir, and they all gave a wonderful performance. Yes, I know I've wandered off again.

Other versions of eisteddfodau are held annually, sometimes in unexpected places. Every October, since 1875 an eisteddfod is organised by the people of Chubut, Patagonia, South America. These are descendants of the original Welsh settlers who arrived there ten years earlier, hoping for a better life in an area with little outside influence which would mean that their culture and language would be preserved. Smaller eisteddfodau occur annually in other communities such as within schools or villages throughout Wales, or organised groups such as the young farmers

Aelwyd Choir at Didsbury Welsh Chapel

club. Often there are small prizes of money given to winners of the different categories, and a model wooden eisteddfod chair is awarded to the winner of the main poetry competition. Llŷn friend Amanda (who will get quite a lot of mention in this book) is the proud owner of one of these, having won one in school. Local eisteddfodau usually take place in the course of one day and a long day that can be. I remember one afternoon several years ago sitting at the back of the old school house in Y Ffôr, watching the afternoon session of a local eisteddfod. I was enjoying watching the children and adults reciting and singing for a couple of hours from my small wooden pew at the back of the building that I think was then serving as the chapel. I began to get a little uncomfortable after a while and wondered when to expect a break but on looking at the programme, I could see that according to the list of contestants, there were many hours to go with no sign of a break. I spied my opportunity and sneaked out. I heard later from a Llŷn friend that these village eisteddfodau can continue beyond midnight. One more eisteddfod that I must mention is the one organised online by Say Something in Welsh, the course I used to learn to speak Welsh. I tend to avoid competitions but in my first year of learning I entered the short story competition and came second. Not bad you may say... but I must confess there were only three entrants.

The Steddfod is the oldest official eisteddfod and also the most important one to most Welsh speakers. Records show that eisteddfodau have been held in Wales from as early as 1176 when it was said that Lord Rhys invited poets and musicians from all over Wales to a grand gathering at his castle in Cardigan. The best poet and musician was said to have been awarded a chair at his table. 'Yr Eisteddfod' (The National Eisteddfod), was established at Denbigh in 1860, and eight annual Eisteddfodau were organised by the council, in different locations in north and south Wales alternately. The first was held in Aberdare and the last in Ruthin in 1868, when debts forced it all to come to an end. In 1880 Hugh Owen established the National Eisteddfod Association which saw the beginning of the current series of Steddfodau, which have continued to be held on an annual basis since then. The venue for the Steddfod continues to rotate each year between different areas of Wales and in 2022, the people of Tregaron in Ceredigion were to host the first Steddfod since the Covid-19 pandemic began in 2020. In 2020 and 2021, the creative people of Wales weren't going to give in to a nasty virus and they managed to put together virtual eisteddfodau, with videos of performances and competitions shared with the public via Facebook and YouTube. They were known as Eisteddfod AmGen – Amgen means alternative. There have been only two other cancellations of the Steddfod, one in 1914 during WW1 and the other in 1940, during WW2 – this one was replaced by a radio broadcasted version. Other variations from the norm have occurred when the Steddfod has been held outside of Wales. This has not occurred since 1929, when it was held in Liverpool for the third time. It has also been held once in Birkenhead and twice in London. It has been suggested over the years, that the Steddfod be held outside of Wales again to help more people understand about the language and culture. What do you think? I feel strongly that the Steddfod should remain in Wales but would love to see other Welsh themed festivals happening all over the world as well. And in fact they already do in some parts of the world.

The motivation behind the development of the Steddfod was to provide a platform on which the people of Wales could display their talent – a celebration of their culture and language. This was thought by many to have been in response to the 1847 education report's assault on the character of Wales. In 1846, the government appointed a commission to enquire into the state of education in Wales and 'especially into the means afforded to the labouring classes of acquiring a knowledge of the English language'. The three commissioners appointed had no knowledge of Welsh or elementary education but they managed to produce three huge blue covered volumes containing the report. These became known as The Blue Books and the implication of the report was that the government should intervene immediately and provide Wales with a network of English-medium elementary schools. At this time, Welsh was the first and only language of the vast majority of the people of Wales. It is thought that although the report had a detrimental effect on the continuity of the Welsh language, it also inspired a growing number of Welsh nationalists, with an aim to defend and strengthen their nation.

The Steddfod is a brilliant way for anyone learning to speak Welsh to fully immerse themselves in the language, either for the full eight days or for just a day or two. There are even opportunities for learners to take part, either for fun or to compete. I'd attended odd days at three Steddfodau and one Urdd (youth) Eisteddfod so far. In 2013, at my first Steddfod, which was in Denbigh, I helped to supervise the Say Something in Welsh (SSIW) stand in Maes D (the learner's tent – **Maes** means field or ground and D for **Dysgwyr** which means learners) for a couple of hours on the day that I was attending. SSIW were sharing the then famous purple couch belonging to Hwb, the S4C (Welsh television channel) platform for learners. I can still remember the incredible feeling that I had after a full day of hearing and speaking only Welsh, albeit broken Welsh with plenty of mistakes on my part. My live experiences of the Steddfod prior to writing this book, have been of watching some of the competitions in the tents, but mostly enjoying favourite musicians and singers performing in the **Tŷ Gwerin** (folk tent) and browsing the hundreds of stalls on the Maes. Traditionally, the Steddfod takes place in August, but I was beginning to realise that there were a lot of interesting things going on behind the scenes for more than a year leading up to the main event. When it was announced that the village of Boduan, only a few miles from our caravan, was to be the venue of the 2023 'Llŷn and Eifionydd National Eisteddfod', I was excited about having this perfect opportunity to witness these things as well as to discover and learn more about the history and relevance of the ceremonies that are a large part of this special festival. One last thing to mention before I move on is that the Royal Welsh Show, always held in Builth Wells in the summer, has nothing to do with eisteddfoddau and is a totally different experience, involving a lot of farm animals and fewer poets. Are you ready for a walk now?

Helping out at the SSIW stand at the 2013 National Eisteddfod

Walk 1
Pen y Garn, Pwllheli
1st October 2021
First Steps

We had wondered whether to walk the hills of Llŷn in any particular order, perhaps starting with the smallest and building up to the highest or vice versa, or in the order of Des' book. But finally, we decided to do them randomly, based on how we were feeling and how far we wanted to walk on that particular day.

This low hill, with easy access from the centre of Pwllheli, was a gentle one to start us off and one that we had never walked up before. We parked on Embankment Road, more often known as The Cob, and walked towards the town centre. As we reached the roundabout at the side of the railway station, we turned left and walked along Y Maes, passing two of my favourite Pwllheli shops – **Glasu** ice-cream shop and café, and **Llên Llŷn** Welsh language book and music shop. We turned right at the next roundabout onto Stryd Moch, with Y Meitr pub on the corner. Stryd Moch is referred to in English as Gaol Street on some maps and it has some interesting old buildings including one that now houses a sportswear shop but was the town jail between 1829 and 1879. **Stryd** means street and **moch** means pigs, but I believe it is purely coincidence that it has this name and is nothing to do with pigs being slang for police. We passed R Gwynedd Evans and Son Ironmongers shop on the corner of Ala Uchaf, a shop we have found useful over the years as it is full to the brim with every household and DIY item that you can imagine. The sign above the door tells us that it was established in 1856 and there's a magic about the place. It's the kind of shop that reminds some of us of a certain age, of times long ago, when, while waiting for mum or dad to purchase some wooden clothes pegs or particular screws and nails, our attention was drawn to all the fascinating tiny drawers, packets and boxes behind the counter. I can imagine that some of the drawers in Evans and Son may still contain useful bits and bobs that have been there since 1856.

At the crossroads, we turned left onto Llŷn Street or Penlon Llŷn. Situated on this corner is another interesting old building –

The Whitehall Pub

Whitehall. Whitehall is a popular pub with the locals, for drinking and for meals. It dates from 1818, is a Grade II listed building and unsurprisingly has an all-white exterior. In Victorian times it was associated with the Conservative Party; the local branch committee used it as a meeting place. In 1871, there was a gas explosion in the hotel, caused by guests who had stayed up late and forgotten to turn off the gas. A maid was injured when she opened the parlour door, which along with part of a wall was damaged in the blast. In 1890, a young Whitehall barmaid Elizabeth Jones was taken to court, accused of sending letters which libeled master mariner Owen Lewis, who was the brother of the hotel proprietor. Her accusations included his having killed his two wives, and that he was a town bully. Elizabeth was found not guilty, but I'm not sure about Mr Lewis.

Off we go again. We trudged up the gradual slope of Penlôn Llŷn, passing rows of terrace houses, then eventually on our right a dry-stone wall with a single wrought iron gateway followed by a wider gateway and gateposts belonging to a larger private house. There was a gradual bend to the right and the road was lined on the right with hedgerows growing on the top of lower dry-stone walls. These are known in Welsh as **cloddiau**. Soon after, the houses on the left also gave way to cloddiau and a kissing gate, and a public footpath sign almost hidden by shrubs appeared on the right. We maneuvered through the gate avoiding the tangle of brambles, and on the other side was the path to Pen y Garn. The low hill was now visible to us for the first time, beyond a metal gate and across a farmer's field. We gradually followed the path around the base of the hill and greeted a group of teenagers who passed us and were chatting loudly with each other. They took a steeper short cut, but we continued along the clearly marked grassy path which eventually brought us to the rocky stretch where we could work our way up to the summit. As we neared the trig point, we got an increasingly excellent view of Pwllheli harbour with a myriad of white masts, and the sea and mountains of Meirionnydd beyond. As we reached the summit we were treated to views of lush green fields and the more distant hills of Llŷn that we had yet to attempt. A small, easy hill to start us off, but I already felt a sense of achievement at having begun our next adventure.

We followed a shorter path heading northeast from the hill for our return. This took us amongst trees and across a field, soon emerging onto the road named Allt Salem, just before the college – Coleg Meirion Dwyfor. **Allt** is derived from **gallt** which means wooded hillside. As we descended back into the town, I was curious about a castellated building and gateway we could see amongst the houses lower down. I later put a message on the Facebook page 'Old Pictures of Pwllheli' and almost immediately received many friendly informative replies. The wonders of the internet! I was told that the castle-like house was called Picton Castle and had been built as a folly in 1810. It had possibly been used as a summer house and hunting lodge by the owners of a larger residence close by.

We arrived back into town in time for lunch – **cinio** – at Caffi Largo, by the promenade. Although it only opened the year before, it had become a popular eating place for locals and visitors and one of my favourite cafés as there is always plenty of Welsh to be heard amongst the staff and regulars, and in the background music. The food is also excellent.

Picton Castle, Pwllheli

The day after this walk, we had a steam train journey booked from Caernarfon to Porthmadog. This had originally been booked for August the previous year as a double celebration – our 30th wedding anniversary and the completion of our coastal path

Caffi Largo

walk from Porthmadog to Caernarfon. We had thought it would be good to complete the circle. But unfortunately, Jim was unwell, and we had to cancel. This time we were both fit and well for the journey, but the weather wasn't. It rained for the whole of the return trip. We enjoyed our luxury hamper of Welsh goods along the journey and the wine helped to ease our disappointment, but it wasn't quite what we hoped for. We'd booked the best seats with the viewing windows at the front of the train but all that we saw was rain and more rain. As if to reinforce the sorry state of the weather, halfway along the journey the jovial guard strolled along the aisles, pointing out to us all where Yr Wyddfa would have been had we been able to see it. We spent a wet two hours in Porthmadog before our return journey and visited St John's Church, to see the memorial stone of RS Thomas, one of my favourite Welsh poets and the excellent little maritime museum close to the harbour and train station. We were compensated for the bad weather by a beautiful rainbow as we arrived home to our caravan.

Pwllheli from Pen y Garn

Walk 2
Mynydd Carreg, near Porthor
28th April 2022
Red Café

As you can see from the date, quite a few months elapsed until we did our second hill walk. At the beginning of November 2021, I suffered a slipped disc with the most horrendously painful sciatica as a result. I continued to walk but couldn't manage long distances and sitting down was almost intolerable for several weeks. I managed to continue working with the help of strong pain killers and by using a rise and fall desk at home which meant I could stand for much of the time, while I interviewed clients via video. I work three days a week for the NHS as an Occupational Therapist, specializing in assessing adults for an Autism Spectrum Condition and our team had already been using video consultation during the Covid-19 lockdowns to avoid face to face contacts. We had returned to seeing people face to face but continued to have the option of using video if people preferred. We'd managed to get to the caravan for visits until it closed for the winter on the 2nd January but had to make many stops on the way to allow me to stand and stretch, and gigs and cinema visits had been out of the question. I did everything advised by the musculoskeletal specialist and more, and eventually the pain began to ease and by the beginning of March, when the caravan reopened, I was able to walk more easily and sit for longer periods of time, but still didn't feel ready to risk any steep hills.

The evening before this walk, we had enjoyed watching the new movie *Belfast* at Pwllheli's cinema. The cinema,

Neuadd Dwyfor

along with a theatre and library is housed in Neuadd Dwyfor, which had only recently reopened in March after extensive modernisation, including new seats and lighting. Neuadd Dwyfor was built as Pwllheli Town and Market Hall in 1900, then used as a theatre since 1902 and as a cinema since 1911. We were glad to see it had kept its original ornate décor and especially pleased that it hadn't been closed down as is happening to so many older small cinemas and libraries around the UK. There are plans for further developments including a roof top viewing point, which I'm looking forward to. We had attended an excellent theatre performance on the first night of opening. This was a one woman show called *The Many Lives of Amy Dillwyn* by the Lighthouse Theatre Company and was about a cigar smoking, novelist, suffragette and philanthropist, born in Swansea in 1845. Quite a character.

I felt excited about this walk as despite being an optimist, I'd begun to wonder if my back would allow me to do any hill walking ever again. We had walked up Mynydd Carreg with the boys many years before and remembered it to be an easy walk and Des promised us this in his book also. Not far from Mynydd Carreg, there was somewhere I had been wanting to visit for some time. Plas Carmel opened towards the end of 2021 and is easy to spot along the winding narrow lane between Rhosirwaun and Anelog as its café – **Caffi Siop Plas** – is painted bright red. It is a community project to restore and revive the old shop, chapel, house and garden. The aim of it is to create a sustainable heritage and cultural site for this rural part of Llŷn. The café is the first part of the project to be completed and is situated in what was the old shop, a single storey metal corrugated building that used to serve the local community between the 1920s and 1980s. One of the first things you notice on the way into the café is an attractive painted map, featuring places of interest in the vicinity. I could recognise the style of the artwork as being that of local artist Ffion Meleri Gwyn. She had produced one of a similar style of Cricieth which is on display in the town and is available as a handy leaflet for visitors. As we entered the café, there was a delicious mix of smells from the food and of the new wood from its cladded interior and we were greeted warmly by local Ffion Enlli and her French partner Coco, who were running this cosy place at the time, both Welsh speakers. The table next to the window with the best view looking straight out to Mynydd Anelog across the fields, was already taken by a small group of people who we soon realised were a working party for the project. They chatted passionately in Welsh about their ideas whilst studying their plans, so I did a bit of ear wigging. We ordered a cuppa and blueberry cheesecake that we had to agree was delicious but would be unlikely to be walked off by our mini hill walk today. After we settled the bill, I asked in Welsh if the old chapel was open to visitors yet. A member of the working party overheard as they were just dispersing, and he offered to unlock and show us around. The Baptist chapel and adjoining house is a plain looking grey stone building. Its interior has hardly changed since it was built about 200 years ago and has been listed as a Grade 11* listed building of special architectural and historic interest by Cadw, the Welsh Government's historic environment service. We could see it was in a state of disrepair, but it was fascinating to see the original boxed pews and beautiful old light fittings. Renovations were to begin shortly, and it is the intention that occasional services and social events will be held here again. The kind gentleman showing us around, pointed out a large red boulder in the car park and explained that this was jasper, which was a stone that had been quarried close by in the past and that often pieces could be found on local beaches. He pointed to the large, corrugated shed, known as **Y Sied Du** – the black shed, due to its black glossy paintwork, and explained that the stone was going to be housed there along with lots of other interesting artifacts and displays about the area, that we would have to return to look at soon. We promised to do that and explained we were off to do a hill walk now. He asked were we going to walk up the nearby Mynydd Anelog, but we explained that we were doing a much smaller hill today but hoping to return to do Anelog and visit Plas Carmel again.

Caffi Siop Plas

Walk 2a

The National Trust car park for Mynydd Carreg was only a few minutes away and as Jim was driving, I admired the bluebells and red campions along the lane as we passed the farmyard close by. Bluebells in Welsh is **clychau'r gog** which means cuckoo's bells, but in Llŷn you will mostly hear them called **bwtsias y gog** which translates as cuckoo's boots or often just **bwtsias**, which sounds a bit like butchers. If you want to learn more Welsh nature words, I recommend a YouTube page which you can subscribe to, which has been created by local Welsh tutor and artist Marian Brosschot. 'Gales con Marian/Welsh with Marian' is its name as Marian also teaches Welsh through the medium of Spanish. She has produced several short videos for learners at different stages of learning and some include walks along country lanes, naming the wildflowers or other wonders of nature that she comes across. I think I was distracted again. The short lane to the free small car park is rather bumpy and gives the impression that it is rarely driven along so take care with your exhaust. The gentle slope across the field towards Mynydd Carreg was clear to see from beyond the small gate as was the village of Anelog at the foot of Mynydd Anelog and the sea to the southwest. We sauntered slowly towards the summit. I wasn't yet up to full speed because of my back and used a walking pole to help. In his book, Des suggests a circular walk around the hill, which looked inviting, but we decided not to push fate. Jim noticed some fresh-looking cow pats on our way, but there were no cows to be seen. We're both wary of cows

The slope of Mynydd Carreg with Mynydd Anelog in the distance

Porthor from the summit shelter

if they are on the same side of the fence as us, after a fairly recent scary experience with a small herd. We soon reached the stone circular shelter at the summit, which was yellow with lichen, and we sheltered inside from the breeze whilst admiring the view. The beach at Porthor was just about visible eastward. As we set off back down the hill, we noticed a group of cows lying in a nearby unfenced field. They were the cow pat culprits and our return walk was much quicker than our outward journey.

We called at Porthor on our journey back to the caravan and enjoyed another cuppa at the beachside Caffi Porthor. I couldn't resist dragging my feet along the sand to hear the squeaking that gives this beach its English name of Whistling Sands. It is said to be one of only two beaches in Europe which can boast this phenomenon, which is thought to be caused by the unique shape of the sand particles. Whilst I was playing, I was also pleasantly surprised to spot some small pieces of red jasper.

Eisteddfod Ramble 1 – 28th April 2022
A Special Visitor at the Caravan

Two days later, we had a visit to the caravan from someone with an important role to play in the Steddfod. Jim and I had woken early on the Saturday morning, and we had decided to give the inside of the caravan a good cleaning. Jim had brought me a **panad**, a cuppa, in bed and I had been pondering something about my previous book that was at that time in the hands of the local publishers Gwasg Carreg Gwalch waiting to be typeset.

Myrddin ap Dafydd is the founder of the **gwasg** (press) and he'd been advising me via emails about my coastal path book. He is also an author with a stream of books to his name and has won major awards for his poetry at the Steddfod, so I felt privileged to have him as my publisher. But more importantly to mention is that at the time of writing this book Myrddin was the current **Archdderwydd** (Archdruid) of Wales. Archdderwydd or Archdruid is the title given to the person presiding over the **Gorsedd**. The Gorsedd – **Yr Orsedd** – is a society of Welsh language poets, writers, musicians and others who have made a contribution to the Welsh language and to public life in Wales and is responsible for the main ceremonies held at the Steddfod.

I had never met Myrddin but had seen him on television on the Welsh language channel S4C as well as at eisteddfodau and other local events. Our Llŷn friend Amanda, who is a great source of information, knew him as a fellow parent at their children's school and had mentioned that he lived not too far away from where our caravan is sited. When I had sent a tentative email to Gwasg Carreg Gwalch about my first book, I'd been surprised and rather nervous at getting a reply from the Archdruid himself. Then after he had read a sample, I was even more surprised and flattered to get a further email saying that he was interested in publishing my story.

I had told him where our caravan was and that if ever he felt we needed to meet face to face about the book, he'd be welcome to visit us when we were there. So anyway, where was I, oh yes in bed with a cuppa and reading over some of the text of my book on my tablet. I spotted an error that I wanted to mention before it was too late and sent an email to Myrddin while I remembered, not expecting a reply until at least after the weekend. He responded almost immediately and asked when we were next at the caravan. I explained that we were there now but were cleaning it this morning and going to a gig the following day, but otherwise we had no other plans. He replied, saying that he would visit us at about 11 that morning. He asked for

A caravan visit by Myrddin ap Dafydd

directions from the outer gate as he would be arriving on his bike. After replying with directions, I gulped down my tea, shot out of bed and following a quick breakfast, we cleaned the caravan from top to bottom then jumped into the shower to clean ourselves.

Then I suddenly wondered… what do you give a visiting Archdruid for elevenses? We were both reducing our cake intake, but I remembered that luckily, we had some **bara brith** and local Welsh cakes in the freezer, which I put on a plate to thaw-perfect. I then paced the caravan nervously, trying to look and feel relaxed. He arrived just before 11 and had walked the last part of the lane, leaving his bike at the gate which was locked. I'd had no need to be nervous as he was ordinary and friendly and chatted easily to both of us about family and work. He had brought a printout of the first chapter of my book to show me, which I was thrilled with, and we discussed a couple of his editing suggestions. I did a small amount of chat with him in Welsh but we spoke mostly in English so that Jim could join in. We were flattered when he said that we were special visitors because of how we try to be involved in the local community as much as possible and because of our respect for the language. He said that he thought that my book would be encouraging to others to have a go at the language, and he wanted to promote it and sell it in places such as the Welsh Language Centre at Nant Gwrtheyrn.

He asked about the gig we were going to and I explained it was to see the band Plu in Caernarfon at the old court building **Hen Lys**. Plu is a local trio band consisting of Elan, Marged and Gwilym Rhys who play alternative Welsh language pop-folk, and being siblings, their voices blend beautifully when they sing in harmony together. We have been to see them, and to Gwilym playing solo many times, including back home near to Manchester. Gwilym, usually known by his full name Gwilym Bowen Rhys, is also carving out a successful solo career and he pops up all over Wales and beyond to perform mostly traditional folk music but with a contemporary feel. Have a listen to them – I think you'll like them. Myrddin was also a fan of Plu and knew that the gig was to launch their new album. Just before he left, I asked him if he would sign a couple of his poetry books that I had in the caravan. Jim took our photo together and shook his head at me in mock disapproval, as I joked that the picture would be for in my next book. I didn't share the picture on Facebook as that's not my way, but I shared it on a text to Tom and Simon and sent it to Amanda via Messenger to cheer her up as she'd been worried lately about her mother being unwell. It did the trick – Amanda responded with **'Archdderwydd yn dy garafan – anghredadwy'**. which means 'Archdruid in your caravan – unbelievable'. and agreed it had put a smile on her face. I also sent a photo from the internet to Tom and Simon to show what Myrddin looks like when in his Archdruid robes and Tom joked and suggested that we'd had a visit from the Welsh equivalent of the pope.

Plu performing at Hen Lys

Eisteddfod Ramble 2 – 13th May 2022
Wales Has Got Talent

A couple of weeks later, we went to another gig, this time at Galeri in Caernarfon. Apologies for so many gig related rambles but I have a passion for music, which I inherited from my late dad who I can still hear singing 'All Through the Night', the English version of Ar Hyd y Nos. The Welsh music scene has contributed greatly to my learning to speak Welsh and one of the many appeals of Llŷn for me is the vast amount of quality music, art and literature to be found there. The repetition in song lyrics along with a catchy tune make a perfect recipe for learning.

This recent gig was another postponed event from pre covid days, with singer songwriter Al Lewis performing songs that he'd composed for a musical show in the 2019 Eisteddfod in Llanrwst, called **Te yn y Grug**. Unfortunately, we hadn't managed to get tickets for the show, but had later seen a recording of it on S4C (Welsh language TV Channel). I was also pleased to have recently managed to read the book, on which the show was based, in its original Welsh. Te yn y Grug (Tea in the Heather) was written by Kate Roberts in the 1950s and was the first book I'd read by a Welsh author, after I'd started to learn the language. I'd had to read an English translated version as I'd found the old-fashioned use of the language and colloquialisms difficult to manage, but I'd vowed to one day read it in Welsh. It's a collection of short stories about the lives of families living and working in and around the village of Rhosgadfan, near Caernarfon and of the poverty suffered by many who were trying to make a living by working in the slate quarries. The gig was a huge success as Al has become quite a name, not only in Wales, but also in the rest of the UK and in America. He was backed by a young mixed choir Côr Dre and also accompanied for some of the songs by Mared Williams, who had managed to take some time off from another exciting commitment.

Mared is a member of the group Welsh of the Westend, who are all young musical theatre performers. They were formed by Steffan Hughes during the first Covid-19 Lockdown in March 2020 and were a huge success, performing together online from their own homes and raising money for the NHS from some of their performances. They were described as a 'viral sensation', – I'm not sure if a pun was intended – and sang their own versions of musical theatre classics. Only a few days after this Al Lewis gig, ten members of Welsh of the Westend appeared on Britain's Got Talent, the popular televised talent programme and successfully auditioned for a place in the contest. This was reported to have been the first time they had all met in person and a few weeks later they reached the semifinal, singing 'You Will be Found', from the Broadway show 'Dear Evan Hansen'. It was great to see that they included a couple of lines of lyrics in Welsh.

Al Lewis and other Te yn y Grug performers

Walk 3

Garn Fadryn, Garn Bach and Moel Caerau, Garnfadryn Village
28th May 2022

A Steep Bare Faced Ramble

A week prior to this walk, I'd been to see the Musculo skeletal specialist about my bulging disc and sciatica. I'd been happy especially with the reduction of pain and stiffness and now being able to do some careful gardening and one small hill walk. She was amazed at the improvement I'd made and said that she'd thought that I was going to need surgery but now it seemed this wasn't the case. I asked about steeper hill walking and emphasised that I thought that it had been regular walking and physio stretches that had helped the improvement. She gave her blessing as long as I listened to my body and eased off if the pain increased.

Exactly a month since our last hill walk, we looked at maps and our Des Marshall hill walking book and decided to have a look at the two small hills next to Garn Fadryn – Moel Caerau and Garn Bach. Des had suggested a route that took in all three hills, but we agreed that Fadryn would be too steep for my back yet.

The hedgerows along our journey looked stunning in the sunshine, still amass with bluebells, cow parsley and red campion.

Garn Fadryn

Pony on the slopes of Garn Fadryn

We parked the car at a layby in the small hamlet of Garnfadryn next to the old chapel, which had been converted into a house and where there still appeared to be work going on with various workmen coming and going as we passed. We noticed that thankfully the attractive house had kept its proper Welsh name Hen Gapel. In Welsh, as in French and many other languages, the adjective usually comes after the noun but old – **hen** – is an exception and comes before the noun. Hen also makes subsequent words which have a particular consonant to take on a soft mutation – **treiglad meddal**. One of those consonants is C, so **capel** becomes **gapel**. There are lots of other situations where words take on mutations in Welsh, but I've always gone with the 'Say Something in Welsh' method, which is to learn them as naturally as possible as you come across them, and to not worry about them. Many first language Welsh speakers don't always use them correctly so learners can definitely be forgiven if they forget. Most of them just begin to sound right and come naturally as you progress with learning the language. I've rambled again.

As we took a left turn just after the chapel, we spotted free range eggs for sale and an honesty box, and I vowed to buy some when we came back down. The sign indicating our route towards Garn Fadryn made us laugh, with the arrow and the image of the walker tilted steeply to warn people of its sharp incline. We remembered that the path for the smaller hills would branch off from this initial single path further along. The path rose quite steeply from the start and behind us we were immediately rewarded with stunning views across farmland to the coast, with the wide bay of Porth Neigwl taking centre stage. There was quite a strong breeze and the clouds cast moving shadows and reflections onto the fields and the sea. A solitary green tractor was ploughing a distant field, with seagulls following behind swooping down to collect the treats that were exposed. The wide path that led up the side of the chapel had a neatly mown grassy strip up its centre. Shortly another sign saying '**Garn**' (hill) with a steeply pointing arrow guided us to a narrower path branching off to the left towards the hills. We could now see why this initial part of the path was so manicured – it also served as a drive to Sweet Tamarind Beauty and Body Therapy and continued to the right through a tunnel of trees, leading to the house. I've rarely visited a beautician's, never mind a beauty and body therapist, and have never worn make up, even on my wedding day, much to the horror of some friends and family. My parents were loving, but strict with me as a teenager, and forbade makeup, and then by my late twenties when I finally felt able to rebel – yes it took me that long – I'd got so used to being barefaced I felt odd wearing it. This walk was my beauty and body therapy today.

The path was now lined with fern, and we reached the point where it divided, with Garn Fadryn to our left, Garn Bach to our right and Moel Caerau ahead of us. We simultaneously commented that Garn Bach didn't look that bach – **bach** means small. The path to Fadryn was clear but the other disappeared into the ferns and with the lack of signs, we were unsure of how to get across to the

Moel Caerau from beneath Garn Fadryn

smaller hills. Des had given clear directions of how to get to both, but I'd forgotten his book. I suggested that we did a slow and careful ascent of Garn Fadryn instead. The path was clearly marked and we couldn't go wrong, I said. Jim smiled, raised his eyebrows then gave me gentle instructions to watch my foothold and stop for rests regularly. Since my spine problem began, we had become better at remembering our walking poles for any uneven walks. The large handle folded down to give a seat to prop on – handy. We laughed at ourselves and our change of plan as we continued along the steep and increasingly stony incline towards the summit. The hill face was covered with ferns, heather (not yet in bloom) and lots of low pale-yellow shrubs with blue-grey ripening berries that looked like tiny blueberries, which I later discovered were bilberries – **llus** in Welsh. We had several long rests on the way up, each time with our back to the slope, so we could admire the views. There was plenty of blue sky but there were low clouds and a haze across the distant hills. My favourite hill range, Yr Eifl, was easy to spot as was the lower hill Foel Fawr, and the small islands of Tudwal (Ynysoedd Tudwal), gradually came into full view close to the headland near Bwlchtocyn. The Llŷn coastline feels even more familiar to us now, having recently walked the coastal path. A solitary white horse interrupted its grass munching to watch us as we passed on the other side of a low dry-stone wall.

One of our resting points was at a large rock. We have walked to the summit of Garn Fadryn at least twice before. Once in 2003, when Tom and Simon were only eight and three and then in 2014 when they were in their teens, to watch a sunset with our friends Amanda and Brian and their teenage children Elain and Owain. My memory isn't that good – I checked on our photos later. We had photos of our young boys leaning on this same rock, that I now leant on while I took in the view. Garn Bach was facing us and looked a stone's throw away and to our left Moel Caerau was, as Des had described in his book, 'a high point in a grassy field'. The only sound to be heard was the tractor, which now looked like a child's toy and the occasional cawing of a couple of rooks soaring above us. As if out of nowhere, I spotted a focused young runner making his way up the zigzagging path towards us. We stood to one side and exchanged a quick hello as he passed, then joked to each other that he'd be back down and home having his breakfast before we got to the summit. The path got steeper as the rocky hillfort on the summit came into clearer view. This Iron Age hillfort was thought to have been built in phases. The first phase dates from about 300 BC when the summit and 12 surrounding acres were enclosed. The area was thought to have been refortified and extended to cover 26 acres about 200 years later. In 1188 a newly built 'castle of the sons of Owain' was documented and was thought to have been the third hillfort on Garn Fadryn. I was glad of our walking poles and the banana I'd brought to keep my energy levels up.

The cross and trig point on Garn Fadryn summit

We found a wider section of path where we propped again and ate our fruit. As expected, the runner soon reappeared on his way down and was able to pass us again.

We eventually came to a fork in the path. The path to the right appeared to lead to two mounds of stones that I presumed had been made recently. We took the path to the left which led more steeply up the slope and towards some ancient circular stone enclosures. We soon began to question if we had done the right thing as the path disappeared and we had to negotiate an uneven and rocky area. But I was glad we had gone this way as we safely reached the low walled enclosures. It was amazing to think that many hundreds of years ago someone had lived or stored their goods or animals within these enclosures. I carefully stepped inside one of them and tried to imagine what it would have been like to live here. As we continued, we joined the alternative path further along and realised it would have been the safer, if less interesting, route. We agreed to return this way later. The path now gave us a clear route towards the summit which was marked by a concrete trig point. This was topped by what appeared to be a wooden cross that we had never seen before and we wondered who had placed it there. There was a strong breeze as we reached the summit and I felt quite exhilarated. The cross wasn't wooden,

Llanfihangel Bachellaeth – St Michael's church

but metal and painted gold, with nails and wire to represent the cross of Christ and it was fixed firmly to the top of the trig point. Needless to say, the views were even more stunning from the top. It was too hazy to make out the Wicklow Hills of Ireland which are meant to be visible on a clear day but we weren't complaining. Yr Eifl hills in one direction and Mynydd Rhiw to the other, with the sea glinting in the sunshine around the isles of Enlli and Tudwal, was a satisfying enough view for me.

On our return, the alternative path was quicker and easier under foot. I spotted a distant circle of white flowers blowing in the breeze. We couldn't get nearer to identify them as the heather was dense and prickly. They looked like poppies but the monocular helped me to identify them as cottongrass. **Plu'r gweunydd** is the Welsh name, which means feathers of the moors. We managed with just one rest on the return and as we perched, we were rewarded with the sight and sound of a beautiful corn bunting, also perched nearby on a low shrub, singing its jangling song. As we continued, we were then serenaded by a wren – **dryw** in Welsh – who was perched on a rock in the midst of bilberry bushes. I imagined he was happy after having his fill of the berries. As we reached the low dry-stone wall and the end of the steepest part of the hill, a family of four approached and the dad jokingly asked if Garn Fadryn was still as steep, and said that each time he walked this hill he forgot how steep it was. As we passed the entry to Sweet Tamarind, I thought that if the owners were to see me now slowly trundling past with my walking pole and with my hair all of a tangle from the sea breeze, they would have thought I was in urgent need of beauty and body therapy. As I collected a dozen eggs and left money in the honesty box on the way back to the car, I felt a real sense of achievement at having managed a higher hill than planned. I now felt that I could take on any of the other hills in Llŷn after all.

As is often the case, I had a few stops planned before we returned to the caravan. The first was just a couple of miles away at a place that no longer exists. Llanfihangel Bachellaeth is a former civil parish that was abolished in 1934 and incorporated into Buan but its old church dedicated to St Michael remains and is well worth a visit. It was thought to have dated from the end of the 17th century but was restored in 1888. Jim and I first visited this church before the boys were born, when I'd read in a small local guidebook that it was situated at the quietest spot on the peninsula. I presumed that the author of the guide had just decided this for himself, but I since learnt that Cynan, the Welsh 20th century, Pwllheli born poet had written a poem about the area including a line saying that it was the quietest place in Llŷn. I'll be saying more about Cynan and his important eisteddfod connections later. It was some years since we had last visited this spot and it appeared even more remote than I had remembered it. The pathway leading to the old rusty gate was overgrown with long grass and gave the impression that the church hadn't been visited for a long time. With some effort, I managed to open the gate and entered the churchyard. Unfortunately, the church was locked but I stood amongst the graves and listened to the silence, interrupted only by a brief chirping from a bird. Yes, I think Cynan was right.

Our next stop was Sarn Meyllteyrn as I had two places that I wanted to visit. The first was Sarn Pottery or **Crochendy**, which is housed in a 16th century stable. It is easily spotted in the village as its stone walls are painted a bright pale blue. It was founded by Oldrich Asenbryl, who is a known and loved character in the area. We have visited and encountered him several times before and remembered his unique sense of humour. As we approached the pottery, there he was in his sandals, sun hat

Sarn Pottery

and long artist's smock, looking as if he'd stepped out of a 19th century painting. A serious stroke in 1983, left him paralyzed in the left side of his body and as we saw him going from the annexe into the pottery, we noticed how slowly he was now walking. We laughed at a sign in the window stating, 'Free parking for Czechs only'.

Oldrich was born in Czechoslovakia, where he trained as a potter and moved to Britain in 1968. His art can be found in many museums around the world. Following his stroke, he adapted his technique to throw his pots one handed, and he glazes them in bright colours inspired by American pop art and by jazz which we could hear playing in the background as we entered cautiously. Oldrich greeted us with a smile as we stepped in and onto the original old, cobbled floor and in response to my 'are you open?' he replied 'of course – that is what it says on the sign'. I said it was good to see that his pottery was still going strong, and I asked how long he had been here now. With a grin, he said that he opened the pottery when I was born 49 years ago and that he had come from Bohemia. I laughed and said that I was actually 61 and Jim a few years older. He said that I looked 49 – the charmer – but then wiped out his compliment by saying to us both 'so you're going on 70, who knows what lies ahead'.

The pottery was bulging with his work which included mugs, jugs, plates and quirky self-pouring teapots, all displayed on tables or hanging on hooks from the low ceiling. I said that I was looking for a mug for myself today and he pointed to the area where most of them were and said that I should find one that spoke to me. He light heartedly suggested I may really want a set of six and asked what we had been doing on this fine day. We told him about our walk, and he said that he could see that we had caught the sun on our faces. He said that he'd heard there was a cross on the summit and asked us to describe it to him. I asked did he know who had put it there, but he didn't reply. Oldrich is a committed Christian and displays his beliefs alongside his stoneware with bible quotes on plaques hanging on the walls. As a lady entered the pottery, he spoke to her and stepped inside a cubicle that I hadn't really taken much notice of, despite it being close to where we were looking. I asked did he accept card and he said that he did and that these days he would exchange his pottery for anything, even items of clothing. He told us goodbye and as he disappeared upwards in what I then realised was a lift, he added 'I've spent my five daughters' inheritance on this gadget, see my wife for your purchase'. What a surreal picture this made – a modern lift in such an old building that didn't look high enough to have a second floor. Oldrich's wife Jenny is also a potter and I expressed my surprise to her at suddenly seeing him disappear in the lift. She explained that it was essential for him now as he had got older. I had chosen a mug with a comfy handle and a red and grey glaze. I had read on the pottery website that the glazes were mixed from locally found materials such as wood ashes and red clay from Porth Neigwl and that copper oxide was used to give the distinctive Sarn Pottery red. I was happy with my new mug, which I added to my small collection of Welsh studio pottery tableware which I like to use when we're at the caravan.

Our next visit was to Sarn Memorial Hall, just across the way, which was where we had parked the car. Over the weekend, a local group of amateur artists **Arlunwyr Sarn**, were holding an exhibition of their work in the hall and today was their opening day. I admire their work each month in the Llŷn local Welsh language newspaper *Llanw Llŷn*, in which they have their own dedicated page and I've visited some of their exhibitions over the years. The standard of their work is high. I am also friendly with two of the members, who I had met at a chat group for Welsh learners in Pwllheli but sadly this group has stopped meeting since the venue Caffi Gwalia closed during the

Sarn Hall Art Exhibition

Sinfonia at Yr Heliwr Nefyn

Covid-19 pandemic. Lesley Jones was one of these and she, along with her husband Howard, were the dedicated organisers of the long running chat group. We meandered through the exhibition, studying the paintings and sketches and were greeted warmly by the artists on duty today. Lesley wasn't here today, but we found some of her work and we were both impressed by her talent at drawing and painting, and I especially liked one of her detailed busy harbour scenes. I was looking for work by Chris Morgan, the other lady I knew and soon easily recognized one of her paintings on the wall as it was of her husband Dave digging. Dave spends a lot of time digging as they are both garden lovers and they also look after a small woodland, dedicated to reintroducing native trees to the area. Chris's painting had captured him well and I wasn't surprised that it wasn't for sale. We enjoy meeting up with Dave and Chris for walks and a cuppa – **panad**, when they are available in between the charitable work they also get involved with and they occasionally pop up on the monthly online Manchester Welsh Learners' chat group, which I organise. Before heading home to the caravan, we had a brief chat with artist Esther Stubbs, whilst sampling her delicious homemade chocolate cake with a panad. Her paintings of scenes and still life were stunning and she said that her work had previously been displayed in the Llŷn art gallery, Oriel Plas Glyn y Weddw.

I went home to the caravan, happy with our hill walking achievement and full of admiration for my new mug and a mini original by Esther showing my favourite Llŷn hill range, Yr Eifl.

The following day was a musical day. It began with a short classical concert in Yr Heliwr pub in Nefyn. This was performed by three female members of Sinfonia Cymru, a large under 30s Welsh orchestra, as part of their 'Mainly Village Halls' tour. I was mesmerised by the harpist, cellist and flautist for a blissful hour in the company of locals. Our evening treat was a show in Cricieth to celebrate 100 years of the memorial hall. **Cofio'r Cant** (remembering the hundred) had been written by Gwyneth Glyn and Twm Morys, two of our favourite Welsh singers and was a bilingual musical comedy drama that raced through 100 years of events that had taken place in or near to the hall. It was performed by Gwyneth, Twm and the people of Cricieth. Prior to the show, I was admiring a long beautiful fabric mural of Cricieth on the wall by the side of where we were sitting for the performance, which until now I had only seen on Facebook. It had been made by a creative group of local people including artist Ffion Gwyn who has also created a painted town plan of Cricieth and the map on display at Plas Carmel as mentioned earlier. As I was looking, Ffion appeared out of nowhere and kindly explained the mural to me and pointed out some of the detail that made up this special piece of work. I recognized her from having chatted to her at a Christmas Craft fair a few years ago, where she was selling her stunningly detailed nature posters. She later appeared as a schoolteacher in the show. So talented this Welsh lot.

Twm Morys, Gwyneth Glyn and other players at the Cricieth Memorial Hall

Eisteddfod Ramble 3 – 10th June 2022
Shanties on the Beach

A couple of weeks later, we found ourselves on Porthdinllaen beach, outside the Tŷ Coch inn, listening to shanties being sung by some local favourite singers/musicians, including Twm Morys, Gwyneth Glyn, Anni Llŷn and Gwenan Gibbard. They were raising money to support the 2023 Steddfod. As you can imagine, due to Wales's proximity to the sea, there are numerous Welsh sea shanties and many of them tell stories of boats and sailors from Llŷn. One name that seems to appear more than any in the local shanties is Huw Puw and you will often hear '**Fflat Huw Puw**', in the lyrics of the songs. There is one shanty with this as its title composed by John Glyn Davies. It means Huw Puw's flat – a flat being a type of shallow boat, used to sail up rivers. Hugh Pugh, as his name is more often spelt, was a mariner, who in the mid-1800s was master of a flat called Ann of Liverpool, which traded between Runcorn and Caernarfon.

'Fflat Huw Puw' is often sung by school children and frequently heard sung in Llŷn and this evening was no exception when it was sung as the finale with the majority of the audience joining in. Gwyneth Glyn is one of my favourite Welsh language folk singers and we've seen her performing live numerous times, mostly in Llŷn, but occasionally also nearer to home. She now recognises us at gigs and sometimes when we're out and about on the peninsula, and always gives a wave or comes over for a little Welsh chat with me. We are always touched by her modesty and how thankful she is for us attending her gigs. Tonight, was no exception as she gave us a lovely wave and smile from the stage. Anni Llŷn, another of the singers this evening, is also a TV presenter and writer and as well as winning the Crown at the Urdd Eisteddfod in 2012, was Wales' Children's Poet Laureate from 2015 to 2017. She also had an important role to play in the 2023 Eisteddfod gorsedd ceremonies, as will be explained soon.

In between the songs, I was lucky to have an interesting Welsh conversation with another learner, called Sally who sat on the beach with us during the gig. She explained her motive for learning the language being her Welsh ancestry including her grandfather

Robert 'Silyn' Roberts, who had been a clergyman, writer, teacher and pacifist and had won the crown at the 1902 Steddfod with his poem 'Trystan ac Esyllt'. The crown is awarded to the winning entrant in the competition for the **Pryddest**, which is poetry written in free verse. Sally had recently moved to the area and was researching her grandfather with the help of Angharad Tomos, the Welsh author and prominent language activist. We also chatted about our experiences of learning to speak Welsh and we had both used the same method – the excellent online course 'Say Something in Welsh', which is now known as Saysomethingin.com, as training in other languages is now offered. Sally had joined a local group of learners, **Dysgwyr Dwyfor** (Welsh Learners in Dwyfor) and was looking for other members as she was new to the group. I was able to point out one of the tutors Marian Broschott (mentioned earlier). This group was led by a married Llŷn couple Martyn and Eluned Croydon, who organised lessons and various activities and chat groups throughout Llŷn, but less is seen of Eluned these days since the arrival of a little one. I'm not an official member of the group as our visits to the area aren't consistent enough to commit to a regular attendance to their lessons or events, but I have been given a warm welcome whenever I've been able to drop into their chat groups from time to time. Martyn is becoming recognised as quite a character in the area, and he won't mind me saying that he is rarely seen without a tie and waistcoat – even on the beach. Martyn originated from Kidderminster, but moved to Llŷn and in 2013, he won **Dysgwr y Flwyddyn**, Welsh learner of the year, at the Steddfod in Denbigh.

Jim enjoying the shanties on Porth Dinllaen beach

Walk 4

Garn Boduan, near Nefyn
12th June 2022
Spitting Frogs

As we got out of the car at the parking area in front of the barrier gate for Garn Boduan and the forest, which is situated along the B4354, just before it joins the A497, we were greeted by the loud and continuous chirping of a chiff chaff, out of view, high up in the trees. Even though we've enjoyed walks to the summit of Garn Boduan several times before, we read Des' description the night before in case there had been any recent changes. It sounded familiar and straightforward.

Though the kissing gate, we followed the wide track through the forest, which is a mix of deciduous and coniferous trees. The path was also lined with shrubs and ferns interspersed with tall purple foxglove in full bloom. The incline began quite gently but we'd both brought our walking poles in preparation for the steeper and uneven parts. We followed the sharp hairpin bend heading to the left and a bright blue sky appeared above the trees.

We reached an information board at the next hairpin. It informed us that the rocky summit of Garn Boduan is a plateau at about 250 metres above sea level crowned by an Iron Age hillfort, measuring about ten hectares – I'm sure I never learnt about

Garn Fadryn from the slopes of Boduan

hectares in school. The hillfort, it continued, contained the remains of about 170 circular stone huts. We were also informed that at the highest eastern end of the hill is a stone citadel which could have been as late as the 7th century and connected with the 6th century Saint Buan, that gave the place the name Boduan – the residence of Buan.

Next to the board was a sign with two yellow arrows. One indicated that we could continue along the track through the forest and the other told us to cut off left to head to the summit, which we did. As we looked back, we could clearly see the small hill Moelypenmaen, but low clouds and haze hid the more distant views. The path became greener, and I noticed that the grass had lots of what I always called frog spit as a child. This is often also known as cuckoo spit (**poer y gwcw** in Welsh) because it appears in spring at a time when the cuckoo can be heard calling. It's a white frothy liquid, secreted by the nymphs of a sap sucking insect, often called a froghopper or spittlebug – **llyffant y gwair** in Welsh (grass frog). Delightful.

We stopped for short rests, each time admiring the gradually emerging views behind us. Garn Fadryn and Garn Bach were the most prominent hills to be seen from the path. Our previous walk had been up the southeastern slope of Fadryn, but today we were gazing at its north eastern side which showed off its woodland Coed Garn Fadryn. We had a visit from our peninsula friends Amanda and Brian the night before this walk and we mentioned our Fadryn walk and laughed about how we were passed twice by a runner. Not surprisingly Amanda knew who he was, knew his wife and knew that he did this run each day. **Byd bach** (small world). Today we were passed along this walk by a man carrying a bulky rucksack with what looked like an aerial sticking out at the top. We exchanged greetings as he marched on. We continued up the clearly marked path and the summit of Boduan gradually came into view. As we reached a spot below a rocky outcrop, we agreed that this was where in 1997 we had left a baby buggy at the edge of the ferns and from where we had continued up a steep path to the top, with Jim carrying Tom. Tom was two at the time but a tall toddler and already in age four clothes, so that was no easy task for Jim. Thankfully today, that path is overgrown, and we continued around and along the current defined path which had now begun

Inside a roundhouse

to level off somewhat. The low remains of stone roundhouses appeared on each side of us. I was struck by how perfectly round they appeared. We reached a short tunnel of low growing trees and had to duck and dodge the branches as we continued. We were almost at the summit, and we trod carefully along the rocky path through the prickly heather, which was beginning to bloom, and the low bilberry bushes and brambles.

As we clambered up the rocks, which we presumed to be part of the hillfort, we could see a family of four people taking selfies on the concrete platform marking the summit. We could hear that they were Welsh speakers. As we reached the platform, they moved along towards the man who had passed us and who was now setting up a large aerial further along the plateau. We noticed that the platform had been graffitied with the words **Cymru Rydd** (Free Wales). We could hear them asking him in English what he was doing but frustratingly didn't hear the reply. Jim agreed we'd need to ask him – he's as nosy as me. It felt chillier than you'd expect for the middle of June, especially with the strong breeze at the summit. We'd heard the occasional bee humming and a few grasshoppers chirping on the way up but not as many as I'd have expected at this time of the year and not a butterfly to be seen. I sheltered in a round house, the top of the existing walls up to about my waist level whilst slowly turning full circle to take photos of the stunning views all around me – Llanbedrog headland, followed by the small hills Foel Fawr, Foel Gron and Carneddol, then the higher Garn Bach and Garn Fadryn. There was a haze across the sea and distant mountains were hidden but we could make out the whole of Porthdinllaen and the beautiful hill range Yr Eifl, with Carnguwch close by.

The wooded slopes of Mynydd Nefyn looked a stone's throw away. We could have spotted our caravan from here if we had remembered our binoculars. We always forget something. So yes of course, we went to ask the man what he was doing on top of Garn Boduan with an aerial. He seemed happy to explain again and told us that he was an amateur radio enthusiast and today he was in a contest which was to see who could have the longest distanced conversation. He said that he'd found the summit of Boduan to be a great place for his VHF radio reception and that he had managed to speak to people in Ireland and even as far as Germany. We wished him luck and joked about how he was likely to be asked many more times what he was doing by the end of the day, then set off back downhill.

On the way down we were startled by the sudden loud barking of two dogs who had run ahead of their owner. They were friendly as was the owner and the two young boys with him who all exchanged greetings with us in Welsh. We strolled slowly back and spent some time marveling at a kestrel hovering quite low, presumably watching its prey. But its prey must have been too quick, or it didn't like people watching it eat, as we didn't see it swoop down for the kill. As we reached the wide path leading to the gate, we heard woodpeckers calling in the trees but couldn't spot them – binoculars would have helped we agreed. As we were almost back at the parking area, the two young boys raced past us and said '**Helo**'. We laughed and I said in Welsh that they had been much quicker than us. They beamed.

We both tend to eat quite healthily, especially as we're getting older and we limit our sugar intake, but we decided that we could have a treat having done a hill walk today. So, after lunch at the caravan, I visited Pwllheli market to the 'Posh Puds' van. For as long as I remember, Pwllheli market has been held every Wednesday and Sunday, but sadly over time the number of stalls has diminished. My two favourite stalls currently are 'Posh Puds' (a company based on Ynys Môn) who specialise in frozen cheesecakes of every variety that you can think of and 'The Farmer and his Wife', who live at the foot of the hill Gyrn Goch and sell various farm products, including eggs and goat's milk soap. I bought a strawberry cheesecake for Jim and a mandarin one for myself. I was informed that the couple who run the 'Farmer and his Wife' stall had been unable to come today due to a puncture in the tyre of their van. I'd have to catch them next time. I also popped into Spar across the road from the market to pick up some of our favourite Welsh cakes that are made locally at Popty Prysur, the bakery at Canolfan y Gwystl, which is a centre for adults with a learning disability. Pwllheli Spar, like the others in Llŷn, are a great place to find locally produced goods. You can even pick your own fresh, live lobster if you like that kind of thing – we're vegetarian. A colleague of mine, stayed in Pwllheli with her children a couple of years ago and she knew how familiar I was with the area. She was overheard by other younger colleagues saying to me 'isn't that Spar in Pwllheli amazing?' They were instantly intrigued but then just as quickly rather disappointed when they realised, we were discussing a shop and not a spa. The cheesecakes were delicious by the way.

The summit

Walk 5

Garn Bentyrch, Llangybi
25th June 2022

A Miraculous Cornish Saint

There was a breezy start to the day and plenty of grey clouds. The forecast didn't look promising but suggested that the morning should at least stay dry. What a change in weather. Only a few days previously, we'd had a couple of days of hot sunshine and our garden was beginning to need a daily watering. We had originally planned to walk to the summit of Moel y Gest from Porthmadog as I wanted to attend an event in the town in the afternoon – the Proclamation Ceremony for Llŷn and Eifionydd National Eisteddfod 2023 – which was to be held on the park on the high street. I'll explain more later. We read in Des' book that Moel y Gest was quite a steep hill and we thought that if the winds got stronger, we may regret it, so we chose a smaller familiar hill. Garn Bentyrch is in clear view from our caravan and has been a favourite walk of ours since the boys were little. Both boys used to love messing around near water and trees and the route to the summit takes you past a historical well and a pleasant, wooded area – perfect.

Dramatic skies over Porthmadog and Moel y Gest

We parked the car on a wide grass verge immediately before the junction where a left turn takes you into the small village of Llangybi, and just past a public footpath sign leading to the beginning of our walk. From here the hill is visible but the summits are hidden by the woodland. We walked back to the sign for **Ffynnon Gybi** – St Cybi's Well, and ventured through the small gate, stopping to read a bilingual information board almost hidden by brambles. This informed us that St Cybi was a sixth century Cornish saint who had refused to become King of Cornwall and after travels to Rome and Jerusalem, had settled in Ynys Môn where he was said to have performed a miracle making water spring out from a rock. Even though it was thought that St Cybi may never have visited this area, its church and well were dedicated to him and pilgrims have been visiting since medieval times. Cornish has a lot of similarities to Welsh as does Breton and the now extinct Cumbric as they all evolved from the same group of Celtic languages known as Brythonic. At the time of the Roman invasion, Brythonic was spoken throughout southern Britain and as far north as parts of Scotland and under the impact of Rome it borrowed words from Latin such as *liber* (book) **llyfr** in Welsh.

St Cybi's church

I've rambled off the path already. We crossed the grassy area that descended towards a further kissing gate and then continued through the gate, following the path alongside some mature trees until we came upon a stone gateway. Through the gateway, the path followed the route of a stream. Two stray sheep stood bravely watching us and allowed us to approach quite closely before turning on their heels (or hooves). We could now see the large, ruined stone well, across the stream and the small field beyond. At the gateway to the well, was a sign warning of the toxic nature of the blue-green algae found in this 'lake water' and a further information board, giving examples of tales of the healing properties of the well. We laughed at the mention of warts having been cured as we remembered our eldest son Tom dipping his hand in the water as a young teen, to see if it would get rid of a wart he happened to have on one of his fingers. About a week later, his wart was still there, and another had joined it. Maybe it was the algae or his skepticism – both of our boys are scientific in their thinking and dismissive of most things unproven. We explored the large rectangular well and went inside the ruins of the attached cottage which the information board had explained was where people had stayed and rested between their 'curing' baths. We wondered about another smaller remains of a building a little downstream and I wondered if it had been the loo. Jim suggested maybe it had been the gift shop.

Through the kissing gate to the well

Behind the well is the gate leading to the path to the hill summit. As we opened the gate, we were reminded of how steep this part of the walk was and of a more gradual way of heading uphill, which was by bearing left and following the edge of a wire fence. So that's what we did until the fern lined path met up with the gate at the other end of the steep section or mountain goat trail as Jim called it. We were now at the start of my favourite section of the walk, which is lined with old, gnarled and stunted trees with their roots spreading across the path and interspersed with moss covered boulders. The path then opened out into a field dotted with more trees and larger mossy rocks. The trunk and branches of a large toppled dead tree had been cleverly converted into a shelter which we admired as we approached the stone wall which divided this field from the next. A sign indicated a space in the wall where we could scramble through, and we could now see the two summits of the hill. We had only ever ventured to the lower of the two summits, the one with the trig point, and according to Des the other summit is only six metres higher, on private land and is beyond a high and loose stone wall – not suitable for us.

Grazing sheep eyed us up curiously beyond the stone wall. Views of other distant hills began to appear towards the west, although many were disguised by the grey clouds which were quickly being blown south westerly towards us. Suddenly the heavens opened. We dashed back to the trees by the edge of the wall and snuggled up in the shelter of the largest one we could find, whilst watching the dark clouds and the rain gradually giving way to blue sky and sunshine. We set off again and with the clouds having blown eastwards could now easily make out Garn Fadryn and Garn Boduan and even the headland at Llanbedrog, Mynydd Tirycwmwd. Moel y Gest was now under a huge blanket of dark clouds, and we could see the heavy rain pouring down on Porthmadog. We had made the right decision about our walk, but we wondered what would happen with the procession that afternoon. We headed diagonally to the right of the field, where we could see a gate at that end of the wall through which we passed, then turned to take in the view. Pwllheli was now visible, and the harbour was glistening in the sunshine.

Another low dry-stone wall cut across the field further ahead and we passed through this gateway where the gate had broken off its hinges. We followed close to the wall to our right, which led us on the final stretch to the summit. My favourite range of hills, Yr Eifl, were finally in view behind the trig point as we worked our way through the ferns where the path was almost overgrown, passing some small iron age roundhouses. I have a terrible sense of direction but by using our monocular, Jim was quickly able to point out our small caravan site from the trig point. We didn't linger long at the summit as the wind was quite strong now.

Our descent was much quicker and when we got to the gate beyond the well, instead of tuning right to follow the stream again, we went straight ahead, remembering this route from a previous visit. This path soon took us to some large stone steps, then after crossing a small field, a few more stone steps and a metal gate brought us into the graveyard of St Cybi's church. This attractive old church was restored in the late 1800s but is said to have some medieval features. The door was locked but as we approached the lychgate or **porth mynwent**, we saw an upright stone with a long cross carved into it. When I Googled later, I discovered that it was thought to be early medieval, and the cross is described as an incised linear Latin cross with clubbing at each end. As we passed through the lychgate we saw an engraved stone set into the wall which read **Catrin Morg, oed 76 1729 Med 3** which means Catrin Morg, age 76 1729 Sept 3. This appears to be a fragment of a gravestone and I presume her surname was Morgan. I hoped to find out more about her and why the stone had been preserved there. We arrived back at the car just in time before the rain started again.

Almost at the summit

Eisteddfod Ramble 4 – 25th June 2022

An Important Proclamation

That afternoon, I headed to Porthmadog for the Proclamation Ceremony **Seremoni'r Cyhoeddi** for the 2023 Steddfod. This is one of the Gorsedd ceremonies held each year. I will mention and explain some others later in the book. The Proclamation ceremony must be held at least a year and a day before the start of the Steddfod. I had never witnessed this ceremony before so was quite excited about the event but also not sure what to expect. Throughout Wales, within a field or park, you will often see a circle of stones with a large flat stone in the centre. This is the Gorsedd Circle and **Maen Llog**, that is used as part of the ceremony. I had seen the one just outside of the centre of Porthmadog and so had expected that this was where the ceremony was to take place this day but discovered that instead some temporary ones had been erected in the park on the high street. After the pouring down rain, I could now understand perhaps why these replica stone circles are often now used, allowing more flexibility and avoiding boggy fields. The rain had eased off in Porthmadog by the time I got there, but whilst grabbing a quick cuppa in a café I overheard a lady saying something about the procession being cancelled.

I checked the Facebook page and saw an update, stating that due to the weather the ceremony was to take place in the high school Ysgol Eifionydd and that the procession through the streets had been cancelled. I dashed off to the school at the other side of Porthmadog and the car park was full of people waiting to go into the school being entertained by a colourful group of people in costume. Some were on stilts and looked like characters from the Mabinogi (ancient mythological Welsh tales) and there were ladies in traditional Welsh costume and singers and musicians brightening up the day. I felt sorry that they had not been able to process through the town as I imagine had been the plan. I enquired in the school if the public were allowed to see the ceremony but was told that due to lack of space it was unlikely unless you had a ticket. Ticket holders appeared to be organisers, those taking part in the ceremony or important local characters, like the local vicar who got in with a smile and a point at his dog collar. I felt disappointed but joined a queue of hopefuls close to the sympathetic steward, who was waving the qualifying people past us towards the school hall. About five minutes before the start of the ceremony, a lady further along the corridor, held up six fingers and shouted **'chwech'**. I was about number eight in the queue that had gradually dwindled to about ten and my heart sank, but as the lady approached, she waved us all in. Along the edge of the corridor were some of the Gorsedd members in their white robes and two men, each with a long trumpet – **corn gwlad** (translates as horn/trumpet of the country) – wearing gold trimmed red suits and fez like hats. At the end of the line was Myrddin ap Dafydd, 'my publisher' in his regal looking cream and gold robes. I knew that he would be central to the whole event as he is the Archdruid, but it still felt rather surreal seeing the man who had cycled to our caravan recently, in all his pomp and finery today. He gave a friendly smile and a Welsh **helo** which I returned in a hurried surprise as I was shepherded to my seat. I was happy to stand anywhere, but the remaining available seats were along the row immediately behind the rows of already seated members of the Gorsedd in their blue, green or white robes. I quickly sent Jim a text message saying 'I'm in'. His response was that he knew I would get in somehow and for me to enjoy.

A Oes Heddwch

People are nominated and granted membership of the Gorsedd according to the type of contribution they have made to **Cymru** and its language **Cymraeg**. Blue robes are worn by honorary members and denote a success in the field of law, science, sports, journalism and media. Green robes are worn by those who have made a contribution to Welsh arts, which could be a degree in literature, music, drama or art or by having won an Eisteddfod literary prize. The white robes are worn only by those who have won one of the main literary competitions at the Steddfod and those with a laurel garland on their headdress are **prifeirdd** (chief bards), plural of **prifardd**, and are previous winners of either the chair or the crown. The chair is a coveted award presented at the Steddfod and given to the poet, judged to have composed the best poem in a particular form called **cynghanedd**, which includes alliteration and rhyme. Cynghanedd is wonderful to listen to even if you don't understand all of the words and you will find Twm Morys reciting some on YouTube if you do a little search. As already mentioned, the crown is given to the poet judged to have written the best poem in free verse – **pryddest**. Ceremonies similar to this one take place at the Steddfod when the main literary prizes are awarded – **cadeirio** is the chairing ceremony, **coroni** is the presentation of the crown and a medal is presented to the winner of the prose competition. I was hoping to witness all of these ceremonies at the 2023 Steddfod and share my experience with you, if I was as lucky as I was today in getting to see them. I felt in awe of this large group of talented people. The only literary awards I have ever won, apart from my O and A Levels in English Literature, are my Blue Peter badge at the age of seven for my poem about snow and my 'writer' badge from brownies – for what I cannot remember. I can still recite the snow poem off by heart, but I will spare you from that. I had a quick chat in Welsh to the lady sitting next to me, Elen from Uwchmynydd, who was also pleased to have got in as her little granddaughter was a 'dancer with roses' in the ceremony.

The stage was set up ready with the Welsh flag as background and a harpist in blue robes played some gentle music as we waited. I suddenly recognised the harpist as being Gwenan Gibbard. As well as having seen and heard her recently on Porth Dinllaen beach as mentioned earlier, we had seen her only the night before this event

Proclamation Concert

as she had been one of the many performers in the Proclamation Concert **Cyngerdd Cyhoeddi** in Neuadd Dwyfor, Pwllheli, which had been staged as an introduction to today's ceremony and to help raise funds for the Steddfod next year. As well as Gwenan Gibbard and some fantastic choirs, one of the highlights for me was to see and hear Dafydd Iwan live for the first time. Dafydd Iwan, aged 78 at the time of this concert, is a singer and nationalist politician and famous especially for his song **'Yma o Hyd'** which means 'still here', and is a rousing patriotic song reminding people that despite all odds the Welsh people and their language remain. It is often sung by the crowds at football matches when Wales are playing and only a couple of weeks before this event, it had reached number one in the iTunes Charts. It had become even more popular than usual after Dafydd Iwan and Wales's beloved winger Gareth Bale had led the team and the supporters to sing it after the defeat of Ukraine, which had booked them a spot at the 2022 World Cup in Qatar. The song was sung at the end of the concert in Pwllheli just before the Welsh National Anthem and even though I only have a tiny amount of Welsh DNA, both songs made my spine tingle as I joined in with the rest of the audience. Now where was I? I've not only rambled away from the hills but I've now also rambled right out of the Proclamation Ceremony.

The procession that should have taken place through the streets of Porthmadog, instead had to be along the corridors then along the aisle between the seats in the school hall. Along came the procession which included the trumpeters, white robed Gorsedd members, the young female dancers in their green dresses

Colourful members of the parade

and floral headdresses, two young ladies in red and gold capes, one carrying a large drinking horn and another carrying a large floral arrangement, two young boys in capes adorned with a red dragon, most members in cream robes and wearing medals (who I later found out were Gorsedd officers including ex archdruids), a white robed man carrying a large sword (known as the keeper of the sword), then the Archdruid and finally some stick bearers in red and gold suits similar to the men with the trumpets. They all took their places on the stage.

I noticed some people had small programmes and I eyed them enviously, taking occasional sneaky peeks at the one that the lady on the other side of me was looking at to try and make more sense of the event. It could take pages to describe the whole ceremony, so I'll try and give my potted version seen through the eyes of a Welsh learner and visitor. Apologies for any bits I've missed out or misinterpreted.

First of all, the trumpeters sounded a fanfare to each of the four sides of the room, which represented the corners of Wales and this was followed by a short prayer sung by local tenor John Eifion. This was followed by a tradition that was familiar to me from seeing **eisteddfod** ceremonies on the TV but one that I'd never seen live before, that of a large sword being unsheathed and held above the bearers' heads while the Archdruid asks 'is there peace?' '**A Oes Heddwch?**' The audience all shout back '**Heddwch!**' – peace. This ritual has to occur three times until the sword can be returned to its sheath and the Archdruid announces the ceremony to be open. I felt excited that I had finally got to participate in this part of the ceremony and responded enthusiastically with the rest of the audience. I later found out that the current keeper of the sword is Robin McBryde, who has a long successful history as a player and coach in rugby union and was invested into the Gorsedd in 2006. Following another hymn, accompanied by a youth brass band, the Archdruid made his address **anerchiad**.

I felt that I managed to grasp most of what Myrddin ap Dafydd said, and my overall impression was that it was sincere but also included humour. He talked of the need to welcome refugees, including those fleeing from the Ukraine since the Russian invasion began in February, and of the importance of sustainable tourism and the support of local businesses for the benefit of the local economy. I began to realise that although from the outside this could appear to be a rather sober ceremony, full of pomp and finery, the participants do not take themselves too seriously and there was plenty of fun going on between the members that created amusement for the audience.

Following the reading of 'Eifionydd', a well-known local poem often learnt and recited by Welsh school children, this humour continued when Twm Morys a long-standing folk/rock singer, but also a master of Welsh cynghanedd and a prifardd, stood up in his white robes and laurel decorated headdress. He looked every part the rock singer as he played his guitar and sang a partly comical song about the areas of Llŷn and Eifionydd and of the village of Boduan especially where the Steddfod is to be held. This song, titled Cymru'n Un (Wales is one) was later to be included on Twm and Gwyneth Glyn's new album which was later launched at the Steddfod. Elen and I shared that we were both fans of Twm's music and Elen jokingly exclaimed that the stage was like a 'Who's Who of Cymru'. We were both loving every minute and I told her that I felt like a child in a sweet shop. I was a little puzzled by the next part of the ceremony, when a lady that I recognized as a singer from our recent gig on the beach, Anni Llŷn, presented a large horn **Corn**

Anni Llŷn and the Corn Hirlas.

Hirlas, also known as the horn of plenty, to the Archdruid, assisted by the two caped page boys. She was wearing a crimson robe and gold lace headdress and I read later that the horn represented the old drinking horn from the courts of the Princes of Wales in the Middle Ages and its presentation was a symbol of welcome **croeso** to the Gorsedd and to the Eisteddfod. The role of presenter of the Corn Hirlas has traditionally been given to a Welsh speaking local mother. As he was presented with the horn, Myrddin ap Dafydd responded with **'Iechyd Da'** which is the equivalent of an English 'cheers', much to the delight of the audience who roared with laughter.

If our Llŷn friend, Amanda hadn't already mentioned it, I would have been surprised at the next performer as it was her colleague and friend Glesni, who I had met briefly a couple of times and she sang a song about the Eisteddfod and Llŷn, that also included some humour, but also touched on the current concern of local young people struggling to buy a house in their home villages due to the increase in second home ownership in the area.

Following this, the booklet **Testunau Llŷn ac Eifionydd 2023**, which contains the list of competitions to be taking place at the Steddfod, was formally handed over to the Archdruid by Michael Strain (one of the stick bearers), the Chairman of the Work's Committee whose role is to organise fundraising for the Steddfod. Michael Strain is also a local solicitor and the Chairman of the local Welsh language newspaper, *Llanw Llŷn*. Following the ceremony, the Testunau were for sale, allowing anyone thinking of entering one of the competitions to see the details. I bought a copy as a souvenir. There are competitions aimed at learners, but at this time I thought I would feel too nervous to attempt or take part in any of these events and that I would much rather watch and admire.

Elen was now excited as it was almost time for her

granddaughter to appear with the other dancers. First of all, a teenage girl, Nansi Glyn Williams, assisted by two younger 'handmaids' presented the flower display known as the **Blodeuged** to the Archdruid, which was a symbol of the dedication of the young people in their commitment to the culture and language of Wales – a gift from the earth. Now it was time for the Flower and Fields Dance performed by a large group of young girls, including Elen's granddaughter. They were wearing garlands of flowers in their hair and carrying a wild flower posy. I had seen an advertisement for local girls or boys from year four or five to audition to join a 'squad' of around 30 who would have to rehearse the dance leading up to the proclamation ceremony then again leading up to the Steddfod. There were no boys present today. I quickly dug out a tissue from my bag for Elen who almost immediately became overwhelmed with pride and happy tears which were playing havoc with her mascara.

The ceremony was closed by a further hymn and an announcement by the Archdruid, followed of course by **Hen Wlad Fy Nhadau**, the Welsh national anthem, which gave me another chance to practise the words – I've almost mastered it. As I waited and watched the Gorsedd members processing out of the hall, I was wishing there was a way of getting hold of a copy of the programme as I wanted a chance to read it to fill in the gaps of my understanding of the event. I glanced on chair seats as the general public began to leave but everyone had taken their programme with them. I then noticed the area where the brass band had been playing, which had been made up mostly, if not all, of teenage boys. There, unsurprisingly, beneath their abandoned chairs were about five programmes left on the floor. I asked one of the ladies who was stacking chairs if I could take one and she replied '**cewch siŵr iawn**', which means of course you can. I left the ceremony buzzing with excitement and keen to tell Jim about my experience, which I can now tick off my bucket list. There had been a full house for this event and for the concert the night before, with only a handful of people wearing masks. It felt good to be able to be more relaxed and enjoy these events, but I hoped that we wouldn't regret this relaxation in the future. I was now hoping that I could witness the other Steddfod ceremonies but would now have to wait for August 2023 for that.

Eisteddfod Ramble 5 – 14th July 2022
A Poet and War Hero

In July, I took two weeks holiday from work and most of the first week was spent on an enjoyable mini-Wales road trip, through Powys, Carmarthenshire and Ceredigion with overnight stops in Airbnbs. Highlights for me had been Laugharne with all of its Dylan Thomas connections including his boathouse and writing shed, where I discovered after all these years that his fictional village of Llareggub made famous in his drama *Under Milkwood* spells 'bugger all' when read backwards. We visited the pretty coastal villages of Aberaeron, Llansteffan, Mwnt and Llangrannog as we headed back northwards to the caravan. We heard Welsh spoken more in Ceredigion than Carmarthenshire and I made the most of a few opportunities to converse in Welsh, mostly in cafés. As expected, I noticed the differences in accents and vocabulary from what we're used to hearing in Llŷn, especially the use of **nawr** rather than **rŵan**. I'm always amused by the use of these two different words, which both mean now. Read either one of them backwards to see why. As we drove through the villages of Ceredigion, we noticed a lot of colourful bunting, banners and posters, advertising the Steddfod, soon to be held in Tregaron. A lot of thought and creativity had gone into making these signs, which included life size collages of the Archdruid and Gorsedd members.

On our last day as we returned to the caravan, we stopped at a place with a special Eisteddfod connection, a few miles off the

Eisteddfod sign in Aberaeron

peninsula, but I feel it needs a mention. Yr Ysgwrn, is an old preserved farmhouse in a picturesque rural area, just outside the village of Trawsfynydd, It was home to a Welsh language poet Ellis Humphrey Evans, known more by his bardic name of Hedd Wyn, which means blessed peace. I cannot do justice to his sad, yet fascinating story here but will give a brief explanation, then highly recommend you visit Yr Ysgwrn and/or watch the Welsh language 1992 film (with subtitles if you like), entitled simply 'Hedd Wyn', to find out more. Hedd Wyn was posthumously awarded the bard's chair at the 1917 Steddfod. He had been killed on the first day of the Battle of Passchendaele during WW1, six weeks prior to the event, which was held in Birkenhead that year. The theme is set for the poems and on this occasion, the subject was **Yr Arwr** – The Hero. Eisteddfod chairs are full size and usually ornately carved in wood, with symbols pertaining to the Welsh language, and the culture of the area where the event is held.

As mentioned, anyone awarded the chair or the crown at the Steddfod is given the title Prifardd (chief bard). Hedd Wyn's nephew, Gerald Williams, had taken on the family farm, since 1954 and, being proud of his uncle's achievement, had kindly allowed visitors from all over the world to visit Yr Ysgwrn, where the chair was, and still is, housed. Gerald handed over the responsibility of the farm to Eryri Authority in 2012, who later funded a three-million-pound refurbishment. In 2017, Yr Ysgwrn reopened as a museum, commemorating the life and community of Hedd Wyn, and we made our first visit there that same year. Gerald continued to live in another house on the estate and was often seen by visitors until he passed away in 2021, aged 92. On this visit to Yr Ysgwrn, we were given an excellent guided tour, by a young university student called Glain, who was working there for the summer. Her passion for all aspects of Hedd Wyn and Yr Ysgwrn was admirable, and we were entranced by her stories of the man, his family and his community. She gave detailed explanations of the symbolism carved into **Y Gadair Ddu**, (the black chair), as it is known, due to the fact that a black cover was draped over it at the chairing ceremony, when it was announced that he was unable to come forward and sit in it as he had died at war, at the young age of 30. Hedd Wyn had won other chairs at local eisteddfodau and these were to be seen in the bedrooms. These days full size chairs do not

Yr Ysgwrn and Hedd Wyn

tend to be awarded at local eisteddfodau, but rather mini model versions. After the tour, Glain happily chatted in Welsh with me – she had done the tour in English so that Jim could understand – and I commented on her obvious passion for the place. She agreed and said that she hoped to return as much as possible to work in her holidays. I was surprised to hear that she was doing a degree in Law and not in Welsh Literature. We were left to explore other parts of the site on our own and watched a short film in the converted barn, which commemorated the many young men of Trawsfynydd, who had lost their lives in WWI, including Hedd Wyn.

Next to the café, an extension housed some interesting artifacts, including a book displaying a sample of each of the twenty-six layers of wallpaper discovered in the kitchen at Yr Ysgwrn during renovation.

Y Gadair Ddu

Our eyes were also drawn to an unusual modern oak bench, with engravings of stars and lines of poetry by Hedd Wyn on its seat. We both immediately recognised it as the work of Miriam Jones, a wood turner from Llŷn, who is known for her creative wooden inscribed bowls, and during the Covid-19 Lockdown for her rainbow tea-light holders, from which she donated profits to organisations supporting people during this difficult time. We have some of her work and keenly watched Miriam making this chair on the S4C programme **Y Stiwdio Grefftau** (the craft studio) in December 2020. Three craft people competed each week having been given a brief by a client, who then chose the best design to suit their requirements. Eryri gave the brief to Miriam and two other competitors, to make a star gazing bench. Miriam lazered mirrored plastic into the ends of the dowels which would make the bench glisten at night and wove plastic strips around the dowels to create a nest effect. Following the show, Miriam was pleased to be told that her bench would be placed at Yr Ysgwrn as it was felt to be more like a piece of artwork. The chair that was chosen to be placed in Eryri was also made by a Llŷn crafter, whose metal work can be seen around the area, including his ornate iron railings as you approach the beach at Nefyn. Chris Brady lives and works as a blacksmith and welder at Hen Siop y Crydd, near Tudweiliog, with his wife Amanda who works as a florist. I'd always presumed that **Crydd** meant blacksmith, so the name of their house being 'the old blacksmith's shop', but on checking the translation whilst writing this, I discover that it in fact means shoemaker. Chris's bench was a huge throne-like metal creation, decorated with constellations and with three built in reclining seats, enabling people to lay back and stargaze. We've yet to find it and try it out.

Miriam Jones's Bench

Walk 6

Foel Fawr and a glimpse of Foel Gron and Comin Mynytho, Mynytho village
16th July 2022
Putting the Fiddle in the Roof

A red warning sign for extreme heat had been issued for the first time in the UK, with two days of temperatures of up to 40 degrees Celsius forecasted to commence two days after this walk in some areas. Today started off cloudy, but we knew that the hot weather was gradually building up and we set off early as we often do, to avoid the hottest part of the day. We'd looked in Des' book for ideas of which hill to do and chose to head to Mynytho where there are three relatively small hills close to one another. We'd walked to the summit of **Foel Gron** and **Foel Fawr** with Tom and Simon about ten years previously but had never been on **Comin Mynytho**. Des warned us, in his humorous way, that unless we were 'hill baggers', Comin Mynytho was best avoided unless we wanted to trip and fall into waist high prickly gorse as the path was heavily overgrown. We decided to heed his warning and just admire this hilly **comin**, common, as we passed by.

We parked the car in the shade of a tree in Mynytho car park, close to the public loos – always welcomed by us both – from where you immediately get a good view of the sea and the two islands of St Tudwal. The beginning of the route up to Foel Gron was via a few steps at the back of the car park as we had recalled, and as Des had described, but it took us a while to find them as they were heavily overgrown with brambles and long grass.

Foel Gron

Foel Fawr behind the play park (above) 1966, with brothers Stephen and Ian in a Colwyn Bay Park (right)

Negotiating the steps was a bit tricky and we both suffered some scratches along the way, and then we could see that the route to the hill was also very overgrown and looked pretty much like Des had described the common, with prickly gorse and pink flowering heather hiding the path. We agreed to turn back and attempt Foel Gron from the other side.

Foel Gron primary school was silent as we passed by as it was a Saturday, but we pondered that it may also now have closed for the long summer holidays, a little earlier than usual, as many schools had done due to the heatwave. Foel Fawr, which means large hill, was visible ahead of us to the right and recognisable from the structure on its summit, the remains of a stone windmill. **Foel Felin Wynt** (windmill hill) and **Foel Tŵr** (tower hill) are other names often given to this hill by local Welsh speakers, and non-Welsh speakers often refer to it as Jam Pot Hill, which describes the shape of the remains. The mill makes this hill easy to spot and identify from miles around. My attention was caught by the play park across the road from the school and especially by an old fashioned red and white rocking horse, which could hold about six children. It brought back childhood memories for me as I remembered playing on similar ones in parks in other parts of North Wales whilst on holiday with my parents and two brothers. I was amazed to see one looking in such good condition but I

The windmill remains

suppose this one would have had a lot less use over the years, than the ones I remembered in the busy resorts of Colwyn Bay and Llanfairfechan in the 1960s. Due to my being distracted in my reverie (which happens often as you may have noticed), we missed the sign indicating a path leading to the shortest route to Foel Gron and continued along the road until we reached the second wooden sign with Foel Gron carved on the post.

Directly across the road from this was a similar post and a stile, which we remembered Des explaining was the way to get across the field to Foel Fawr. I noticed a blue sticker with an anchor on the signs that told us we were also on the **Llwybr Morwyr** (mariner's path), which I later discovered was a coast to coast 16 km linear route between Nefyn and Abersoch... mm maybe our next adventure. We turned left at the sign and followed the wide, even path which was lined with ferns, grass, blooming brambles and thistles. **Garn Fadryn** and **Carneddol** were the most prominent hills to our right. We continued until we reached the entry to a white house **Tŷ Uchaf,**

Jim shading inside the mill

batting away horseflies as we went. At this point we turned left between the stone wall and a large pampas grass plant. Keeping the wall to our left, we headed up the narrower, gradually inclining track. We greeted Comin Mynytho as we passed, and could see what Des had meant as there was no obvious pain free route to the rocky summit of this gorse and heather covered hill. The information board at the car park had said that the common had been a busy place in the past, when local residents had collected the heather and gorse. The heather was used for roofing material for the cottages or bundled together to make brooms. Residents with commoners' rights were allowed to graze their animals and gather firewood there. Maybe if a few goats were introduced to the common now, the paths to the summit would reappear. We worked our way to Foel Gron, which looked a perfectly even shaped hill with a pinkish tinge from the heather. We could see the steep winding path to the summit, and I hoped, as is sometimes the case, that it wasn't as steep as it looked from a distance. We took a detour along a path leading off to the right of our main path to take in the stunning views of the wide bay, **Porth Neigwl**, then returned again to continue.

    The clouds were clearing now, and we were beginning to feel hotter. As we reached the path to the summit, we were both hesitant as it was bone dry and its surface was made up of loose stones, which felt risky under foot for a couple of over 60s with dodgy knees. I felt I could have made it up, but would have probably had to scramble down on my bum and I didn't fancy spending the evening pulling out gorse needles. So, here's the explanation for the unusual title of this chapter – **rhoi'r ffidil yn y to** is a Welsh idiom which translates to 'put the fiddle in the roof', and is the equivalent of the English 'throwing the towel' in or giving up. And that's just what we did. So that was none out of three hills so far. I just hoped we could manage Foel Fawr now.

    We trod along the path that followed the base of the hill and we were soon back on the road opposite the park, at the previously missed sign. As we had continued to be plagued by horseflies, but amazingly only Jim had suffered one bite, we decided to continue along the road rather than cross the field which was full of grazing sheep. Do sheep attract horseflies? We weren't risking it. As you will have seen by now, we're not big risk takers. My attention was taken by a loud clack clacking sound and at the top of a small rowan tree was a beautiful orange breasted stonechat. Stonechats get their names in English and Welsh from their call, which sounds like two pebbles being banged together. The Welsh name is **clochdar y cerrig**, meaning stone cackle or cluck.

At the corner of the field, we turned right along another road, passing a large farmhouse, which was for sale. The sheep which surrounded an old, ruined farmhouse in the field, were making themselves heard. Maybe they didn't like the heat which was becoming quite intense. Swallows and martins swooped low across the fields, and dragonflies and butterflies skimmed us as they passed. Crickets or grasshoppers chirped in the long grass alongside the path. At the wooden kissing gate was a National Trust sign telling us we were approaching Foel Felin Wynt. Ferns and patches of low flowering gorse and heather lined the dry, wide path that gently took us to the summit and the windmill remains. We both instinctively stepped inside the windmill and gave relieved smiles at its coolness, guzzling water from our bottles and munching on our snack. We propped on our walking pole seats admiring the views through the two large doorways. Pwllheli was in a haze and Cricieth and the mountains of Meirionnydd were barely visible beyond. When we eventually stepped back into the heat, we were able to admire the southerly views of Abersoch and the Isles of St Tudwal, then immediately ahead, we looked down on Llanbedrog headland. We'd finally managed to reach the summit of a hill. We slowly made our way back to the car, and relaxed for a while in its coolness, feeling smug that we'd left it in the shade of the trees.

Gorse covered slopes of Comin Mynytho

Eisteddfod Ramble 6 – 19th July 2022
Fallen Oak Trees and a Special Chair

We agreed that it would be foolish to do a hill walk on what was probably going to be the two hottest days in the UK this year, so we found cooler things to do – in both senses of the word. A walk along the banks of the river Dwyfor on the first day, then an early morning swim in the sea in Cricieth, followed by a stroll along the tree lined lane **Lôn Goed** the following day were perfect ways to keep active but avoid the heat of the sun. So, what has all that got to do with an eisteddfod? I'm getting there. I did warn you it was a ramble.

As I was struggling to figure out the pay by phone machine at Cricieth sea front before our swim, a familiar voice gave a friendly greeting in Welsh. It was Gwyneth Glyn, the musician and poet mentioned earlier, taking her dog for an early morning walk. I still get star struck when I see my favourite performers in Llŷn and they seem to pop up quite regularly as it's such a small area. I tried to look calm and relaxed as we chatted in Welsh about the recent shanty evening, and I mentioned that Jim and I were looking forward to her gig with her recently formed all female band **Pedair** in Cricieth later this week. Pedair is the female form of the word four (pedwar is the male form) and the group consists of four Welsh female singers, three from north Wales – Gwyneth, Gwenan Gibbard and Meinir Gwilym – and one from mid-Wales – Siân James. They are all established and popular singers who first

A refreshing swim at Cricieth

Cooling off at river Dwyfor

performed together at the Ynys Môn Steddfod in 2017. They then got together digitally during the Covid – 19 pandemic and released **Cân y Clo** (lockdown song), which was about a longing for a better world after the dark days of the 2020 lockdown.

The song was a huge success and was one of the highlights of the AmGen Eisteddfod in 2020. Pedair continued to write and perform songs together and on the 8th July, released their first album, which meant that my first shop to visit as we arrived in Llŷn on this holiday, was Llên Llŷn in Pwllheli, to buy the C.D. Yes, I know CDs are old fashioned these days and I do download a lot of music, but I like the little booklets with lyrics, and I also like to support smaller bands or artists who get more for selling a CD than they do for an iTunes download. Gwyneth explained that Sian had been ill with covid, but they were hoping that she would be well enough to be at the gig or otherwise they would be **Tair** (three) and not Pedair.

Gwyneth continued on her way, and we had our wonderfully cool swim, under the watch of Cricieth castle. Following an obligatory ice cream from Cadwalader's, we popped to one of the local shops to buy a print that I had seen advertised on Facebook that was being sold to help raise funds towards next year's Steddfod. The large square print was of an illustrated map of Cricieth created by Ffion Meleri Gwyn, a local artist mentioned earlier who also created the map at Plas Carmel. The map, which is adorned with birds and sea-life had already been made available by Cricieth council to the public in the form of a free leaflet, but it looked even more stunning in print form and it was perfect for a space on our extension wall at home. We had already planned to continue on to Lôn Goed after our swim so it was rather a coincidence that we had seen Gwyneth Glyn earlier. Lôn Goed is a special place on the peninsula and in fact we can thank Gwyneth for our discovery of it. I was watching a TV programme on S4C about ten years ago and a video appeared of her singing a popular song of hers, called **Eifionydd**, whilst sitting on a wooden bench along a beautiful leafy lane. We later discovered from Llŷn friend Amanda that it was Lôn Goed, and she explained where it was situated. It has been a regular walk of ours ever since – especially on hot days like this one. Gwyneth co-wrote Eifionydd with Twm Morys, the poet and musician mentioned earlier who is now her partner in life and often in music. Various video versions are available of Gwyneth performing this song online and it features on her album Cainc, which is tricky to find on CD now, but is available to download on Bandcamp, where you will find some of her other earlier albums. Lôn Goed was immortalised by the poet R Williams Parry in his poem **Eifionydd**, which is often recited by school children on the peninsula. Parry won the chair at the 1910 Steddfod for his poem **Yr Haf** (the summer) and is also remembered for his **englyn** (four line verse) in cynghanedd form to lament the death of Hedd Wyn. It had already been announced that the chair to be presented at the 2023 Steddfod would be made from an oak tree from Lôn Goed, that had been blown down during Storm Darwin in 2014. On our walk, we saw what we discovered later was this very tree, already cut into pieces and ready to be transported and transformed. Lôn Goed was built initially to enable farmers to transport lime to their inland farms from the sea, and for quite a distance the sea is visible running parallel to the lane which on our walk gave us a much-appreciated sea breeze.

Lôn Goed, and the fallen tree to be used for the Eisteddfod Chair

Walk 7

Mynydd Tirycwmwd, Llanbedrog
21st July 2022
Prickles, Mini Beasts and Heroes

As we set off for our walk wearing light jackets, it was difficult to believe that only two days earlier, the UK had the hottest weather it had experienced since records began. We had coped well with the help of sea breezes, but we had been concerned about Tom and Simon. Tom luckily works in an office with a decent air conditioning system, but he sent us a picture of his car thermometer registering at 44 degrees Celsius as he set off for his home. Thankfully Simon wasn't in work on those days and managed to stay reasonably cool and kept our garden alive with regular watering. Today it was quite overcast with a lovely cool breeze. I'd suggested a Llanbedrog hill to Jim, as I'd read in the local Welsh language paper *Llanw Llŷn*, that the summer exhibition had just started at the art gallery, **Oriel** Plas Glyn y Weddw. We left the car at a handy parking space in the village on the road, Pentre Llan, and followed the road past St Pedrog's church until we came to the gateway for Plas Glyn y Weddw, the hall that houses the art gallery and sits at the edge of woodlands at the foot of the hill we were about to walk. Des speaks more of the history of this stunning gothic building in his book as did I in my previous book, as the initial part of this hill walk is along part of the Llŷn coastal path. It's well worth a visit. We noticed a bright blue and white temporary gazebo set up at the side of the hall, ready to receive children attending the many art workshops being offered during the school holidays. The gallery wasn't yet open for the day, but there was plenty of activity and noise in this usually peaceful

Oriel Plas Glyn y Weddw

place. Builders were working on the new café, the old conservatory one having been demolished recently. The plans and model on display in the gallery show the new one to be a silver dome shaped, rather space-age looking building and we could see it was beginning to take shape. We followed the tarmac path in front of the amphitheatre, where there were colourful posters advertising the plays that were to be performed there over the summer. These are almost always performed by an English travelling theatre group, in order to ensure non-Welsh speaking visitors are included over the school holidays. I was hoping that we may catch the Peter Pan one in August, but also hoped to see some Welsh language performances on offer later in the year. The initial climb takes you through the woodlands via stone steps, that gradually increase in steepness and from where you get glimpses of the sea and Llanbedrog beach below. We could also see the long row of brightly coloured beach huts, finally lined up on the sand after being redundant for the two previous summers because of Covid-19. We bore left at the wooden finger post, where there was an information board that told us that **Mynydd Tirycwmwd** is an excellent example of a coastal heathland and a site of Special Scientific Interest. It also explained that the cliffs are the remains of three disused granite quarries, that were worked for almost a century until 1950, producing setts for paving streets and chippings. Further steep steps took us to the cliff edge where we greeted a familiar guy that we have met many times over the years

New café under construction

Oriel Plas Glyn y Weddw

Jim at the toposcope with the islands of St Tudwal behind

with Tom and Simon. He is known as the iron man and is the third statue to be in position here, looking across at the stunning view of Llanbedrog bay, and beyond the fields and several hills including Foel Fawr and Garn Fadryn, which we had recently walked. He is larger than life and made of strips of iron, bolted and welded together and now rusting, and on a windy day he whistles but despite the breeze today he remained silent. Today, I noticed that someone had left a blue and yellow painted rock by his base, representing the Ukraine flag, a symbol of ongoing support.

This has usually been our turning back point apart from on a couple of occasions, including on our coastal walk, when we continued and circumnavigated the hill. We muttered together in disbelief that we had never diverted from the outer path and followed one of the many paths leading across the blooming heather and gorse to the summit. Some of the original paths were heavily overgrown and after our recent battles with gorse, we decided to look for a clearer route and continued along the dry stony coastal path, which continued to gradually incline. We saw an occasional bee and butterfly and heard an odd cricket or grasshopper, but we noticed and commented on how so far this summer, despite the warm weather, there had been a lack of mini beasts. The large stretches of heather looked pretty in varying shades, from an unusually pale pink to a deep mauve. Jim helped me to navigate across some large uneven rocks along the path after which we got a clearer view of the sea and the two St Tudwal's islands.

Soon after this point, we turned off onto a narrower path that gave us a short cut across the headland. This was initially overgrown and prickly which set Jim off grumbling and saying that we should have a machete with us or at least scythes on the base of our walking poles so we could cut through the prickles as we went. I tried not to laugh. As we reached the coastal path again, there was another immediate path leading to the summit, which thankfully was wider this time – my ears could take no more. This gently took us up to the summit and the gorse and heather lining the path gradually gave way to much softer ferns, with an occasional small mountain ash or holly tree. The trig point at the summit was soon in sight, along with a mound of stones that looked recently built, but first we headed to an attractive crescent shaped stone viewing platform with slate engraved diagrams identifying the hills, mountains and bays to be viewed, including Yr Wyddfa and the other mountains of **Eryri**, Pwllheli, Abersoch and the wide bay of Porth Neigwl. Des explained this structure was called a toposcope. Llŷn friend Amanda and I often share 'guess where we are' photos via Messenger and I sent one to her of our view from the toposcope and she replied saying that she knew the person who had made this structure – Gwilym Roberts of Pwllheli who was related to her by marriage.

A family of three were seated at the nearby bench having a drink from their flask. The breeze was strong and it felt quite chilly. I was envious of their hot drinks and joked about this with them as we walked the last few steps to the summit, drinking cold water from our bottles. We had a choice of two paths to return to the coastal path and chose the right one as Jim's navigational gadget showed it was the shortest. The path gradually merged with a narrow road with access to houses along it. We turned right and continued the steep downwards walk, passing houses for about half a mile, passing through a tunnel of trees and a campsite called Bolmynydd. We saw several wooden poles with Mynydd Tirycwmwd engraved along the length and arrows directing to other paths to the summit. The road took us back down into the

The iron man and the plas in the background

village, emerging at the side of St Pedrog's church hall. At the car, we changed out of our walking boots and retrod our steps back to the gallery, which was now open.

I enjoy the summer exhibition at the gallery, because rather than focusing on three or four artists' work, it displays the art of many local people, with a wide variety of styles to be admired or criticised. We recognised a painting by Esther Stubbs, the lady we'd spoken to recently at the art display in Sarn. This was a colourful and detailed painting of a local National Trust gardens at Plas yn Rhiw. There were a couple of local views by one of my favourite Llŷn artists Tess Urbanska, who uses collage to give her buildings and boats a raised effect and uses lovely shades of blue for the sea and the sky. We noticed a couple of pieces by Russ Chester, who had recently exhibited a large collection of his work here. We, like many others, had been blown away by his incredibly detailed paintings in the exhibition 'The Journey in my Heart' which he explained explored light, textures, mood and colours of the Welsh countryside of Gwynedd and Môn. This exhibition had now moved on to Oriel Môn, the art gallery in Llangefni, Ynys Môn.

As we headed up the grand Jacobean gallery staircase, we admired the colourful dramatic oil paintings of award-winning artist Meinir Mathias, displayed along the walls of the landing. Her exhibition was called **Arwriaeth** (heroism) and featured portraits and figurative paintings representing symbols from Welsh folklore and political protest. I especially liked one of Catrin Glyndŵr, the daughter of Owain Glyndŵr the 14th century hero and the last native-born Welshman to hold the title prince of Wales. In 1409, during Glyndŵr's fight for the freedom of Wales, Catrin was captured at Harlech and taken, along with her children and mother, as hostages, to the Tower of London. It is unknown how they died four years later, but their burial at St Swithin's was recorded in Exchequer documents. We completed our gallery visit with a **panad** – cuppa – of course, one of the upstairs art spaces being successfully used as the café for now until the new one was completed.

Eisteddfod Ramble 7 – 21st July 2022
A Cultural Evening Stroll

On the evening following our last hill walk, I joined a small group of other Welsh learners on a ramble led by the poet and musician Twm Morys (mentioned earlier) and arranged by **Hunaniaith** a Gwynedd language initiative, which aims to increase opportunities for people to use the Welsh language in all aspects of their lives. Since completing all the lessons on the *Say Something in Welsh*, course several years ago, I'm constantly on the lookout for opportunities of this kind to practise using the language as much as possible. In addition to this, I listen to Radio Cymru and Welsh podcasts as much as possible and watch TV programmes on S4C that grab my interest. One of my favourite podcasts is **Colli'r Plot** (losing the plot) because it's a discussion of books – Welsh and English ones – by four different authors Bethan Gwanas, Manon Steffan Ros, Siân Northey and Dafydd Llywelyn. I'm more familiar with Bethan and Manon, having read several of their books for learners and then later those for more fluent speakers. **Hunaniaeth** means identity, but Ifan, the organiser of the walk pointed out to me that there is a play on words for the name of the organisation as the letter 'e' is changed to an 'i' altering the last part of the name to **iaith** which means language. The walk began at the village hall in Pentrefelin and as I arrived, I was pleasantly surprised to see that Gwyneth Glyn was also joining the walk with her dog Nico. As well as Twm, Gwyneth and Ifan, there were three other learners, and two local first language speakers who contributed to Twm's vast knowledge of the area

Twm Morys at the grave of Dafydd y Garreg Wen

St Cynhaearn's church

Stained glass window with St David and harp

and its history. It was a most enjoyable and interesting evening with Twm telling us the stories of two local characters Dafydd y Garreg Wen and John Ystumllyn and taking us to see associated places. Dafydd was an 18th century harpist and composer, who I rambled on about in my previous book and he and John, who was often referred to as Jack Black were both buried in St Cynhaearn's churchyard in Pentrefelin. It was a cloudy yet bright evening, as we headed to the church and Moel y Gest, the hill between Porthmadog and Borth-y-gest, was lit up by the evening sunshine. Carys, the local lady asked if I'd ever walked up this hill and I explained that Jim and I were intending climbing it soon. She reassured me that it was an easy climb, if we did it from the Porthmadog side – I hoped she was right. Jim and I had visited this church, as part of our coastal walk, a couple of years ago, after hearing about its Dafydd y Garreg Wen connection from singer Cerys Matthews in an episode of an S4C series about folk music called **Y Goeden Faled** (the ballad tree). Soon after, we also saw Twm giving a similar talk for an S4C programme called Pethe. If you Google 'Twm Morys, Dafydd y Garreg Wen', you should still

Plas Ystumllyn

find the video online to hear the tale – worth a watch and good Welsh listening practice. The church had been left unlocked this evening, so we were able to take a peek, something Jim and I had been unable to do on our visit. Gwyneth pointed out to Twm the stained-glass window of St David who was holding a harp; Twm is also a skilled harpist. A harp is also engraved on the flat slate grave of Dafydd y Garreg Wen which Twm stood by as he gave his history. He then moved on to the simple upright grave, marking the burial spot of John Ystumllyn. John was thought to have been born in Africa about 1738 and eventually ended up in the West Indies, probably a victim of the slave trade. He was kidnapped and brought to Wales and to the Wynn family at their Ystumllyn estate in Pentrefelin, from where he was given his name. It was said that John had recounted his memories of the day that he was snatched as he was distracted trying to catch a moorhen and that he had screamed out for his mother. He was taught to speak Welsh and English and became a skilled gardener, but no one ever knew his real identity and name. He married a local maid Margaret Gruffydd and they had seven children, and died in 1786. Several people in the area claim to be descendants of John and in 2021, a yellow rose (representing friendship) was named after him. This is the first rose to be named after a person of colour in the UK and shortly there will be one growing in our tiny caravan garden. From the church, we ambled across a field to visit the Ystumllyn estate, where we had been given permission to view the outside of the hall where John had lived with the Wynn family.

So what has any of this got to do with eisteddfodau I hear you say. Well let me see... Really I just wanted an excuse to share this experience but there is a tentative connection. Twm Morys and Gwyneth Glyn, who I felt privileged, although rather nervous, to have been able to practise my Welsh with, are both winners of Eisteddfod awards. In 2003, Twm won the chair of the Steddfod in

Meifod, and became a prifardd for his poem in cynghanedd. Writing under his pseudonym Heilyn, he won with a poem linking the themes of doors, the past and future opportunities. He was presented with his prize by the previous year's chair winner at the Steddfod in St David's, Pembrokeshire... Myrddin ap Dafydd. Myrddin also won the chair in 1990 in the Steddfod held in Rhymney Valley. Myrddin was the first **Bardd Plant Cymru** (Welsh children's poet laureate) in 2000 to 2001 and Twm took this position in 2009 to 2010. I imagine the two of them are friends as they can regularly be seen locally at cisteddfodau competing in fun bardic contests, called Stomp alongside other local poets, hoping to win the vote of the crowd. I find understanding poetry in the Welsh language more challenging than songs, but love to listen to them as they always sound so musical to the ears. Myrddin and Gwyneth Glyn have published poetry books for children, that I find are easier for me to manage and recommend other learners who enjoy poetry to try them. Gwyneth Glyn was Bardd Plant Cymru for 2006 to 2007 and won the Crown at the 1998 **Eisteddfod Genedlaethol Urdd Gobaith Cymru** at the age of 18. More often known simply as the **Urdd, Urdd Gobaith Cymru**, is a national voluntary youth organisation with members aged eight to 25 years old. It celebrated its centenary in January 2022 and provides opportunities for young people to take part in a range of experiences through the medium of Welsh. Its mascot is Mistar Urdd, an egg-shaped character made up of the Welsh flag colours of white, red and green, who is often seen around on posters or models. The Eisteddfod Genedlaethol Urdd Gobaith Cymru, is the annual National Eisteddfod for young people, traditionally held in the May/June half term school holidays. It was first hosted in 1929 in Corwen, Denbighshire. Children and young adults can also compete in the Steddfod, so they get double the opportunities. Eisteddfodau are a large part of the lives of many Welsh people and create a lot of hard work and fun for the competitors from what I have seen and heard, but you do occasionally hear tales of pushy 'Eisteddfod Mams' (who could perhaps be seen as equivalents to pushy 'Football Dads') who will do anything to ensure their child gets onto the stage at the Eisteddfod.

Walk 8
Mynydd Nefyn and a wave to Carreglefain, Nefyn
22nd July 2022
A Back to Front Walk

For many years, Nefyn was our special area in Llŷn where we stayed with some lovely locals in their caravans or chalets and we treasure memories of long sunny days playing in the sea and on the beach with Tom and Simon. When the tide was in, we would often enjoy a hill walk and Mynydd Nefyn was an area we headed to on a couple of occasions. The woodland Coed Mynydd Nefyn, on its slopes is great for shelter on a hot sunny day and this was where we always thought of as the summit. We were surprised when we referred to maps and Des' book before heading off to this walk, that the summit was the disused quarry beyond the woodland. We considered continuing on to the summit of the other adjacent disused quarry Carreglefain as suggested by Des, but we decided to see how we felt when we got there.

We parked the car in the car park Parc y Ddôl on Stryd y Plas in Nefyn, from where the woodlands are visible. Turning left out of the car park onto the road, we then bore left onto the narrow and steep road Bryn Glas. We'd discussed taking the car to a parking space at the end of this road and starting from there as this was described by Des as a pleasant afternoon or evening stroll. But on checking Google earth, Jim saw that this was a narrow road with few passing places and these kinds of roads make him rather grumpy, so we

Watch out for frogs in Nefyn!

Heading towards Mynydd Nefyn woodlands

Quarry hills Gwylwyr and Carreglefain

opted to walk up to reduce the risk of my getting earache. Instead, I became grumpy, and Jim got the earache from me grumbling about my knees aching as the road was steeper than we'd anticipated. We were amused on the way up by an official road warning sign showing a frog, but none leapt out at us on the way. I looked back at the grey rooftops of Nefyn. I've always had a fondness for the town. Unlike the beach, it can't be described as picturesque, but I like how it hasn't been taken over by tourism and has retained its ordinariness. The village school remains open thank goodness, as so many are shutting on the peninsula due to the high proportion of housing now being second homes. Llanaelhaearn is the nearest village to where our caravan is sited, and its primary school has recently had to close as it had only 12 pupils attending. Children now have to travel six miles each way to attend a primary school in Chwilog. As we left the town behind us, we passed various cottages, and harebells were plentiful on the roadside, blowing gently in the breeze. Despite the greyness of the day, we gained a clear view of the bays of Nefyn and Morfa Nefyn as we looked back beyond the town.

We continued on the road for some time and ignored other public footpath signs as advised by Des, until we reached a rectangular convex viewing mirror on a pole on the right of the road, next to a farm gateway with a **preifat** / private sign. We turned left here onto another narrow road and plodded on, passing occasional houses and farms with fields lying next to the grassy and wooded slopes of Mynydd Nefyn. From a distance the woodlands looked to be mostly made up of pine trees, but there is

Smiley hay bales

also a small woodland on the slopes, cared for by the Woodlands Trust, called Short's Wood, where native trees such as sycamore, ash, oak and yew have been planted. We were greeted by a mass of smiley faces from one of the farmers' fields – hay bales wrapped in black had been decorated with white paint. We passed slate signs naming the various houses hidden off the main lane and it was great to see they all had Welsh names. The Welsh language society **Cymdeithas yr Iaith** launched a scheme in 2021 called **Diogelwn** (we will protect). The scheme encourages people to ask their solicitor to include a clause when selling their house to prevent the buyers and their successors from changing the name. This idea has now been extended to include names of land after **Banc Cornicyll** in Gorslas was renamed Hakuna Matata on an OS map. I'm proud of a solicitor friend of mine, Simon Chandler, who originates from London, but has learnt to speak Welsh fluently. He organises evening chat groups in Manchester for first language or advanced learners which he calls **Sgwrs a Pheint** (chat and a pint). He is a member of Cymdeithas yr Iaith and led the campaign for Diogelwn and created a set of legal covenants for property owners to use to prevent the change of house names. The Welsh language, history and culture needs to be protected not eroded in this way.

The lane became narrower, but thankfully also levelled off somewhat and my knees gave a cheer. Immediately ahead of us was the rocky summit of Carreglefain and to its left another quarry hill Gwylwyr, that we've walked across on our coastal path walk, and with Tom and Simon in the past. We arrived at the parking place where we could have taken the car and I couldn't resist reminding Jim of the fact. A wide kissing gate led out of the parking area and onto another path, with Carreglefain and the rocky outcrop at the end of Mynydd Nefyn looming closer.

We continued along the narrowing path which was lined with

tall ferns and a man and dog emerged from knee high gorse to our right along an almost hidden path that Des had described as an option to use at this point. We greeted one another and he headed back towards the parking area. We opted to continue ahead to see if we could avoid the gorse, we'd been prickled enough on these hill walks so far. The grassy path became steeper still and led up to the ruined quarry building next to the rocky outcrop. Jim climbed up into the ruins and explored the grey stone remains. Many of the distant hills and mountains were hidden by the mist, but Yr Eifl hill range and Carnguwch to the northeast of us looked beautiful despite the haze. Jim managed to locate the steep path leading up towards the summit opposite the ruin – the summit is still hidden at this point. We realised we were doing Des's route back to front and this was where he described returning down from the summit to continue to Carreglefain, from where we could now hear a lot of loud cawing from the rooks. By now we had decided that we wouldn't be continuing on to Carreglefain and that we would be satisfied with giving it a wave. I heard the sound of a stonechat and was quite pleased with myself that I had been able to identify it with its song but not so pleased that I had already forgotten its Welsh name – **clochdar y cerrig**. The final short trek to the summit was steep and rocky but there were plenty of foot holds and it was dry underfoot. It had been raining on the southern side of the peninsula so we'd been lucky this morning. A heap of stones came

Jim at the summit with Garn Boduan and Fadryn behind

into view, marking one of the lower summits of Mynydd Nefyn and we made it to the highest summit – a wider, flat rocky area with no trig point or marker.

It was time to prop on our poles, catch our breath and have a snack, continuing to admire the views. We could now see Garn Boduan and Garn Fadryn beyond Coed Mynydd Nefyn and the beautiful bays of Nefyn and Porthdinllaen were now more visible with the sun shining down on them. I was looking forward to a panad on the beach in Nefyn soon. We decided to work our way down through the gorse after all – a couple of bees were humming and collecting pollen from the bright yellow flowers. We headed towards the low, long stone wall, searching for our path which at times was barely definable. Without too many scratches and only a couple of horsefly bites, we emerged eventually onto a clearer path and turned right with the quarry hill Gwylwyr straight ahead of us. This eventually took us onto the path we'd come up on and we slowly made our way back into Nefyn.

Almost at the summit with Gwylwyr behind

Eisteddfod Ramble 8 – 23rd July 2022
A Hall of Fame

What a perfect end to our fortnight's holiday – a gig at Cricieth Memorial Hall. Tickets for the gig had been sold in aid of the 2023 Steddfod appeal and by the looks of the hall when we arrived on the Saturday evening, they were fully booked. The seats were set out cabaret style and we sat at a large table close to the stage and were soon joined by a family group of friendly local people. I chatted in Welsh to one of the ladies, who asked where we were from. Jim and I joked that we were possibly the only non-Welsh people in the building. Across the room at another table was Twm Morys with family members and he gave a wave. When I went to get drinks from the bar, he also came over and wanted to correct a detail from his talk on the learners' walk two evenings ago. He had said that John Ystumllyn was likely to have originated from Bali before arriving in the West Indies but he had meant to say Mali. I said not to worry as my geography wasn't the best. I cheated and said geography in English as the Welsh word is tricky and contains more vowels than should be allowed in a single word – **daearyddiaeth**. I said that I was looking forward to hearing Pedair and he confirmed that thankfully they were Pedair tonight and not Tair as Siân James was now well enough to join them. I said that I loved the sound of their voices together and got a bit tongue tied over the word **lleisiau**, which means voices and it came out more like **llysiau**, which means vegetables. Thankfully he saw the funny side and laughed with me about it. On the way back to my seat, I spotted Myrddin ap Dafydd with his family in the audience and he also gave a smile and a wave. The place was full of Welsh celebs.

    The lady who introduced Pedair, mentioned that the band was on the front cover of the weekly Welsh language magazine *Golwg* (view) and that they had been described as a supergroup, as the four members were all talented and successful singers and musicians in their own right. By the way, the producers of *Golwg*, also produce a bi-monthly magazine for learners, called **Lingo Newydd** (new language), which has graded articles aimed at learners at different levels and vocabulary lists to help. Well, Pedair proved *Golwg* right. They gave an amazing performance, which

Pedair

they divided into three sets and their blend of voices sounded beautiful, along with varying accompaniments. Gwyneth played guitar, harmonica and rhythm instruments, Meinir played guitar and drum, Gwenan played the harp and Sian keyboard and harp. In the first set, they sang songs from their newly released album, **Mae 'na Olau** which means there is light. Songs included ones about their feelings and experiences during the Covid-19 Lockdown as well as some adapted traditional folk songs. In the second set, they took turns to lead with one of their own songs, but also accompanied by the other three, then they returned to songs from their album for the third set.

They received a well-deserved standing ovation and thrilled the audience with an encore of the popular song **Calon Lân**, which means pure heart and is almost used like an anthem, sometimes even heard at football and rugby matches. It was hard to believe that Calon Lân was written in the 1890s as it sounded so modern when they sang it. Daniel James wrote the words, and the original music was written by John Hughes but it is often sung to different tunes. That night Pedair sang it to the tune of another old traditional song, that after much research (and eventually asking people on a Facebook page dedicated to Welsh music), I discovered was called Deio Bach. They invited the audience to join in and commented that there were plenty of other singers in the audience and Gwyneth Glyn pointed to some people on our table.

What a moving experience – the whole hall erupted into song, with not a note out of tune and I was left wondering who we had shared the table with that night. I love to sing as long as no-one else is listening as I have a terrible singing voice. I'm not being overly self-critical or modest – I've had it confirmed. When I started at the girls' grammar school at the age of 11, every pupil had to be auditioned for the choir. About four or five notes of my chosen hymn had escaped my mouth, when the kind but honest music teacher, told me with a shake of her head that I could leave. So yes, I joined in with Calon Lân but I mimed. Music and singing is definitely in the blood of the Welsh, and my four percent Welsh DNA perhaps contributes to my mediocre piano and low D whistle playing but doesn't quite stretch to my singing voice.

Eisteddfod Ramble 9
30th July to 4th August 2022
A Steddfod Part 1

The Steddfod 2022, was held in Tregaron between Saturday 30th July and Saturday 6th August. Due to work and family commitments, I was unable to attend, but I didn't feel too sad about this as I was anticipating the 2023 one on the peninsula and we were able to watch the highlights of the event on S4C at home and then from the caravan when we returned for a long weekend on the Thursday evening. The Steddfod is a huge event, so I'll just describe some of the highlights.

I feel I need to mention a matter of pronunciation at this point. Like most non-Welsh speakers, before I learnt to speak the language, I made up my own way of pronouncing most Welsh words, sometimes influenced by how I heard others saying them or just by guessing. Since I've learnt to speak Welsh, I've found that it's difficult to unlearn pronunciations of certain words that are engrained in my skull from my pre learning days. One of these is 'eisteddfod'. I would always pronounce the 'ei' part of the word to rhyme with the word 'pie', the 'dd' the same as a single 'd' in English and the 'f' as said in English. The Welsh 'ei' sound actually rhymes with 'say', the double 'd' in the middle of the word sounds like a soft 'th' as in 'the' and the f like an English 'v'. I'm improving but I can still find myself reverting back to the incorrect pronunciation on occasions. Be careful if Googling to hear correct pronunciations on audio or video clips as there are many incorrect ones out there. As mentioned earlier the YouTube videos of Marian Brosschot are to be recommended for their accuracy as is anything that Martyn Croydon shares on Facebook on his Dysgwyr Dwyfor page.

There are many ceremonies as part of the Steddfod, in order to present awards to the winners of the various competitions held there, including those in the field of literature, music, art, drama, dance and science and technology and of course learning of the Welsh language. Not all of these involve the Gorsedd. There are six Gorsedd ceremonies as part of a Steddfod. The first of these is the proclamation ceremony as I described earlier and the order and format of each Gorsedd ceremony is similar to this one, with the same characters involved including the Archdruid, the harpist, trumpeters, keeper of the sword, the ladies with the Corn Gwlad and the Blodeuged, page boys, hand maidens, flower dancers and current members of the Gorsedd who have applied to be in the audience. The Tregaron proclamation ceremony had taken place in June 2019 in Aberteifi, with everyone involved having no idea of course that the Steddfod wouldn't be happening the following year and that they would have to wait for just over three years. Myrddin ap Dafydd was welcomed as the new Archdruid at this ceremony.

The other five Gorsedd ceremonies are spread out throughout the Steddfod week and are held either in the large pavilion or in the outdoor space (weather permitting) on the **Maes** where a set of Gorsedd Stones (**Cerrig yr Orsedd**) are installed. The Maes is the name of the Steddfod site, and I'll explain more about what happens where, when describing the 2023 event.

I enjoyed watching clips on S4C of the various competitions and events as well as catching glimpses of some of my favourite Welsh performers, including Pedair, who were entertaining visitors in my favourite tent on the Maes, the **Tŷ Gwerin** (folk tent). This was then interspersed with the Gorsedd and other award giving ceremonies, once the judging had taken place and the winners announced.

The second and sixth of the Gorsedd Ceremonies are called the **Cyhoeddi Urddau'r Orsedd Eisteddfod** – announcement of the order of the Gorsedd. This is where new members are honoured and welcomed into the Gorsedd. Weather permitting these take place outdoors, allowing a procession of the current Gorsedd members across the Maes to the **cylch** – the stone circle, where the ceremony then takes place. Those who take part in the first of these ceremonies are people who have succeeded in the Gorsedd examination or are eligible because of their degree in literature, music, drama or art, as well as the winner of the Osborne Roberts Memorial prize and winners of the Urdd Crown and Chair. They are entitled to wear green robes. White robes are awarded to the winners of the Steddfod main prizes as mentioned earlier. I will explain about those who take part in the second **Urddau** ceremony later.

Thankfully the weather was fine on the Monday for this first Urddau ceremony. Watching it on the TV, gave a different perspective and allowed the audience to see things that wouldn't have been seen live on the Maes. This included behind the scenes interviews with the Archdruid and new members, and aerial views of the procession which looked impressive with a snake of green, white and blue Gorsedd members, led by the Archdruid and the colourfully dressed procession members, working their way to the cylch and then seated in their blocks of colour. As mentioned, the order of the ceremony seemed similar to the Porthmadog proclamation ceremony, but the ladies with the Corn Gwlad and the Blodeuged, the page boys, hand maidens and flower dancers were all selected from the Ceredigion area. New Gorsedd members included winners from the last live Steddfod in 2019 as well as those from the alternative (Amgen) eisteddfodau held in 2020 and 2021 because of covid 19. This included the **Dysgwr y Flwyddyn** – learner of the year – for these three years. In 2020, a reduced Steddfod took place virtually, and the Gorsedd competitions and ceremonies were postponed – a lot of the video content can still be found on YouTube. In 2021, the Gorsedd competitions took place, and the ceremonies were held in the BBC building in Cardiff, with masks, social distancing, a tiny audience, and no dancing or singing. This year, it was great to see Fiona Collins, who had won Dysgwr y Flwyddyn in 2019, as she is familiar to me from the online Welsh storytelling sessions that she organises monthly and that I attend when possible.

The crowning of the bard (**Coroni**) ceremony is always held on the Monday afternoon. The three Gorsedd award ceremonies, including the crowning, are held inside the Pavilion. The remit for this competition had been a collection of poems, not in cynghanedd, of less than 250 lines on the subject of **gwres** – heat or warmth. Again a similar ceremony took place and began with the Gorsedd members parading onto the stage and taking their seats, with the Archdruid leading the ceremony as usual. At this ceremony I was surprised to see representatives of **Gorseddau** (more than one Gorsedd) and other national festivals from Cornwall, Patagonia, Scotland, Ireland and Isle of Man. They were also welcomed onto the stage, with apologies being given from Brittany – I hadn't realised there were Gorseddau in so many other countries. A *nom de plume* (**ffugenw** in Welsh – **ffug** = false, **enw**=name) is used by each competitor to keep their identity a secret until the award ceremony. The Archdruid announced the ffugenw 'Samiwel' and requested the winner to stand. Searchlights shone across the audience, where the winner would be sitting somewhere, perhaps with friends and family. Even watching on the TV, I could feel the tension and excitement of the crowd. A lady stood and smiled modestly and was then helped on with a purple gown by three Gorsedd members, including the **Arwyddfardd** (Head Bard) who then escorted her to the stage. As she approached the stage, the audience all stood and clapped in time to marching music that sounded familiar to me, having heard my dad singing along to a record of it when I was a child. I knew it as Men of Harlech, but it was first published without words in 1794 as **Gorhoffedd Gwŷr Harlech** – March of the Men of Harlech. The lady looked emotional, and it was moving to watch as she was invited to sit on the 2022 Eisteddfod Chair, which was still to be awarded at the chairing ceremony later in the week.

The winner's real name was revealed – Esyllt Maelor, from Morfa Nefyn in Llŷn. The Archdruid gave some of her history, including that she had been the first woman to win the Urdd Eisteddfod chair in 1977 and that she had worked as a teacher in Edern and Botwnnog in Llŷn as well as being a writer. She had written several books and her volume of stories for learners was about to be published. The ceremony continued with the sword bearer unsheathing and sheathing the sword above Esyllt's head as the crowd responded loudly with 'Heddwch'. to the question of 'A oes heddwch?' as described earlier. Two young girls brought the crown on a cushion for the archdruid to place on her head announcing her the winner to the delight of the crowd. A short film was then shown on a screen with actress Rhian Blythe reciting one of the poems in Esyllt's winning collection. Then Esyllt was honoured and entertained by a poetry recital and a variety of performances of music, singing and dancing as seen at the previous ceremonies with the Corn Hirlas and Blodeuged being presented to her by the young ladies. The ceremony ended with the National Anthem of course and the Gorsedd processed out of the pavilion. Esyllt was then escorted across the Maes to the building where the S4C TV crew were, in order to be interviewed. The crown was large and tricky for her to balance as she was walking and being interviewed by reporters on the way. It seemed like a long walk, and I couldn't help wondering – what if she needs the loo.

She sat on the couch to be interviewed by TV presenter, Nia Roberts and still looked emotional. She was able to remove her crown and relax as she answered questions put to her. Her family – husband and grown-up son and daughter were interviewed and filmed outside on the Maes so she could see their proud reactions to her win. In a moving conversation, Esyllt shared with Nia that her winning poems included themes of loss as only a few years earlier she had lost her young adult son in a tragic road accident. She explained that the theme of warmth came into the poems as this was what she had felt from her son whilst writing them. The prize, the crown was an impressive looking piece of art and was a celebration of the culture of Ceredigion. It was made up of 12 stained glass facades including images representing the area such as Aberteifi castle, the river Teifi, the National Library and red kites. I could understand why the red kite featured as on our recent trip through Ceredigion, we had spotted many of them, and realised how common they were in the area.

On the Tuesday, I watched the awarding of the Daniel Owen Memorial Medal – Gwobr Goffa Daniel Owen. Daniel Owen was an 1800s Welsh novelist and regarded as the first significant novelist to write in Welsh and the foremost Welsh language novelist of the 19th century. Competitors were challenged to write a novel with a strong storyline of no less than 50,000 words. The ceremony was less formal than those with a Gorsedd presence, but the pavilion appeared just as full and the atmosphere as exciting. A large crowd of children created the backdrop on the stage. One of the three judges for this award was Manon Steffan Ros, who is one of my favourite Welsh language authors, having written books for fluent Welsh speakers and learners. She won the Prose Medal in 2018 for her book *Llyfr Glas Nebo*, which tells the emotional post-apocalyptic tale of a mother and her two children. Jim and I watched a powerful dramatised version of the story at the theatre Pontio, Bangor, ironically just before the first Covid 19 Lockdown in 2020. Manon is also a talented singer and one half of the duo **Blodau Gwylltion** (wild flowers). She introduced the ceremony and I was surprised at how much she shared of her opinions and those of the other two judges about the winning book *Capten* (Captain) by Polly Preston (ffugenw). She said that the strength of the characters and their relationship with their communities had reminded her of the style of Kate Roberts and that the novel was **'hyfryd, hyfryd, hyfryd'** – lovely, lovely, lovely.

The searchlights went out across the audience and Polly Preston was invited to stand up, whilst a small brass band played. Jim and I were both taken by surprise at the familiar looking smiling lady who stood up – Meinir Pierce Jones. We had always referred to her as the friendly lady in charge of the Maritime Museum in Nefyn, where we have been regular visitors for years. We had then recently read in the local paper that she had retired from the museum and that she was now working as an editor for the press **Gwasg y Bwthyn** in Caernarfon. I had also become aware of her having written some novels for children and adults and had intended having a go at reading one of them. Meinir was helped on with her purple robe, by officials and accompanied to the stage, again to handclapping and the same Men of Harlech tune. Whilst seated on the Eisteddfod chair, her true name was revealed and a mention that she, like the winner of the crown, was from Morfa Nefyn, Llŷn. The crowd, and we in the caravan, were delighted for her and for Llŷn. Megan Llŷn, from Pwllheli, who had won an award for recitation at the 2019 Steddfod, had aptly been chosen to read an excerpt from Meinir's book, accompanied by some video footage of sea scenes on the large screen. This was followed by a short film of Meinir herself, introducing the book and saying how pleased she was to have won this award. I was surprised as I had thought that the winners were unaware until it was announced on the stage. She explained that many of her ideas for the book, which is based on the lives of seafaring families living in and around Nefyn and Morfa Nefyn in the 1800s, had come from her time working in the museum. The medal was placed around Meinir's neck and she was presented with a hardback copy of her book, published by the press where she is employed. It was announced that the book was available from the Maes, immediately following the ceremony. A few months later, I contacted Meinir to ask her if winners of the main awards knew in advance and she explained that she found out a few months before the ceremony as time was needed for editing, proof reading and arranging the cover of the book. She thought that the winner of the chair and crown got to know a couple of months in advance also. She shared how exciting it was to receive the phone call letting her know she had won.

Meinir and the audience were then entertained by various singers and musicians including the large Ceredigion School choir, standing behind her, who ended the ceremony with a lively song. Meinir was also interviewed by Nia Roberts and the author Bethan Gwanas was seated with them in the studio. Bethan is familiar to Welsh learners who have used the Say Something in Welsh (SSIW) method, as her books for learners were often recommended in discussions in the forum, especially the Blodwen Jones trilogy, which are funny and were my first experience of reading a novel in Welsh. They have been compared to the Bridget Jones stories by Helen Fielding. Bethan has also written many novels for fluent speakers as well as some non-fiction books and has created some interesting and comical discussions for listening practice for advance learners on the SSIW course. At this interview, she asked Meinir if her book would make the reader cry as she liked a good cry. Meinir said that it may do. I knew then that a trip was needed to Llên Llŷn bookshop in Pwllheli as soon as possible.

Wednesday was the day for awarding of the Prose Medal – **Y Fedal Ryddiaith**, which involved another Gorsedd ceremony. The remit for this competition was a volume of creative prose to be written of no more than 40,000 words on the subject of **Dianc** – Escape. It was announced that the ffugenw of the winner was 'Mesen' and a young lady stood and was clapped to the Men of Harlech tune to the stage. When seated on the Eisteddfod chair, it was revealed that Mesen was 24 years old Sioned Erin Hughes, from Boduan. There were cries of delight and amusement from the audience and the Gorsedd members as Myrddin ap Dafydd, the Archdruid, explained for those not familiar with the area, that Boduan was not far at all from Morfa Nefyn in Llŷn. It was also the area planning to host the Llŷn and Eifionydd Steddfod in a year's time. The Archdruid explained that Sioned had won the Crown at the Urdd Eisteddfod in 2018, had come second in the Drama medal at this year's Urdd Eisteddfod and had recently written a children's book. The medal was placed around Sioned's neck and she was presented with a hardback copy of her book which was called *Rhyngom*, which means between us. People were reminded that the book would be available to buy immediately following the ceremony. I was glad that my pay cheque had recently gone in the bank. A film was shown on the screen, based on one of the short stories in the book and called '**I Fod yn Fam**', which means 'to be a mother'. It was an emotional watch about a midwife's attempt to start her own family, through IVF. The ceremony was similar to the other Gorsedd ceremonies already mentioned, with the Gorsedd members and their 'team' present and following similar procedures and performances, including the unsheathing of the sword and the presenting of the Corn Hirlas and flowers to Sioned. Instead of being entertained with the flower dance by the young female dancers, Sioned was presented with a mixed sex group of children who performed a lively clog dance.

Dysgwr y Flwyddyn (Learner of the Year) was the Wednesday afternoon ceremony and the quietest event I'd witnessed so far in the pavilion. Four judges were seated on the stage and a film was shown on the screen of the four finalists out of the 18 entrants. Each gave a short account of their experience of learning Welsh and what the language meant to them. The four were then invited to join the judges on the stage. One of the judges, Cyril Jones gave a speech, which included mention of the high standard of the entrants and of the admiration of the judges for how they had learnt and were using the language in their lives. He also suggested that at future Steddfodau, Wednesdays should be dedicated to learners of the language and be called 'Learners' Day', and free entry should be given on that day to all Welsh learners. The audience roared in agreement. The winner was revealed to be Joe Healy, who was from Wimbledon, but had settled in Cardiff after moving there to study at the university. He looked stunned, tearful but thrilled at the announcement. He was invited to sit in the Steddfod chair and gave a huge grin and thumbs up to his friends in the audience. He was presented with an attractive stained-glass trophy that looked like an ammonite and the three runners up won similar smaller trophies. All winners at the Steddfod also receive prizes of money donated by various organisations. On this occasion, the winner won £300 donated by the Masonic Province of West Wales. Joe was also reminded that he would now be welcomed into the Gorsedd. At his interview later, Joe joked with the previous year's winner of the award about having to choose a bardic name. A bardic name is different to a ffugenw, as it is known to others and a ffugenw has to be changed for each competition so that the person remains anonymous until the judging has taken place. As mentioned earlier, was the bardic name of Ellis Humphrey Evans and he was often known as that by friends and family but the ffugenw that was called out but not responded to on that tragic day at the 1917 Steddfod, was Fleur de Lys.

The following evening, we headed to the caravan for a long weekend stay, once I'd finished work. I was feeling even more ready than usual to be in Llŷn, after watching the Eisteddfod events on TV – I needed to get to that bookshop. I was also feeling ready to do some more hill walking.

Walk 9
Moel Tŷ-gwyn, Pistyll
5th August 2022
Almost a Hill Walk

Some friends had recently stayed in a cottage in Pistyll, not many miles from the caravan and we had enjoyed a meet up and a walk with them. When they arrived home they discovered they'd left their pressure cooker at the cottage. It was this incident that helped us decide on our next hill walk as we arranged to collect it for them and Moel Tŷ-gwyn is near to the cottage. I also wanted to see if there was a notice at St Beuno's church in Pistyll about the Lammas service, which I had heard was held at this beautiful old church on the first Sunday of August each year. Lammas is also known as Loaf Mass Day and is a festival to mark the blessing of the first fruits of harvest, with a loaf of bread brought to the church for this purpose. I'd remembered visiting the church a few years ago and seeing a lady preparing the floor of the church for Lammas, by laying down hay or straw.

Des had described a circular walk incorporating a climb to the summit but we decided to cut it shorter and just head to the summit from the parking area which is a layby on the B4417 close to the road leading down to Pistyll church. About 100 metres across the grass verge, heading towards Nefyn from the layby, we

View from the slopes

Excavations and the quarry hills

could see the public footpath sign and a few steps leading to a gate at the foot of the hill. We bore left as we walked up the field as Des had suggested, then diagonally right across another field dodging thistles – more prickles but I suppose it made a change from gorse. Dotted between the thistles, the flowers of which were mostly over by now, were some suspiciously fresh cow pats. We continued slowly up the gentle slope, with our eyes peeled. Higher up in the field we could see two bright yellow diggers, with no sign of any operators and we realised that a lot of excavation had already taken place, changing the look of the area since Des described it. We followed a newly levelled off wide dirt path and hoped to find how to continue to the summit. Carreglefain and Gwylwyr, the two quarry hills that we'd encountered on our previous walk were clearly visible ahead of us. Behind us we already had good views of Pistyll church, the cottages at 'Nature's Point' (shame it wasn't **Pwynt Natur**), where we were calling later, and a beautiful turquoise sea beyond. Unfortunately, the view towards the summit wasn't as pleasing – on the horizon we could make out the silhouette of a row of cows. We stopped in our tracks and although rather disappointed, we agreed to call it a day and head back. This idea was reinforced further by the sight of one of the cows beginning to make its way down towards us – we were soon back at the gate.

On the way to the cottages, I was pleased to see a notice about the Lammas service which was to be held in two days' time. We chatted to the owner of the cottages when we collected the pressure cooker, who said that he'd heard the farmer was improving access for his cows on the hill. He told us other ways of getting to the summit and seemed amused at our wariness of cows, but as the cows appeared to be on or close to the summit, we decided to tick Moel Tŷ-gwyn off our list.

Eisteddfod Ramble 10
5th to 6th August 2022
A Steddfod Part 2

Friday 5th August, saw the 2nd of the Urddau ceremonies. The word ceremony in Welsh is nice and easy by the way – it's **seremoni** and sounds similar. Again, this event was held outdoors in the cylch and included the same processing and order to the previous ceremony. People who were welcomed into the Gorsedd on this occasion were those who are described as honorary members and are seen to have made a significant contribution to Wales and/or the language and culture. They are all presented individually, to the archdruid, and are already wearing their new green or blue robes depending on their field of interest. The green robes signify contribution to the arts and the blue are worn by those who have succeeded in law, science, sports, journalism, media or local/national activities. Mark Drakeford, Wales's First Minister received blue robes. If you're interested in seeing any of these ceremonies, you are likely to still be able to find at least the highlights of some of them on YouTube but seeing them live will always be best, which at this stage I was hoping to do in 2023.

The final and what is often seen as the main ceremony at the Steddfod is the **Cadeirio** – the chairing. This is the awarding of the chair, which is presented for a poem in cynghanedd – known as an **awdl** – or a collection of these poems. The remit for this year's competition was that it should be of no more than 250 lines in total and on the subject of **Traeth** – beach. The T.V. cameramen zoomed in on the huge queues of people waiting to go into the pavilion via the various doors. It made me wonder if I had any chance of seeing the ceremony live at the Steddfod next year – I hoped so. Again, a similar procedure was followed, beginning with the Gorsedd processing into the huge pavilion. There were three judges for this competition and Twm Morys was one of them. Another judge, Idris Reynolds, gave a long introduction before announcing the winner. He explained to the audience that the closing date for this competition and the first Covid-19 lockdown had coincided, but it was decided not to extend the deadline. He had been concerned that this had been a mistake, but on looking at the fourteen entries, which was the largest number received for over thirty years, he realised he needn't have worried, as all fourteen deserved credit for their efforts. There have been years where the prize of the chair has been withheld due to a high enough standard not having been reached by the competitors, the 2013 Denbigh Steddfod being the most recent occurrence of this kind. This had been the first Steddfod I had ever attended, but at this time I was oblivious about ceremonies and chairs and spent the day browsing the myriad of stalls and listening to music in the various tents. Idris explained that they had selected five finalists for serious consideration but that the collection of poems that they judged to be the winning ones, had been written and submitted by the poet with the amusing ffugenw **Cnwt Gwirion** (stupid nut). He explained that the collection of thirteen poems told of the story of parents and their two-year-old son, spending the day on Llangrannog beach and described the usual seaside holiday activities such as buying ice-cream and building sandcastles but that it also brought in more serious and concerning subjects such as climate change and the decline of the Welsh language. The Archdruid announced the name formally, the searchlight went out across the audience and a pleased looking young man stood up to the trumpeting sound of the Corn Gwlad, and after being robed in purple was brought to the stage, accompanied by the crowd clapping to the Men of Harlech tune. Myrddin ap Dafydd, the Archdruid, announced that the real name of the winner was Llŷr Gwyn Lewis and then laughed as he added that although he was now living in Cardiff, he originated from Caernarfon which is also within the area where next years' Steddfod would be taking place – Llŷn and Eifionydd. As Llŷr sat in the chair, which he would later be taking home with him, a short film was shown for all to see, showing seaside views, with his voice in the background reading out some of his verses.

    The beautiful carved wooden chair had been shown in detail on S4C earlier and it had been explained that it was made with ancient bog wood local to the area and the curious lettering carved into the back below a large red kite, read 'Ceredigion' in **'Coelbren y beirdd'**, which is a script that was created in the late 18th century by the literary forger and founder of the Gorsedd, Edward Williams, better known as Iolo Morganwg. I spotted a symbol on

Zoom chat in Pwllheli

the chair that I had begun to notice on various eisteddfod related items. It is called the **Nod Cyfrin**, which means the Mystic Mark, and sometimes known as the Mark of the Ray of Light. The symbol was devised, yet again, by Iolo Morganwg and the three lines are said to represent Love, Justice and Truth.

The following day, the final day of the Steddfod and a Saturday, I headed into Pwllheli for two reasons. Unusually, throughout the weekend, we'd had poor Wi-Fi signals at the caravan but had noticed that this was much better in Pwllheli. That morning I was meant to be at the Manchester Welsh Learners' Chat group on Zoom (video conferencing platform). I found a discrete place on a bench overlooking the harbour, and conveniently close to Caffi Largo and I managed to log into the session on my iPad, much to the amusement of the group. Other members of the group had also been following the Steddfod on S4C and this took up much of our conversation that morning. My second reason for visiting Pwllheli of course was Llên Llŷn book shop, to buy the books *Capten* and *Rhyngom*. I also bought the **Cyfansoddiadau a Beirniadaethau 2022** (compositions and judgements 2022), which includes information about the winners of many of this year's competitions and gives surprisingly detailed accounts of the discussions between the judges before they came to make their final decisions. More importantly it also includes the poems of the winners of the crown and the chair. I'd initially been amazed at how quickly these books were printed and made available not only in the shops but on the Steddfod Maes but now realised that a lot of work had been

Detail on Hedd Wyn's chair showing the Nod Cyfrin

going on for weeks before the general public knew who the winners were. None of these books would be easy reading for me, but I wanted to give them a go. By the way, Caffi Largo has eisteddfod connections too. Largo was named after one of the characters in a poem by Cynan (bardic name of Albert Evans-Jones), who was born in Pwllheli. Cynan was hugely influential in the modernisation of the Steddfod and was the Archdruid twice. He won the crown three times at Steddfodau, the first in 1921 at Caernarfon for a poem which told of his World War I experiences. In 1924, he won the Chair at Pontypool and he also adjudicated at many other eisteddfodau.

On the Saturday evening, I did more Steddfod viewing in the caravan and watched an interview with Myrddin ap Dafydd, now looking like he did when he visited us wearing his shorts and T-shirt rather than his Archdruid robes. It was explained that he would be continuing as Archdruid until after the 2023 Steddfod, which of course was to be held in his '**milltir sgwâr**' (locality – literal meaning square mile). He joked that he'd had no influence at all on the outcome of the main competitions, which had all been won by people from Llŷn. He mentioned his own close connections with Ceredigion and how he had experienced nothing but warmth from the people there throughout the week. When asked what the highlight had been for him, he replied that one of them had been watching Pedair in the **Tŷ Gwerin** (folk tent) and how he had especially enjoyed the blend of their voices with three other Gaelic musicians who had joined them – Gwen Mairi (Scottish/Welsh) on the harp, Jenna Reid (Scottish) on the fiddle and Deirdre Hurley (Irish) on the flute. Until that point, I'd felt that watching the Steddfod on the TV had been a good second best to seeing it live, but I then realised I'd missed something special. Luckily, I managed to find a recording of the session on BBC

Sounds, so at least I got to listen to them... and they were excellent of course. Gwyneth Glyn, of Pedair, especially is used to collaborating with other singers and musicians from all over the world. Jim and I had been entranced a few years ago, by a live performance of hers with Seckou Keita, a singer, kora player and drummer from Senegal, that we attended at a folk venue in Bury, nearer to home. And the sound of her collaboration with Mumbai singer and musician Tauseef Akhtar, which was called Ghazalaw, is enchanting and can be heard on the album of the same name. Ghazal is the name for a popular type of Indian music and **alaw** means tune in Welsh.

There was a sad tinge to the Steddfod this year, due to the recent sudden death of popular singer and actor Dyfrig Evans at the age of 43. A touching tribute was shown in the midst of the highlights on S4C. I imagine he would have been a regular at on the Maes with his band Topper in previous years.

By that evening, I felt I'd been well and truly Steddfoded (made up English verb) this week. I now felt even more excited about the 2023 event and finally placed an order for one of the attractive T-shirts specially designed by Sioned Williams, which I'd heard were selling like hot cakes. Sioned works under the name of her company Dylunio Swi Designs and examples of her work can be seen around Llŷn, including the signs for the community pub in Nefyn, Yr Heliwr, which depict a fisherman and fisherwoman. Nefyn was farmed for centuries for its herrings, and Heliwr means hunter. Talking of Nefyn – that night I also made a slow start on reading *Capten*, which is based mostly around the Nefyn area.

Yr Heliwr Pub sign

Walk 10

Mynydd Carnguwch, near Llithfaen
7th August 2022
Wobbly and Weary on Booby Hill

I'd been looking forward to walking this hill as it has been a favourite of mine for many years. In fact, I used to say that Mynydd Carnguwch was my favourite hill and Yr Eifl were my favourite mountains. I then discovered that Yr Eifl was a hill range and not mountains at all, so I had a dilemma. We're fortunate to be able to see Carnguwch and Yr Eifl from our caravan, one of the deciding factors when choosing where to have it sited in 2017. We have walked up this hill a few times in the past and have some special memories associated with it and if asked by other visitors for suggestions of a hill to walk, we have often suggested Carnguwch as being an easy walk with fantastic views. When I later checked with our photographs, I could see that the four of us climbed the hill in 2010, and then again in 2011 but this time with our Llŷn friend Amanda, whose caravan we used to stay in on the family farm in Llannor. Carnguwch is the backdrop to their farm, but this was the first time she had walked to the summit. A special memory for me was in 2014, when Jim, Tom and myself crept out quietly before dawn and walked to the summit to watch a stunning sunrise, leaving Simon fast asleep in the caravan at Llannor – at 14, his sleep was more important than a spectacular view.

Carnguwch

We could see Carnguwch for most of our short car journey through Llanaelhaearn, its patches of heather glowing pink in the sunshine. On our previous walks to the summit, we've left the car in a parking area close to the foot of the hill, but this time Jim had been looking at maps and had found somewhere just over a mile away from that area that looked as if it would allow a pleasant flat walk before we started on the incline. This was a grass verge close to the sign for Llithfaen when approaching from Llanaelhaearn and today the sign had a large Welsh flag draped across it. It was a warm summer's morning, with a clear blue sky broken by a few fluffy white clouds. We strode out enthusiastically down the narrower road forking off left from the main B4417 road. Even at this stage, we had excellent views of many of the hills that we had already climbed this year – Garn Fadryn, Boduan, the now familiar flat summit of Mynydd Nefyn and the other stony quarry hills Carreglefain and Gwylwyr.

Blackberries were ripening on the brambles, that were tangled with blooming honeysuckle along the roadside, and an occasional clump of harebells took me by surprise. There were regular chirping sounds from crickets or grasshoppers and a few bees buzzed past us or stopped to get pollen from low yellow gorse flowers. There were more butterflies around today, but I commented to Jim that I still thought there were less bees and butterflies than you expect to see on a sunny day in August. Or maybe this is what happens to your memory as you get older, like remembering that every Christmas it snowed or every school holiday was sunny. We soon realised that the road wasn't as flat as Jim had expected it to be and we were beginning to feel the heat. I tried not to comment or grumble too much.

We were soon looking down on the small village of Llithfaen, a place I always think of as the Welshest village in Wales, with its community pub Tafarn y Fic, that regularly hosts gigs and rugby match viewings. The Tudwal islands and Llanbedrog headland all looked hazy in the distance. Thick clumps of heather in various shades of pink were dotted along the grass verge. We turned left when we reached a crossroads and continued along the narrow lane, passing gateways for an occasional house and as the road curved, we were finally facing Carnguwch. Jim commented at some cows behind a fence 'where they should be', in a field alongside the lane. It was almost silent but for the sound of swallows as they swooped down onto the slopes of the hill and a buzzard mewed as it hovered high above. We passed a sign saying '**Tai Uchaf**', which means 'upper houses'. One house is **tŷ** but more than one is **tai**. Plurals can be tricky in Welsh and although not in this case, are often a shorter word than the singular, so **aderyn** is bird but birds is **adar**. We came across two cattle grids and went through the adjoining gates to continue along the lane. Jim's navigational gadget identified the lake that appeared below to our right as Carnguwch lake, and it looked inviting as we were feeling quite hot now. The dry grass on the lower slope of the hill shone golden in the sunshine and a few shading sheep bleated as we passed.

We passed the house called Ty'n y Mynydd and carefully stepped across the nearby cattle grid as the gate was padlocked. We were at the parking area where we both by now agreed that we should have started from, and began to head up the hill across the grass. There were thistles again, but these were easily avoided as we headed steadily upwards, the summit now out of view. Sheep were lazily grazing as we passed, and we agreed to stop regularly for rests and drinks of water as the slope was much steeper than we had remembered, and our hearts were pounding. We heard a cockerel crowing and the loud noise of a cow or a bull, both sounded as if coming from the direction of our caravan and we could just about make out the position of the site. We stepped through clumps of flowering gorse and remembered from previous walks to keep the wall close to our left. The summit remained out of view, but we aimed for the visible ridge of the hill then stopped for a rest where we could then see the next one.

I began to feel a bit dizzy and sick. Jim wondered if it was heat stroke even though I was wearing a hat and had been drinking plenty of water. I thought it was more likely related to the medication I'd had to take that morning for my osteoporosis. I sat down in the midst of the long grass and tried to distract from the wooziness by looking at the view and eating one of our emergency nutrition bars that we always carry. When Jim was satisfied that I was fit to be left for a couple of minutes, he went to the top of the next ridge to see if he could tell how much further there was to go. The sugar was helping but I felt rather emotional as I reminisced about striding up this hill with ease with Tom and Simon in the past and wondered if I'd even make it to the summit today or in fact ever again. Jim reported back that you could see the summit from the ridge, and it wasn't too much further. He checked and double checked, as he does, that I was ok to continue and he helped me back up onto my feet.

Jim on top of the cairn

It was great to see the cairn at the summit which is made of hundreds of large loose stones and it didn't take us too long to reach it. The cairn gives the hill its distinctive shape and the reason why we have always called it booby hill. I saw the look of relief on Jim's face when I said that I wouldn't be climbing to the top of the cairn this time. I was satisfied with walking around it, while Jim clambered to the top and was rewarded with a spectacular view of the sea and the hills lying north of Carnguwch including Yr Eifl. When Jim came back down, we looked through the monocular and were able to see our caravan. We remembered on our walk here with Amanda 11 years ago, Jim had been able to locate the farmhouse where she lived with her family, by finding a distinctive

View from the summit

Inside of Pistyll Church

The leper window

solitary pine tree at the edge of one of their fields, but sadly this came down in a recent storm, so we were unsuccessful in spotting the house today.

We slowly made our way down the hill and the walk felt much easier than the incline, although we were both tired by the time we reached the car. We agreed that from now on we would reserve our energy for the hills, and we'd try and park the car as close as we could to the start of slopes. I joked that if I wrote about any future adventures, it would be *A Welsh Learner's Ramble on the Flat, Even Lanes of Llŷn*. But since then, I've had a better idea of *A Welsh Learner's Ramble into the Cafés of Llŷn*.

On returning to the caravan, I just had time to grab lunch before setting off for Pistyll to attend the Lammas service, which started at 3pm. I arrived early, which gave me time to look around the outside and inside of this beautiful building. This church is along the Pilgrim's Way and is said to be on the site where Beuno, the 7th century missionary, later made a saint, used to go for solace. The current church is said to date mostly from the 15th century with parts possibly from the 12th. A thatched roof was replaced by tiles in the early 20th century. I especially wanted to have a look at an interesting window. There is evidence of lepers visiting the church in the Middle Ages, looking for a cure and during communion they would receive the Host through a tiny window, now known as the leper's window. The first thing I noticed as I entered the building was the peaceful atmosphere created by delicious smell of herbs and hay strewn on the stone floor and the glowing candles adding to the sunlight which was beaming through the window behind the altar. I had a look at the window and was greeted by the minister and a lady who I recognised as being the one who'd been preparing the church for Lammas on a previous visit. She was also the bell ringer and the keyboard player. While waiting for the service to start, I chatted to a man on the pew in front of me who introduced himself as Dafydd and husband of the minister. He was surprised that I responded in Welsh, and we continued a short chat before the service started. A second minister arrived and gradually a small congregation gathered, including Lisbeth, a lady I knew from nearby Llanaelhaearn church. Following the short bilingual service, where delicious fresh bread was offered for communion, I chatted to people outside. I learnt that both ministers were Welsh learners and the male minister, who originated from Sheffield, had been having lessons with Martyn Croydon, mentioned earlier. I caught up with local and family news with Lisbeth as the last time I'd visited Llanaelhaearn church was pre-covid. She informed me that services had started up again and I said that I hoped to visit and see her again soon.

Pistyll church

Walk 11

Mynydd Anelog, Uwchmynydd and a Glimpse of Mynydd Ystum
20th August 2022
Confidence Renewed

We had decided on Mynydd Ystum for our next walk as it wasn't too far from Rhosirwaun where Felin Uchaf is situated and where there was to be an open day. I'll tell you more about this special place later. We parked along the grass verge along the B4413, between Rhosirwaun and Aberdaron and could see this small hill as we walked along the road to reach the opening for the farm track that led to it. After my difficulties last time, this seemed a good one to test out my current hill walking abilities. I was looking forward to spotting the remains of an ancient hillfort Castell Odo

Starting point at Uwchmynydd

as described by Des in his book and also a boulder which he explained is known as Carreg Samson. The legend says that this had been thrown from Uwchmynydd by a giant called Odo Gawr and that there is now a pot of gold beneath it. But sadly, we weren't to reach the pot of gold, as further up

Mynydd Ystum

View from Anelog summit

the lane there was a closed gate and just beyond that we spotted several fresh-looking large cow pats. Quick turnaround and back to the car for us.

Mynydd Anelog seemed the natural plan B, as it wasn't much further away, but it was higher and a longer walk. The outline of Mynydd Anelog is familiar to us, especially from our recent coastal path walk and from frequent visits to Aberdaron, but we had never ventured to the summit. We had Des' book in the car, so we followed his suggested route which began from the Calvinistic Chapel at Uwchmynydd, where we parked our car on the rough grassy parking area. It was built in 1904, which was at the height of the Welsh religious revival, but it now appeared to be a private residence. We exited the parking area and after about 10 metres along the road, we turned right up the narrower dead-end lane. We soon realised how windy it was as we headed uphill along the lane and my unruly hair became even more unruly. We soon arrived at a wide gate with a sign bearing the name of the cottage beyond, 'Talcen Foel', and a yellow arrow indicating we should head towards it. Views behind us quickly opened up with Mynydd Mawr, the Gwylan

Admiring Anelog from Plas Carmel

islands and the isle of Enlli. It was pleasant having a wide clear path to follow for a change, after all the dense heather we'd been fighting recently. As we passed through a second wide gate, we were able to see Mynydd Anelog ahead of us and we continued to white Talcen Foel cottage which appeared inhabited. The path turned right in front of the cottage and continued between a wire fence and a wide grassy mound. We heard the familiar cry of choughs and I was delighted to see several of them playing about in the wind with their wing feathers blowing like kites. We reached a small gate near some thick gorse bushes and the track became steeper as it continued beyond this. We approached another white cottage, but this looked deserted, with rusting corrugated outbuildings. The path took us above and behind this and we stopped again to admire the view behind us and the sun reflecting in the sea. The path now led steeply up the dry slope of Anelog, via a rough, uneven path which snaked its way through... yes more low prickly gorse bushes. The wind was whipping my hair into my face but it felt lovely and cool and made the walk feel more manageable than our recent Carnguwch one. We reached the summit more quickly than I'd expected and stood admiring the views whilst laughing and trying to keep our balance in the wind. I felt pleased with myself at having reached the summit and it was a boost to my confidence which had been knocked by the previous walk. The summit cairn made of loose stones, was much smaller than the pictures I'd seen of it but the views of the surrounding hills, farmland and the sea with her islands were spectacular.

Mynydd Anelog and colourful cottages

We looked down on a familiar stretch of coastal path near Braich Anelog, that we both remembered from our walk as being the most challenging for our knees and stamina, but with the reward of stunning views. We spotted a blob of red not too far away that we recognised as the café at Plas Carmel, and we agreed this would be a great spot for lunch before we continued to Felin Uchaf. A young couple joined us on the summit and the dad was carrying a baby in a backpack. He spoke in Welsh and commented on how windy it was '**Mae'n wyntog, tydy?**' I continued in Welsh with him, and I got the usual surprised but pleased response at being from near to Manchester yet speaking Welsh – '**Da iawn chdi**'. They explained they were staying in a nearby caravan park and were from Caernarfon. We empathized with carrying babies in backpacks on hill walks as we (well mostly Jim) had done this with both of our boys many years ago. I was asked to take a picture of the three of them on the summit and tried to get the baby to look towards the camera, so asked her name so I could call to her as I took it. She was called Gwen and as I called out, I was amused as I realised her name, with the addition of a little accent which stretches the 'e' would be **gwên** which means smile. They thanked us and we enviously admired their agility as they headed quickly downhill. After taking a rare selfie – we didn't think to ask them to return the favour – we followed slowly and noticed how dry much of the farmland looked. We took the narrow heather lined path down and around the northern slope, which then led to a wider grassy path heading southwards again. This was extremely dry, perfect for the ferns and gorse which were thriving there. The whole of the UK hadn't seen much rain for some time now and we'd had a recent second heat wave. The sea in Aberdaron Bay and surrounding the Gwylan islands was glowing in the bright sunshine, and we were more sheltered from the wind now. We approached the same deserted cottage from earlier and from this side we could see now how

Summit selfie

derelict it was. There were attractive metal bird sculptures on poles attached to the fence and gate and a large slate plaque, outside of the gate had a long message in English that appeared to have been made by the use of a drill, which recorded an event that had taken place there. 'Craft View Cottage was blessed to keep it safe by night and day by Pastor Peter Sayer and Charles Bramble of the Christian Adventist camp site, Coventry camp, the manager Les Simpson. The cottage was full with the camp playing guitars and singing songs. It brought the cottage back to life after being derelict for 30 years with storm damage'. I wondered how long ago this happened and was it this group that made the sculptures. All I could find when researching later was a small description of the cottage on the Coflein website. Coflein is the online database for the National Monuments Record of Wales (NMRW) and contains details of many thousands of archaeological sites, monuments, buildings and maritime sites in Wales. The name is derived from the Welsh **cof** (memory) and **lein** (line). The stone cottage was described by them as being post medieval and a 'small single storey cottage built on the margins, probable encroachment on common land'. **Bwlch Uchaf** was the name recorded on the map, which was presumably the original name of the cottage. We passed through a wooden gateway with the gate in pieces on the ground and along the path which led down the side of a further two semidetached single storey old stone cottages. As we passed by the front of them, we could see that one was white but were taken by surprise that the other which had a window missing, was painted a vivid pale blue with dark blue patches. Beyond the gateway were two fields joined by a kissing gate that we had to cross to reach a narrow-overgrown path beyond a second kissing gate. After a few minutes of fighting our way through prickly brambles, stinging nettles and high ferns and the sound of Jim grumbling and comparing it to a jungle, we finally emerged onto a lawn at the side of a house which was attached to the chapel where we had started.

    As we were changing our shoes at the car, I was surprised to see Martyn Croydon, who jumped from his car to take a photo of the chapel. I called out a good morning '**bore da Martyn**'. I had recently sent him a message on Facebook, asking could I join his learner's chat group to be held four days following this and as always, he'd said I'd be welcome. We joked that he looked informal today without a tie. He explained when I next saw him that his photo was something he was using for his students on his Facebook page about the pronunciation of Welsh placenames, as Uwchmynydd, which can be a bit tricky to learn, was written in large letters on the front of the chapel. Jim drove us to Plas Carmel so we could have lunch at the café Caffi Plas, as planned. We were surprised to see the young couple from the summit, who had just arrived on foot and we greeted them again. There was a lovely atmosphere inside the café. The sun was shining and we had a seat by the window so we could gaze back at Mynydd Anelog, and the background music was lively and cheerful – a mix of French and Welsh – as are the young couple running the place. After a delicious lunch including home baked sourdough bread, we headed back to Felin Uchaf. Felin Uchaf needs to be visited to be appreciated, but is a unique place on Llŷn, run by Dafydd Davies Hughes and his family. Dafydd is a carpenter and storyteller and has made many attractive carved oak gates and benches throughout Gwynedd but especially in Llŷn, including a small gate attached to our decking at the caravan. For many years, they have welcomed volunteers from around the world, who stay throughout the summer to learn traditional skills such as thatching, carpentry and boat building and help to build and develop the area, which includes an organic garden and thatched roundhouses. In the largest of the roundhouses, we had all regularly been captivated by Dafydd or a visiting storyteller during sessions held around the open fire during the warmer months.

    Since the 2020 main covid – 19 lockdown, things had become much quieter at Felin Uchaf, but volunteers were beginning to return and the storytelling sessions had finally recommenced. We hadn't yet managed to get to one of them, but were happy to be able to visit the open day, where a whole range of activities were on offer, such as spoon carving and weaving, nature walks and talks about the stars in the observatory. The café was still being developed and we'd been happy to make a contribution to the Crowdfunding campaign that was set up to help to support this. In return there is now a slate tile, carved with '**teulu** Brandwood' (Brandwood family) on the wall around the outside of the café building, amongst those of other contributors. We went to have a look at this before sampling some fresh coffee and home-made cakes in the 'pop up' café which was there today. We did not see Dafydd on this occasion, but I heard the gentle sound of harp music from the room above the café and wondered if it was the man himself practicing for the evening musical and storytelling event that we were sad not to be able to attend on this occasion.

Our slate at Felin Uchaf

Felin Uchaf

Eisteddfod Ramble 11
21st August 2022
A talented young musician and a whole village of talent

The day after our Anelog walk, I attended the church service at Llanaelhaearn church, where I met with Lisbeth again who I'd seen at the Lammas service. It was lovely to see the other familiar faces of this small but welcoming congregation again after so long, including Sian who plays the keyboard, Lynda who makes amazing cakes and Rose, who always supports me with my Welsh speaking. Rose is after all the mother-in-law of Aran the founder of Say Something in Welsh (SSIW), the course I have to thank for teaching me this wonderful language. Her daughter Catrin is the SSIW events manager and female voice of the northern lessons. It was announced at the service, that later on that evening there was to be a musical performance in the church by local teenager Lea Roberts, so that was my next gig sorted. It was lovely to see the church so full of people that evening, many being friends and family of Lea but I was also made to feel welcome amongst them. The audience was charmed by Lea's renditions of classical, popular and folk tunes on piano, saxophone and clarinet.

Lynda and I chatted in the interval about our taste in music and about how talented this young lady was already at the age of fourteen. I joked that like myself, Lea had begun piano lessons at the age of eight (I may have been seven), but she was a lot more advanced than me already. It was mentioned that Lea had won awards including some at recent Urdd Eisteddfodau and that she had been on the stage at the recent Steddfod in Tregaron competing for the **Rhuban Glas** (blue ribbon) – under 16s instrumental award.

Lea Roberts in Llanaelhaearn church

I asked Lynda about the colourful painted mural that had appeared in Llanaelhaearn recently, which was mostly made up of faces of people who had strong connections with the village and had made their mark in some way on the area or on Welsh culture. The mural had been created by SJW Graphics and Signs as part of the villagers' attempts to boost the village, which had sadly seen the closure of their primary school in 2020, after many years of fighting to keep it open. I had recognised some of the faces on the mural which is on the wall of the **Antur Aelhaearn** building, which I often stand close to whilst waiting for our pizzas from the van of our favourite local pizza makers, HM Catering or Helena and Mitch as we know them. **Antur** (meaning venture) **Aelhaearn** (the name of the saint of this parish) evolved in the 1970s, and was the first community co-operative in the UK, and this rather unassuming looking building has been the meeting place and workshop for various creative activities for many years. I asked Lynda about some of the faces on the mural that I was unsure of, and shortly after this a key was added to the mural, identifying all of the different characters. Lynda appeared to be one of the current driving forces behind the continuation of the Antur, who were currently working hard to develop a community shop and allotments. Founding members of the Antur are featured on the mural including Dr Carl Clowes who had been a rural GP in the village, Beti Hughes, William Arthur Evans and Emrys Williams, husband of Rose mentioned earlier. Carl Clowes, who sadly died in 2021 also led the trust that transformed the deserted quarry village of Nant Gwrtheyrn into a Welsh language centre. At the recent Steddfod in Tregaron, a session was held in the learners' area, **Maes D**, to acknowledge this contribution and included audio clips of Carl himself talking about some of the principal milestones.

There are some other eisteddfod connections on the mural including Robert Lambert Gapper who was a sculptor and artist, closely associated with the development of art and craft at the Steddfod, for which he designed the prestigious Gold Medal for Art. Musicians Dafydd Ieuan and Cian Ciaran, sons of Carl Clowes and his wife Dorothy and famous for being members of the band Super Furry Animals, who formed in 1993, also feature on the mural. They reached the UK charts and promoted the Welsh language through their music. Places and features of historical interest are also depicted, including something that was proudly pointed out to me by the minister on my first visit to the church. The Allortus Elmetiaco stone was found in a field close to the church in 1865 and is now displayed on the wall of the north transept within the church. It dates from the fifth or sixth century and bears an inscription in Roman 'here lies Allertus, the man from Elmet'. Elmet was a Brythonic kingdom at that time in west Yorkshire close to where Leeds is today. I wondered why a simple small touring caravan was depicted on the mural, but this caravan was the home of the first workshop for the Antur and was used for knitting clothes. It's well worth stopping to look at the mural to find out more about this seemingly unassuming little village, which is nestled at the foot of Tre'r Ceiri, the smallest of the range of hills Yr Eifl. There's also a delightful short YouTube film called 'Antur Aelhaearn 1978', which tells you more about the development of the Antur and the local characters who made it all happen.

Llanaelhaearn Mural

Walk 12

Moel Ednyfed, Criccieth
23rd August 2022
Cow Pats and Roses

We arose to a grey drizzly Tuesday morning, but decided to go ahead with a walk. Rain in Welsh is **glaw** and drizzle is **glaw mân**. We looked at Des' description for this hill on the outskirts of Criccieth and it sounded straightforward. The skies were brightening and the rain had eased as we parked up at our regular spot near the castle. I communicate regularly in Welsh with Llŷn friend Amanda, usually via Messenger, whether at home or at the caravan and she had asked what our plans had been for today. She reminded us to look out for the John Ystumllyn bench and roses as she'd heard about my recent walk and my interest in this character. She thought it was near the library somewhere, so we decided to look for it at the end of our walk. From the town centre, we crossed the High Street opposite the Prince of Wales pub, passing a pillar box decorated with a bright blue and white crocheted 'hat' decorated with birds and sunflowers. This one and at least two other postboxes around the town had been decorated in a similar way for several weeks now and demonstrated the talents of the members of a local creative group **Criccieth Creadigol**, whose artwork

John Ystumllyn roses, bench and info board

Moel Ednyfed

appears and delights locals and visitors on a regular basis. We strode out along Lôn Ednyfed, passing the side of the memorial hall, now proudly displaying its new slate plaque to commemorate its centenary. This was an unexplored part of Cricieth for us, despite having visited the town regularly. Jim and I chatted about this and how one of the interesting things about these hill walks and our previous coastal path walks was that they had taken us to parts of the peninsula that we hadn't come upon before, despite us feeling that by now we knew the area inside out. The lane passed Cricieth Family church, then turned right at St Catherine's church. We passed various large

Crocheted postbox hat and Cricieth Memorial Hall

Lôn Ednyfed and St Catherine's church

private residences and fields with sheep grazing peacefully and as the lane began a gradual incline the weather was beginning to feel muggy or **mwll** as they say here, and we threw off our coats. The lane levelled off as we reached a wide gate which led to a rough open area, which had been the golf club car park. As we passed through the gate, we noticed the old clubhouse which we heard later was due to be demolished soon. Cricieth Golf Club was formed in 1905 and one of its founding members was prime minister David Lloyd George, who lived in Cricieth and was said to have played there with locals and on at least one occasion, with Prime Ministers Winston Churchill and Andrew Bonar Law. The club closed in 2017. We followed the gravel path that led towards the slope of this small hill. There was plenty of evidence of sheep having trod the path which was fine as we feel happy amongst sheep, but oh no not again – fresh cow pats. We continued uncertainly and began to clamber up the slope and there on the other side of the slope, with no fence between us, were several brown cows staring back at us with their large cow eyes. Jim did an immediate about turn and headed downhill and I was sure he was expecting me to do the same. But as I thought the summit only appeared to be a few more strides away, I continued quickly and defiantly, with an occasional glance towards the cows who for now remained motionless. As I reached what I thought was the summit, I realised there was another slightly higher mound beyond a wall with a boulder. This was the true summit, but I would need to walk past the cows to get to this and there was now a cow by the wall looking at me rather menacingly. I satisfied myself with a quick look at the view of the castle, the town and the surrounding hills, all looking rather grey in the distance, then quickly followed Jim who by now was looking back at me with a scowl and a disbelieving look on his face. On the way back into the town, we got an excellent view of the hill Moel y Gest near Porthmadog, another hill waiting to be walked by us.

Soon after our return into the town, we found ourselves seated on a bench near the lifeboat station, eating a child sized portion of chips and peas from Castle Fish and Chips – we hadn't walked far enough to earn a full portion. This chip shop is popular with locals and visitors and considered by many to be one of the best on the peninsula. We have many memories of having a tasty chippy lunch with the boys and their friends in the café at the back, which has still not reopened since the Covid-19 lockdown. I noticed others were doing the same and I suddenly felt like a pensioner having my small portion on a bench watching the sea. I suppose I'm not so far off that and after all, Jim is now the proud owner of a pensioner's bus pass, being a few years older than me.

When the boys were younger, we were known to walk out of the chippy café and straight into Cadwalader's the famous ice-cream shop for dessert. We most definitely hadn't walked enough steps to do that today! An elderly lady walked towards us and said quite loudly 'we just missed it!' and I realised she meant the bench we were sitting on and that she was shouting back to a younger man who could have been her son. He looked embarrassed and tried to shush her but I moved up and invited her to sit next to me and said that we were almost finished and would be going shortly. The man stood at one side and explained that another family member was bringing their fish chips soon and the lady added that this was where they usually sat to eat theirs. I jokingly apologized for taking their usual place and she joked back and said she'd forgive us. She told us that they had a caravan further along the peninsula and that, like us, she and her family had been coming to this area and this chip shop for years. We said our goodbyes and went on our way towards the library. Along the high street, we passed the old attractive brick library building, which was built in the early 1900s and was funded by Scot-American entrepreneur Andrew Carnegie, who was said to have had a fondness for Wales, having come across Welsh Quaker immigrants in Pennsylvania where he lived and made his fortune. He funded 35 libraries across Wales and I'm ashamed to say, I have only recently discovered, since its threat of closure, that my own local library back home, is also a Carnegie library. I'm happy to say that this library that I have used since childhood, has been saved from closure, thanks to campaigns by locals.

Criccieth library is currently housed in the Encil y Coed centre – a white one storey building, plain in comparison to the original building and situated across the road from it. In front of the modern library building was a square rose garden filled with yellow John Ystumllyn roses in various stages of blooming. Looking over the garden was the brightly painted blue memorial bench, decorated with his name, yellow roses and images of old-fashioned gardening implements of the kind he may have used. A plaque close by gave some of John's history and recorded that he was known locally as Jac Blac. The attractive information board was designed by local artist Ffion Gwyn, who had designed the Criccieth and Plas Carmel maps and included a photograph of Zehra Zaidi and an image taken from a painting of John. Zehra is the founder of 'We Too Built Britain' which campaigns to raise awareness of underrepresented groups. She had approached Harkness Roses in the wake of the Black Lives Matter protest in the summer of 2020 and they had agreed to create the John Ystumllyn rose

One of Ffion Gwyn's town maps

in 2021. The friendship bench was designed and painted by students Sophie Williams and Elin Williams from Coleg Meirion Dwyfor.

Following this walk, I found a short film on Facebook, showing a ceremony held a week earlier at the pavilion at Cae Crwn, Cricieth's community garden, which has recently been developed with the help of grants from the National Lottery and the Welsh Government. This was an event to commemorate the life of John Ystumllyn. Five of the 25 roses donated to Cricieth had been planted in this garden – the other 20 being in the library garden. The gathering was welcomed by Councilor Sian Williams, Chairwoman of Cricieth Town Council. Twm Morys and Gwyneth Glyn sang a song they had composed about John and his rose and it included a verse from his gravestone. Lowri Ann Richards, who is now a local councillor entertained the small audience with a humorous Welsh rap written by chaired poet Aneirin Karadog, that also demonstrated cynghanedd. Lowri Ann is a trained actress and has appeared on the stage and on television and in the 1980s she was also in the pop business and claimed two top ten hits with the group Tight Fit. There was an address by Plaid Cymru M.P. Liz Saville Roberts, who had campaigned and raised awareness about John for several years. Zehra Zaidi also gave a speech as did the couple Peregrine and Caroline Armstrong Jones. Peregrine is the half-brother of Anthony Armstrong Jones who was the husband of the Queen's sister Princess Margaret. He had brought a painting of John that had belonged to his ancestors. He wasn't sure how it had come into his family but said that it was thought to have first belonged to Captain Thomas Jones a seafarer in Porthmadog and over time had been passed down to his descendants. Captain Thomas Jones is buried in the same graveyard as John at St Cynhaearn's church.

A few weeks following this we had a wander through Cricieth Nature Garden and then to Cae Crwn community garden to see the other five roses. Along the way we came across several of Ffion Gwyn's Cricieth town maps and other display boards designed by her showing the flora and fauna of the area. In total 5000 John Ystumllyn roses had been donated and delivered to communities across Britain including one to Buckingham Palace.

Walk 13

Garn Fôr, Yr Eifl, Llithfaen
25th August 2022
127 Steps

Today was our 31st wedding anniversary and we had thought that it would have been good to have climbed the highest of Llŷn's hills, Garn Ganol, situated in the middle of the range of hills called Yr Eifl, near Llithfaen, of which I'm fond. We don't make a big fuss about our anniversary and don't even buy cards anymore but instead dig out our first anniversary cards and display these. Instead of gifts we usually arrange to do something special and this year we had booked another steam train journey on the Ffestiniog Railway in a first-class luxury Pullman carriage between Caernarfon and Porthmadog for the day after. We hoped to have better luck than last October when it had rained throughout the whole trip. As the forecast was saying cloudy and wet once more for tomorrow, we cancelled our anniversary trip, not wanting to relive that experience. We rebooked it for the next available slot which ominously was October. We are lucky to have views of Yr Eifl, Yr Wyddfa and Mynydd Carnguwch from the caravan. This morning we could see that they were all in cloud apart from Garn Fôr, the 2nd highest of the three Yr Eifl hills and the one closest to the sea (**fôr** is a mutated form of the word **môr**, which means sea). Tre'r Ceiri is the smallest and I'm hoping you'll hear of that one soon too. Today's forecast said dry with clouds, so we headed out to the car park above Nant Gwrtheyrn Welsh Language Centre, hoping the

Dodging puddles with cloudy Garn Ganol in the background

Approching Garn Fôr

clouds may have shifted from the summit of Garn Ganol by the time we got there. As we collected our well stocked rucksacks and our walking poles, there was a cool breeze and the clouds were shifting but Garn Fôr was still the only one of the range that was cloud free, so we decided to play it safe and head for that one.

Garn Fôr was a working quarry in the past and it's often referred to as **Mynydd Gwaith** 'quarry mountain'. As we strode out of the car park, we passed three decorated granite pillars, which are a memorial to the quarrymen who worked in the three local quarries Chwarel Cae'r Nant, Porth y Nant and Chwarel Carreg y Llam. We cut across the grass towards the obvious tarmac path which leads to the foot of Garn Ganol and onward to Garn Fôr and reminisced about the last time we had walked here. This had been as part of our coastal path walk adventure last year when we had crossed the **bwlch** (passage) between these two hills to head towards the village of

Selfie from Garn Fôr with Trefor behind

Trefor. There are lots of interesting tales and legends associated with this area around Nant Gwrtheyrn, some of which I mentioned in my coastal path walk book and more information can also be discovered about these by visiting the museum, café and quarry worker's house at the Welsh Language Centre. It's also an excellent place to book in for Welsh lessons of course. The heathland on either side of the path was carpeted with blooming pink heather (at its best now in August), bright yellow gorse and low bilberry bushes with few remaining berries – the birds must have been feasting.

Slippery slab and rocks on Garn Fôr

As we sauntered up the gently sloping path with Garn Ganol facing us, the clouds were still sitting heavily on the summit. We dodged the large puddles along the way – we'd had a mix of sunshine and heavy rain so far this week. We were

Steps on Garn Fôr

surrounded by spectacular views with Garn Ganol now to our right, views of the quarry side and Nant Gwrtheyrn village to our left and westwards we could see some of the hills we had already climbed including Boduan, Fadryn and Mynydd Nefyn with the bays of Porth Dinllaen and our favourite Nefyn gradually appearing into view. There was a thin veil of cloud on the summit of Garn Fôr as we approached the hill which is easily identified with its tall mast and communication centre partway up its slopes. The path levelled off as we reached the start of the bwlch and we were able to see the rather 'mountainous' (as Des accurately describes them) looking hills at the other side – Gyrn Goch, Gyrn Du and Moel Penllechog. For this adventure we had decided to only climb hills to the west of Yr Eifl, which meant we would not be attempting these – **diolch byth** (thank goodness). Garn Ganol is higher than all three of the Yr Eifl hills, but we had read that they were much more challenging to climb, and we thought probably beyond the capabilities of our knees. As we turned left up the obvious grassy track towards Garn Fôr, with the high slope of Garn Ganol behind us, we noticed that the cloud had dispersed thankfully. We were surprised to have not spotted any of the feral goats often seen grazing around these parts. The ruined quarry buildings below the communication centre were clearly visible and we reached the long flight of concrete steps leading to the mast. Jim reached the top quite quickly and as I gripped the metal handrails to help me up, he announced that there were 127 steps. My knees were feeling it by the time I reached the mast, but I was greeted by great views of Trefor village and the sea. I'd remembered Des describing the next stretch of the hill which was mostly made up of rocks and a concrete slab that we would have to scramble across. He had written 'CARE' at this point in the book. We both looked at the slab that was damp from earlier rain and pondered if we should attempt it. We were feeling doubtful when a group of four people appeared behind us. They looked to be parents of a similar age to us with their two sporty looking adult daughters. They also wondered about this next part. The mother tried to dissuade them all from doing it, but the father continued with one of the daughters behind him. He then slipped and fell, thankfully unhurt, and that decided them both to return, much to the mother's relief. We decided we would not attempt it either. The family headed back down the steps but we decided to walk around the rocky part of the summit through some dense heather with a hint of a path where others had done the same. This gave us further views of Trefor's beaches, the pier and the sea. We both agreed we were satisfied to leave it there and made our slow return back down and to the car park. The sun was shining on our return, and we were entertained by choughs, some distant feral goats and lots of buzzing bees in the gorse.

 We drove down to Caffi Meinir at the language centre at Nant Gwrtheyrn for lunch and were greeted by a familiar smiling face.

It was our young friend Elain, daughter of Llŷn friends Amanda and Brian. Elain has worked at this café for years with regular intervals allowing her to jet off to enjoy adventures in foreign lands. She told us that it was her last ever week at the café as she was going to be starting work full time at a local vet's surgery whilst training to be a veterinary assistant. After a tasty lunch and saying our goodbyes, we went on to Pant Du vineyard near Pen y Groes to continue our anniversary celebration.

It was turning out to be a gloriously sunny day and Pant Du was busy with what sounded to be mostly locals, perhaps getting away from all the visitors who would be sunning themselves on the beaches. We were surprised to see Mitch and Helena from the pizza van and stopped for a little chat. Our celebratory treat wasn't wine as you would expect as neither of us like the stuff. Pant Du also has orchards, so we ordered delicious apple juice to go with our Lemon cheesecake and took a bottle of their cider back to the caravan to have with our tea. As we strolled back to the carpark above the vineyard, we could see Garn Fôr clearly in the distance, now with cloud settling on the summit.

Garn Fôr from the Pant Du Vineyard

Eisteddfod Ramble 12
8th to 12th September 2022
The Queen and the National Poet of Wales

We were back at the caravan for a long weekend, and we'd agreed that we'd be unlikely to do any hill walks as the forecast was mostly rain and I was still suffering with vertigo as well as stiff knees – not a good combination. On the Thursday evening, the 8th September, as we journeyed to the caravan, we'd heard that the Royal Family had been summoned to the Queen's side at Balmoral. We knew that meant she did not have long to live or that she may have already passed away. As we pulled away from Chester Services – one of our regular loo stops – we noticed the large news board now had a black and white image of the Queen with her years '1926 – 2022', so we realised the sad news must have been confirmed.

I'm not a staunch royalist but as for many people it still came as a bit of a shock as she had been there for all of my 61 years, and I felt for her family. Two days after the death of the Queen, it was reported that the now King Charles III had announced that his son William was to be prince of Wales. I was quite shocked as I knew that a lot of Welsh people hoped that this position would be abolished or at least discussed with the Welsh people. Since the days of the true Welsh Princes, the title has been held exclusively by Englishmen and many feel that this has continued to be a symbol of dominance over Wales and is an insult. The royal title was originally given to Edward II of Caernarfon, son of Edward 1 who conquered Wales. This was a way of confirming that the **Tywysog Cymru** (prince of Wales) title was subservient to that of the King of England. Plaid Cymru's leader Adam Price expressed unhappiness but said that the time to oppose would be after the period of national mourning. It was announced that the Queen's funeral was to be on 19th September 2022. So how can this be an eisteddfod ramble you say? I'm sure I can link it in somehow. Oh yes, the Queen was a member of the Gorsedd of the Bards. She was invested as an honorary ovate at the Steddfod in 1946. Ovate (or **ofydd** in Welsh) is the name sometimes used to define a member of what was seen as the lowest rank of the Gorsedd and the wearer of the green robes. But more recently the Gorsedd has come away from ideas of hierarchy and all members are seen as equals. In 2019, it was suggested that the Queen was now ineligible as it was made clear in 2006 that to be a member of the Gorsedd you had to be able to speak Welsh which the Queen did not.

On the Saturday of our long weekend, we had a gig booked for the evening at Galeri in Caernarfon and I wanted to attend the Caernarfon chat group for Welsh learners in the morning at Palas Print book shop. I had been on the mailing list for this group for quite a while now, but had never been able to attend. I had received a recent email from Bethan Glyn, the organiser explaining that this was the first face to face meet up for the group since the Covid-19 lockdown. Palas Print were also celebrating 20 years of having been opened and there were other events going on during the day including the launch of Meinir Pierce Jones's book *Capten*, which I was also keen to attend. So, Jim and I decided that we'd both spend the whole day in Caernarfon and that I would dip in and out of the Palas Print events but meet back with Jim for lunch.

I was greeted in the cosy area at the back of the shop by Ffion Ellis, who told me that she was a tutor and we chatted in Welsh as others began to arrive for the chat group. Bethan Glyn arrived and I realised that I recognised her from previous events that I'd been to and that she wasn't the owner of Palas Print book shop, as I had thought, but that she was also a Welsh tutor and the wife of Ifor ap Glyn, the current National Poet of Wales. Bethan greeted me and other learners and then in walked Ifor. I was surprised and a little star struck when he joined the group and then especially when I was included in a conversation with him and Bethan. I remembered having met them several years ago at the home of an acquaintance, who had organised a poetry recital charity evening where Ifor had been the poet for the evening. I mentioned this and they also recalled the event. I tried to remember the book of Ifor's that I'd purchased that evening and had to confess that it was still on my 'to be read' shelf, but that it would definitely be my next Welsh read. I have two of these shelves – one for Welsh books and one for books in English – and they're both beginning to sag in the middle. Whilst I was recounting the event, I'd used the phrase **'amser maith yn ôl'** to mean a long time ago, a phrase I had pondered about a few times as I'd also heard it used in children's books at the beginning of a tale in the same way that 'once upon a time' is used in English. I asked Ifor if it could be used in the context that I'd used it without sounding like the introduction to a fairy story and he reassured me that it could. I heard an entertaining tale from the shop manager, who I discovered was called Eirian and not Bethan as I had thought. She overheard me chatting to another member of the group about how it can be tricky sometimes deciding whether to use **ti** or **chi**, when talking to someone. As in French and some other languages, Welsh has two different words for you, ti being used usually with children or with people who you are familiar with and chi with people older or less familiar. Say Something in Welsh is an informal and friendly course and tends to use ti a lot more than chi, so I have a tendency to use ti quite often with people, then sometimes worry that I've been too familiar. Eirian told us a tale of a poet, who thought himself distinguished, being referred to as **ti** by one of his readers and how he had been annoyed by this and had corrected them and reminded them of his importance. The reader had retorted in Welsh 'if it's good enough for God, it's good enough for you'. This is because in the Welsh bible, God (**Duw**) is always referred to as **ti**.

Following the chat group, Jim and I had a light lunch at Caffi Tŷ Winsh, which is close to the harbour and will always be remembered by us as the café we visited to celebrate the end of our Llŷn coastal path walk. Pat, the owner, knew that my book about that adventure was to be published soon and we chatted to her about it and about her and her husband now selling the café so they could retire and have more time to do coastal path walks themselves. Pat asked me to bring her one of my books when it was released and I promised I would.

I returned to Palas Print for the book launch, which was being held in the garden at the back of the shop, with a canopy in case of rain but it was a fine, warm afternoon. I was greeted by Bethan again who kindly invited me to join her and some of her family seated in the audience, awaiting the arrival of the author. Bethan and I chatted about the book *Capten* and I said how I was enjoying it but also finding it difficult in parts and that sometimes I stopped to look up words in the dictionary but where possible I just tried to keep going as long as I was getting the gist. Bethan said that she felt that this was the best thing to do when reading in Welsh, so that it was an enjoyable experience and didn't become tedious. Meinir

Meinir Pierce Jones's book launch

arrived and greeted her friends as she headed to her seat at the front. I was touched that she remembered me and said **helo** as she passed. I knew her from our frequent visits with Tom and Simon to Nefyn maritime museum where she used to work. I was enthralled listening to her being interviewed in Welsh and I managed to understand most of what was being said. She was asked about how she felt when one of the three judges at the Steddfod had commented that she had used too much English in the book and whether now on hindsight she would change it. The audience, including me, cheered when she said that she wouldn't. The other two judges had agreed that the way the English had been used, highlighted the threat to the communities at the time as a result of the use of it, and that it in fact emphasised the importance and beauty of the Welsh language. On chatting to some other members of the audience at the end of this interesting session, I was disappointed when I realised that whilst having lunch with Jim, I'd missed a historical event at Palas Print. The session prior to the launch of *Capten*, had been a discussion and a handing over of the title National Poet of Wales from Ifor ap Glyn to Hanan Issa. But I consoled myself with the knowledge that I'd had the opportunity to practise my Welsh with the National Poet of Wales, only an hour before he relinquished his title, after serving in this position for six years. Ifor ap Glyn, who was born in London to a Welsh speaking family, also has Steddfod connections, having won the Crown in 1999 and 2013. He is also a television presenter and is familiar to many Welsh learners, having presented programmes and short videos with useful tips to aid learning. You can find quite a few of these if you search on YouTube.

In the afternoon, Jim and I had a wander around Caernarfon and were surprised to see a familiar smiling face on a young lady approaching us. It was Eve Goodman, who was to have been the supporting act for the band we had booked to see in Galeri that evening. We have frequently been to watch this talented singer songwriter and both of us love her clear, gentle voice. She offered a hug to us both and we had a brief chat in Welsh and English to include Jim. She told us that sadly, she was unable to be at the gig tonight due to illness in the family and we wished her and her family well and said that we hoped to see her again soon. We wandered across towards the harbour and to Cei Llechi, a redevelopment project which has included the transformation of the old Harbour Office and adjoining derelict buildings into workspaces for local artisan and craft manufacturers. It was turning out to be a beautiful sunny day, so we knew just where to head to help keep cool. We sampled the delicious ice cream from the recently opened Red Boat Ice Cream Parlour at Cei Llechi and devoured this whilst taking in the views of the harbour and the castle.

A table had been booked at the Villa Marina, Italian Restaurant and we enjoyed a delicious meal there before heading off to the gig at Galeri. The band we were to see was Tapestri made up of two singer songwriters, Sarah Zyborksa (or Sera as she is often known) from north Wales and Lowri Evans from Pembrokeshire. We had seen both perform individually before, Lowri Evans especially, who we had even commissioned to write and record a song for us when she was offering this service a few years previously. This gig was part of their much anticipated first UK tour and was accompanied by the release of an E.P. with their intention of following up shortly with an album. We had originally booked to see them at Galeri in February 2020, but Storm Ciara hit Caernarfon hard and damaged the roof of the building, then of course Covid – 19 arrived... We got a prime seat at one of the tables near to the stage and I was surprised at how small the audience was – people didn't know what they were missing. The gig began with Alis Glyn , who had stepped in for Eve Goodman. She is a teenage singer songwriter from Caernarfon, who we hadn't heard of before, but we were both impressed with her confidence and her clear, bold voice as she sang and accompanied herself on the keyboard. We're expecting to hear a lot more of her in the future. Tapestri followed, with Lowri on guitar and Sarah on keyboard both singing in English and in Welsh, as they also do when performing individually. They were accompanied as always by Lee Mason on guitar, Lowri's partner in life and music, and another guitarist on bass. They describe their genres as Roots and Americana and the blend of their voices together is a joy to the ears. We stopped to say hi to them on our way out as they were selling their E.P.s near the exit, and Lowri jokingly greeted us as her 'superfans'.

Alis Glyn performing at Galeri

The following day was mostly grey and wet, but I managed to buy some plants, including a John Ystumllyn rosebush from nearby Tyddyn Sachau nursery, and planted these in our tiny caravan garden just before the rain came lashing down.

Tapestri performing at Galeri (above)

Jean, the super fan looking a little over excited (right)

Interlude September to November 2022

Mostly due to health issues and the weather, we were unable to attempt any hill walks between September and the middle of November, but still managed to get to the caravan for short breaks and to Dublin for a mini break.

We still managed to do the following:

Alys Williams gig at Yr Heliwr, Nefyn

Another gig at Yr Heliwr with Geraint Lovgreen a'r Enw Da

An evening of entertainment in Dylan's Cricieth, with Gwyneth Glyn and Twm Morys

Posing with my first book on sale in my favourite Welsh book shop Llên Llŷn in Pwllheli

Admiring signs in Pwllheli promoting fundraising for the 2023 Steddfod

Eisteddfod fundraising promotion poster in Pwllheli

Admiring the giant Welsh bucket hat on the square in Caernarfon

(left) Discovering a disused Welsh Chapel on Talbot Street in Dublin

Stargazing with Tom and Simon from the caravan decking. Tom took the images of Saturn and Jupiter through his telescope

145

Walk 14
Mynydd y Gwyddel, Uwchmynydd and a wave to Mynydd Mawr
13th November 2022
The Hills at the End of the World

One mild and sunny day in the middle of November, we were feeling ready for a short excursion so we drove down to a favourite café in Uwchmynydd, at Tŷ Newydd campsite, for a cuppa. This is about a forty-minute drive from our caravan and one of my favourite routes on the peninsula, following the B4417 through Morfa Nefyn, Tudweiliog and Penllech, with frequent peeks of the sea across stretches of flat farmland. As we arrived at the café, we smiled at the large sign at the front of the café, facing the road, which reads **'Pen Draw'r Byd'**, which means the end of the world. Uwchmynydd is often referred to as the Lands' End of north Wales and can rightly be known as Pen Llŷn. Pen Llŷn is often the name used for the whole of the peninsula by locals and visitors alike, but I have it on good authority that as it means the head of Llŷn, it really only refers to this most westerly point. We were greeted warmly by Marian the owner and I presented her with a copy of my book about our coastal path walk and told her that I'd included a

Mynydd y Gwyddel

Enlli from Mynydd y Gwyddel

tale in the book that was as familiar to her as to us. Just over two years ago, when we were over halfway along completing the whole of the Llŷn coastal path walk without having suffered any injuries, I lost my footing in Tŷ Newydd café outdoor seating area whilst trying to catch a fly away serviette. I injured my ankle and passed out and Marian had called for an ambulance. She and her daughter had been very kind and attentive until it arrived, something I'll always remember and be grateful for. Marian joked and said I should sit down carefully and they would bring our drinks and scones to us. The café was looking great after having been extended and modernized and Marian said that they were trialing staying open over the colder months and that so far, they were still having a steady flow of visitors. She chatted proudly about her ten grandchildren and some holidays they'd had together as a family. Marian was more than happy for us to leave our car in the car park while we had a little walk, which was needed after her generous sized scones with jam and cream.

From the car park and camping area at Tŷ Newydd Café, you are able to see the sea and a tantalizing hint of the island Ynys Enlli peeping out from behind the small hill Mynydd y Gwyddel. Some people describe Ynys Enlli as looking like a turtle floating on its belly. Using this description, from the café you can see its fat bum but not its slim neck and head. Strolling along the road towards

Ty Newydd Campsite and Café, Uwchmynydd

the hill, that we recalled having walked past on our coastal path walk, we very soon were able to see Ynys Enlli in its entirety. We saw the inviting wide grassy path leading to the summit and agreed, that even our stiff old knees could manage this short gentle incline. The walk was very easy and worthwhile. There was Enlli looking glorious, with the pale low sun creating a shining pool of light around it in the **Swnt**. Swnt means sound and is the name given to the stretch of strong tidal waters between Aberdaron and Enlli. From Mynydd y Gwyddel we could see Mynydd Mawr and the old coastguard lookout buildings on its summit, where we have visited often by car to get the stunning view of Enlli, and once on foot as part of our coastal path walk, just before I injured my foot at the café. Gwyddel now means Irishman, but in old Welsh it is said to have meant pirate and this part of Wales, as with much of the western coast of Britain, was said to have been visited frequently by Irish pirates.

Four days after this walk, we were pleased to hear that the Snowdonia National Park Committee members voted to use the Welsh names of Eryri (Snowdonia) and Yr Wyddfa (Snowdon), in both Welsh and English context. Yr Wyddfa is the highest mountain in Wales and attracts thousands of visitors from all over the world each year. It was hoped that this change would continue to help share the Welsh language and culture with them.

Eisteddfod Ramble 13
December 2022 and January 2023
Welsh Goings on in Manchester

Winter was now upon us; the weather was getting much colder and we had to plan the shut down and winterizing of our caravan as the site closes each year for January and February. Our final visit to the caravan for 2022 was a long weekend in mid-December as we had plans to meet up with family nearer to Christmas. High winds and icy weather meant that all of our planned excursions and gigs were cancelled. We dared a trip to Pwllheli, buying a few essentials from the shops, things to take home to help me with my hiraeth over the next couple of months. Hiraeth is a wonderful Welsh word that means a deep longing for something or somewhere that feels like home. We headed to Pwllheli Spar for local eggs, Dwyfor filter coffee and a loaf of delicious oaty bread from the Llanaelhaearn bakery, Becws Glanrhyd. Llên Llŷn bookshop was our next stop for the local monthly Welsh papers, with a quick glance to see if my book was still on the shelves and I was thrilled to see that it was. I read the posters in Llên Llŷn window and took a photo of one advertising a Bob Delyn a'r Ebillion gig at the end of January. Jim commented that the caravan would be shut then. I gave him a cheeky smile and he smiled back but rolled his eyes and shook his head, knowing already that I would be plotting something over the next couple of weeks. Before the new year began, I had booked three nights in a sea front flat in Cricieth at the end of January for Jim and I, plus tickets for the Bob Delyn a'r Ebillion gig in the memorial hall.

Just before Christmas, I was flattered to see the Facebook page for the Welsh learner magazine **Lingo Newydd**, featured an article about my coastal path book and I was told that something similar would be printed in the next edition of the physical and digital copy of the magazine itself. Whilst browsing Facebook, I also spotted a request from the Facebook page for **Merched y Wawr** (the Welsh equivalent of the Women's Institute), asking people for stories of acts of kindness from any of their members. I immediately thought of a friend that I always refer to as 'eBay Ann' as I knew she was an active and very popular member of this

With eBay Ann at Plas Glyn y Weddw

organisation. In 2013, about a year after I'd started to learn Welsh, I was buying an item from eBay and I noticed that the seller's eBay name was Ann Pedair. Presuming that the seller spoke Welsh, I thanked her on the eBay message in Welsh and explained that I was learning the language. Ann (real name Williams) was indeed a first language Welsh speaker, a retired primary school teacher from Penmachno and she sent me a friendly reply and suggested that we exchange email addresses so we could continue to 'chat' more easily. For about a year, Ann emailed me daily with short messages about the weather and bits of news and I replied back in Welsh. I was by now learning to read and write in Welsh and this was a huge help on my learning journey. Ann and I have met face to face a couple of times and we now send occasional emails, but I will always be grateful for her kindness and patience. I wrote and told our story and it soon appeared on Facebook, and the following day I received an email from Ann, who'd been surprised at seeing the story. We caught up with some chatty emails and I told her I was writing this book and asked her about her eisteddfod experiences. I discovered she'd been even more involved than I'd realised and had also accompanied folk dancers on the piano at various eisteddfodau and competed in several different choirs. I was very impressed to discover that she'd been in the large choir who'd made up the 'mountain' in the Te yn y Grug show at the Llanrwst eisteddfod and following this was one of several members of the choir who'd backed Al Lewis in Sain studios when he recorded all of his songs from the show for his new album. This year she had been singing with the **Cerdd Dant** choir from Trillyn at the Tregaron Steddfod and was hoping they would qualify to be able to compete in the Llŷn and Eifionydd 2023 Steddfod next year. Cerdd Dant is a particular kind of singing, has a long tradition in Wales and is seen as an art form. A melody is played on the harp, and a poem is then sung to a tune that is different to the accompanying one from the harp. The idea sounds strange, but the music doesn't. Ann explained to me the process of the competitions in eisteddfodau. In the urdd (youth) eisteddfodau, competitors from all the different categories (music, dance, recitation etc) go through various heats. Initially they compete in their own district around February, with qualifiers going on to compete in their county eisteddfod about mid-March and the winners from that are able to then compete in the Urdd Eisteddfod which is always held in the Whitsun holidays at the end of May/beginning of June. In the Steddfod, Ann explained, anyone can compete but there is a preliminary round where the judge chooses three from each category to go on stage. I'd heard from various sources that people often use the expressions '**cael llwyfan**', which means get to go on the stage or '**cael cam**' which means to be 'wronged' but used to convey the feelings around not having got a place on the stage. Such are the strong emotions around competition time at eisteddfodau. I hoped that Ann and her choir would 'cael llwyfan'.

In the new year 2023, it was great to meet up with Welsh speaking friends in Manchester and across Zoom. The learner group continues to meet in Manchester Art Gallery Café, where the fantastic staff are by now getting used to our monthly appearance and some of them even having a little go at '**bore da**' and '**diolch**' (good morning and thank you). We were also very lucky that Rhianwen was often on duty on Saturday mornings. Rhianwen comes from north Wales, is first language Welsh and enjoys a bit of chat with us when she can in between serving people. She is also an artist and her art work can be seen on Instagram – Rhianwenart. The Sgwrs a Pheint (chat and a pint) group, for fluent speakers, met for the first time in its new venue, Mamucium cocktail bar in the Northern Quarter of Manchester, and was more suitable for the meet up as it was quieter than the city centre bar we'd been meeting in recently, and we could hear each other speak. Friends kindly asked how the book launch had gone in November (this had been held at Nant Gwrtheyrn) and teased about whether I'd managed without an alcoholic drink. I reported back that I'd managed with a hot chocolate, and that on reflection felt that this was the sensible thing to have done as I'd probably have broken down sobbing rather than just gulping back tears, if my inhibitions had been let loose by half a cider. I'd taken the local papers from Llŷn and a book to give to Peter, a friend at the group who originates from Pwllheli and with whom we'd not yet managed to meet up with in Llŷn – he often returns to visit friends and family but hadn't managed to get there in December. I'd just finished reading Jos Simon's book *On Bonfires, Butlins and Being Welsh*, which is a collection of the author's memories and those of others from his generation who grew up in and around Pwllheli in the 1950s and 1960s. I thought this would be of interest to Peter as he was born in the 1950s. Butlins was the name of the holiday park a few miles outside of Pwllheli, now called **Hafan y Môr** (or Haven to non-Welsh speakers). Peter told me that he had spent a lot of time there enjoying the pool and even working there for a while and that they sometimes held eisteddfodau there for employees.

Welsh Learner Group Manchester

Eisteddfod Ramble 14
January 2023
Creative Cricieth

This chapter rambles all over the place but mostly around Cricieth and just about qualifies to be called an Eisteddfod Ramble, but be warned I do go off on many non-eisteddfod tangents.

The end of January was soon upon us, and we joined the tail end of the work traffic on a cold Friday morning after saying goodbye to Simon, who was working from home that day. I couldn't wait to be in Llŷn again. On the way we called at our regular stop off – La Parisienne French bakery in Colwyn Bay for baguettes for tea and asked Guy about his winter back in Paris. Next stop was Caernarfon and Caffi Tŷ Winsh for a delicious lunch, where Marek greeted us warmly and told us that business was going quite well. We arrived in Cricieth too early to get into our sea front flat, but we had plenty of errands to fill our time while we waited for 4 o'clock. Once Jim had parked the car close to the memorial hall, we wandered into **Y Deli Newydd** (The New Deli) on the high street and collected our saved tickets for the Bob Delyn a'r Ebillion gig for the following night. While there we browsed the shelves in this treasure of a shop, which were crammed with goods from a myriad of local producers, such as beers from Cwrw Llŷn in Nefyn, ciders from the vineyard Pant Du and jams and chutneys from Welsh Lady Preserves. We bought some of our favourite Welsh cakes from Popty Prysur, then headed further along the high street to collect some bread and croissants from Idris Bakery and the local Welsh language newspapers from the newsagents close by. We returned to the car and I browsed the papers and within minutes something very interesting caught my eye. It was an Irish-Welsh event of music, story and art at Llŷn's art gallery at Plas Glyn y Weddw and it was on that evening – how had I missed that until now? I described it enthusiastically and managed to sell the

Plas Glyn y Weddw Café

idea to Jim, which is fortunate as I'd already clicked on 'book tickets' by then. In *Y Ffynnon* (the Eifionydd newspaper) I was interested to read about Stephen Faherty, originally from Porthmadog, the craftsman who had been chosen to create the Steddfod chair. The chair is being sponsored by the family of the late Dafydd Orwig, in memory of his contribution to Gwynedd, where for many years he was a councillor and a strong campaigner for the Welsh language. The tree, which is over 200 years old, was donated by Eifion and Ann Williams, whose farm Tyddyn Heilyn in Chwilog, is situated by the woodland lane Lôn Goed, where it fell. I read another news article a few weeks later that explained that Stephen would be carving the chair from one solid piece of wood, rather than cutting the wood into pieces and that he would also be adding slate slabs from Ireland, at the request of the Orwig family. Dafydd Orwig spent many years living in County Wicklow where his father worked as manager of a slate quarry. Stephen's own father was born and raised in the county of Connemara in the west of Ireland but in the 1960s had travelled to Wales to work on the Trawsfynydd power station. Stephen was looking forward to visiting Ireland with the Orwig family to select the slate. I found out that Stephen's first carving was of William Madocks on the Cob in Porthmadog, so this was now on my list of things to get around to looking at.

Our first-floor flat on Marine Terrace overlooking the western beach was cosy and gave us great views across the bay of Ceredigion with Harlech Castle and the hills of Meirionydd southeastwards, and northwestwards some of our hilly conquests from last year including Garn Fadryn. The block of flats was named The Towers, because of its conical roof but I was pleased that each individual flat had a Welsh name and ours was Ardudwy. Guy's baguettes went down well for our tea and it was soon time to head off to Plas Glyn y Weddw.

As we drove into the art gallery car park, the first thing we noticed adjoining the plas was the new circular café which was now completed and looked like Cinderella's coach, silver and glinting under the dark and rather cloudy sky. The gig was held in the entrance to this beautiful gothic hall, a great setting for the event. As we took our seat, we were delighted to see Dafydd, the storyteller from Felin Uchaf and maker of our beautiful carved wooden gate at the caravan. We exchanged greetings and Dafydd joined the audience with his family and friends. In the first half of the gig, we were entertained by Irish singer-songwriter Padraig Jack, who sang in English and Gaelic and accompanied himself on guitar. He explained that he was from the largest of the Aran Islands Inis Mor, which had featured in the movie *The Banshees of Inisherin*, which, along with a recent Irish language film *The Quiet Girl*, was getting a lot of public attention and had recently won several awards. He joked about having the same first name as the main character but also having a little more intelligence. About a week earlier we'd seen and enjoyed this quirky film, which is said to be a metaphor for the Irish Civil War and similar conflicts. I hadn't realised until then how to pronounce Padraig, which I'd always thought was said how it appears to us English (a little like Patrick), but had been surprised to discover it sounds more like Porick. Padraig charmed us all with his Irish humour and singing and I especially enjoyed hearing him singing in his own first language. By coincidence, some of his songs referred to Connemara which has close links to the Aran Islands. **Byd bach** – small world. He agreed with others' suggestions that his island had a lot of similarities to Llŷn, including a determination by its people to hold onto the language. I wondered if this event had any connection with the Ecoamgueddfa, as Plas Glyn y Weddw is one of the partners involved in this project, although Padraig wasn't from the part of Ireland that was being twinned with Llŷn.

The second half of the gig was a bi-lingual performance by a group of four people who called themselves **Gorllewinwynt**, which means western wind. Nikolaz Davalan was from Brittany and played the double bass, Meic Llewellyn from Ceredigion was the main storyteller, Catrin O'Neill from Gwynedd, sang, played guitar and bodhran and helped to tell the story, and Nicky Arscott, artist from Powys created charcoal murals to illustrate the story as it unfolded. The folk tale was set in Ceredigion and taken from the ancient stories of the Mabinogi. It told the story of a small boy Gwion Bach and his encounters with the enchantress Ceridwen. The cast were all dressed with a hint of the medieval to help create the right atmosphere. In between accompanying the singing, the stern double bassist sat down, with his arms folded and his hood almost over his eyes. When we chatted about it later, Jim and I shared that we had both expected this character to eventually be the antagonist of the story and to leap out and make us all jump but this never

Snowdrops at Plas yn Rhiw

happened. We wondered if he was just tired and perhaps cold as he was sitting near the doorway of the plas. The group were to continue their tour in Aberystwyth the following evening while we would be at the memorial hall for the Bob Delyn gig, which Jim heard one member of the group refer to. The whole evening had been very enjoyable and entertaining and we returned to the flat with another two CDs for the collection.

The following day, we did a quick check of our caravan and I was thrilled to see a small clump of snowdrops in full bloom in our mini garden. We were less thrilled to see that the mini murmuration of starlings that often land in the field in front of the caravan had splattered the French windows with their droppings as they had taken flight. A regular occurrence but a small price to pay for the fortune of having a caravan in such a stunning location. The caravan seemed to have survived the coldest of the weather so we happily returned to Cricieth for now.

We have visited Cricieth often but it felt different viewing it through the eyes of temporary residents with more time to explore this attractive little town, which is what we did for the majority of the remainder of the day. Where Pwllheli feels very Welsh, with rarely an English word to be heard on the streets out of the tourist season, Cricieth feels a little less so, but an interesting place nonetheless and to my eyes is an open-air art gallery, with something to see and admire wherever you look. The town has a strong creative element to it and a lot of that is down to local artist, tutor and councillor Ffion Meleri Gwyn – mentioned previously – and the Cricieth Creadigol group. Ffion's wonderful work can be seen around the town on maps and signs showing the local flora and fauna, especially around the nature walk area between the high street and the castle. Cricieth Creadigol had changed the woollen toppers on the three red pillar boxes in the town, with the knitted lifeboat coxswain who I believe is called Brian adorning the one near the lifeboat station. The other two were now keeping up with the season and were dedicated to the theme of love, as St Dwynwen's day had been on the 25th January and it wasn't long until St Valentine's Day. St Dwynwen is the 5th century Welsh patron saint of lovers, who came from Ynys Môn and there are several variations of her tale, none of them very cheery. Jim and I don't send cards to each other for any events these days, as part of being more eco-friendly and not adding to our clutter. I'm very sentimental and find it difficult to part with any offerings from loved ones. Jim isn't romantic in the hearts and flowers sense but shows his love in very thoughtful and practical ways. His first gift to me not long after we met was a long metal shoe horn that he made by hand, after he'd seen me struggling to pull my boots on. Now that's the kind of romance I like.

We went to look at another recent piece of art work that had evolved from a project led by Ffion Gwyn and had been created by her college art students. Lining the front drive of the memorial hall are ceramic tiles, mostly in monochrome with various images and words in Welsh or English which seemed to mostly be concerned with the theme of peace **'heddwch'**. I later discovered that it was called 'The Path of Peace', and had been installed as part of the

Nature boards by Ffion Gwyn

commemoration of the centenary of the hall. Not far from the tiles within the gardens was an object I'd heard about but never seen. Caged in what looked like a small rabbit hutch, was a boulder. Close by a sign explained that this was **'Y Garreg Orchest'** or 'The Stone of Strength', and that it weighed about 170kg. The stone was thought to have originally stood outside the old town hall at the foot of the castle and used to mount horses, having been known as the **Carreg Cam** (step stone). It was moved to its current place in 1927 after many years of having been used as a focal point by campaigning politicians, possibly including David Lloyd George, who would stand by it or on it to give their speeches. More recently it has been used as a 'feat stone', with strong men attempting to lift the stone and

The Stone of Strength, Cricieth

from 2014 it became an annual sponsored event in Cricieth, with prize money for those who succeeded to lift it. Although this didn't last long due to covid 19 and it hasn't taken place again since 2019. If you're interested, individuals can contact the memorial hall caretaker to attempt to lift the stone and have it recorded in the guestbook. There are three levels of lift, the first being 'breaking the ground', which is defined as putting wind beneath the stone, then there's 'to the chest' and 'to the shoulder'. So far only one man has shouldered the stone – Wales's Mark Jeanes. Jim and I decided to not bother for now.

There was another piece of art work that I had somehow missed in the town, that I wanted to see and find out more about and it was on the grassed area by the Memorial Hall. It's a rather unusual looking stone sculpture with four parts to it – a structure with a cut out and three unevenly shaped, decorated boulders positioned on the grass in front which can be viewed through this 'window'. This was created by Howard Bowcott and is called the 'Welsh Incident', representing a light hearted poem of the same name written by Robert Graves and published in 1929. The poem describes a vision of mysterious creatures emerging from the sea caves of Cricieth, which are 'very strange, un-Welsh, utterly peculiar things'. We went to see the sculpture of course and as many have done before me, I took photos of the boulders through the 'window'. I looked back on Facebook and could see that there'd been a special festival in Cricieth called 'The Creative Incident' on the 3rd August 2019. This had included poetry, song, storytelling by Dafydd from Felin Uchaf, lots of workshops and demonstrations from various local artists and producers and an exhibition of the work of Howard Bowcott and his ideas for the sculpture which was expected to be in place by November of that year. The sculpture was unveiled on the 2nd November 2019, with Gwyneth Glyn and Twm Morys reciting the poem in its original form and then in a translated Welsh form. The video of this can be found on the Cricieth Creadigol Facebook page.

The full poem can be found on a board on a wall at the train station, surrounded by other interesting art and information boards. I wondered how I'd managed to miss both events, which I'd have been keen to see. I looked back at photographs and found that on the 3rd August we were at the Steddfod in Llanrwst and on the 2nd November we were on our way home from Aberystwyth after a weekend of Welsh music and storytelling. After we'd booked tickets for the Bob Delyn gig, I'd seen posters for two other favourite singers Steve Eaves and Meinir Gwilym, all three performing on the same night. These Welsh folk need to coordinate their diaries so I don't miss anything.

The Bob Delyn a'r Ebillion gig was a lively memorable event if not a bit of a Deja vu experience after having been to see Twm Morys (the lead singer of the band) and Gwyneth Glyn perform quite recently. The hall was packed out and tonight Gwyneth was in the audience amongst a lot of other faces that were beginning to look familiar, having seen them at other recent events in Cricieth. Jim and I were possibly the only non-Welsh people in the place. There is always a strong sense of community at events we've attended in Cricieth, but we are always welcomed warmly and never made to feel like outsiders. We were taken by surprise by a member of the band who played guitar and... double bass. Yes, the Breton guy from the night before, now looking much warmer and cheerier, but clearly having abandoned Gorllewinwynt for that night. Not long after this gig, I discovered that Nikolaz Davalan was the very same "Daval Donc" whose Facebook page I had started following recently, where he offers lessons and tips to Welsh learners and is known to his students as 'Mr D!' Jim and I commented simultaneously on another member of the band who played saxophone, stating that we'd seen him many times over the years performing for different bands. I later discovered that his name was Edwin Humphreys and that Welsh news magazine *Golwg* had nicknamed him Edwin **'Chwarae fo powb'**, (plays with everyone) Humphreys. His wife Einir should have the nickname **'Canu fo pawb'** (sings with everyone) as she is a backing singer who is seen frequently with many bands including at this gig tonight.

The gig was in three sets and the final set was the liveliest and people got up and danced near the stage and also did a repeat of the conga line dance to the 'Trên Bach y Sgwarnogod', song as we'd seen at Dylan's earlier in the year. I've not got up and danced (apart from when guided at a Ceilidh and in Zumba classes) since my twenties as I've got two left feet, and Jim just doesn't do dancing despite his Irish ancestry, but I love to see people dancing. The end of the gig was the best I've ever seen and such a brilliant idea. Throughout the gig, Twm often sang instead of speaking, for example to ask one of the band members to come to the stage or to tease the guitarist as he tuned his guitar in between each song. We knew the gig was approaching the end but I think all were taken by surprise when he suddenly started to sing the Welsh National Anthem. Of course, everyone stood up, the dancers stopped and all joined in with the words. He then began to speed up the singing of the anthem and added a catchier rhythm so the dancers returned to dancing and the rest of the audience continued to sing but also started to either dance or at least jiggle about a bit – even Jim tapped his feet. Twm then sang repeated lines of **'diolch yn fawr'** (thank you very much), then **'am wrando arnoni'** (for listening to us) and finally **'nos da, nos da'** (goodnight, goodnight).

The lights went up and that was it, without any ideas of clapping for an encore as the finale had been created already. Brilliant! On the walk back to the flat, we took a detour to see the castle lit up in the dark. It looked stunning but at that time there was some controversy about whether Cadw who the castle is entrusted to, should be illuminating their buildings at night, because of light pollution and to save power.

The following day, we drove down to Plas yn Rhiw, a National Trust property not far from Aberdaron. To our good fortune, it happened to be snowdrop weekend there, the one weekend in the winter when the gardens are open to the public enabling them to admire the carpets of snowdrops growing in the woodland area. Our little clump at the caravan had grown from a single snowdrop that we'd purchased from the shop on a previous visit a few years ago. The snowdrops looked beautiful and the views of Porth Neigwl equally so, although we could see that a large piece of cliff that had looked precarious at the time of our coastal walk was now lying across the beach. After a delicious lunch in the tearoom – yes yet another café – we headed back towards the caravan but Jim took a detour before we got to Botwnnog. I had given a strong hint about wanting to visit a church that I had recently been admiring on the front cover of one of my books ***Englynion Mynwentydd Gwlad Llŷn*** (verses of the cemeteries of Llŷn) – wonderful bedtime reading! The book catalogues the graves across the peninsula where there is an **englyn** (a traditional Welsh short poem)

Llandygwnning Church

inscribed as part of the dedication. Today I just wanted a closer look at Llandygwnning church as it looked unlike any other I'd seen on the peninsula – its conical tower and old stone structure giving it an almost medieval appearance. An inscription on a slate sign on the tower informed me however that it was rebuilt as recently as 1840 and another sign by the locked door that it was now a local history centre in the care of the 'Friends of Llandegwning', but it was well worth a mini detour. Notice the different spelling of the village name which seems to have evolved over the years.

We walked off our lunch back in Cricieth on the western beach close to our flat, dodging the wooden breakers as the tide was on its way out. Picture postcard pretty Cricieth Castle, which is perched high on its own rocky headland, divides the beach into two. On the western side of the headland which has small caves and inlets, the locals suggest there is a face in the rocks which perhaps inspired Graves to write his poem. From the pebbly beach we could also admire the whole of the pretty multicoloured terrace of houses including the blue 'tower' where our flat was. As we worked our way to the headland, we kept our eyes open for seals, dolphins or porpoises which are said to frequently appear there. We didn't observe any 'Welsh incidents' on our walk – not

Face in the rock at Cricieth

a creature in sight – neither ordinary nor mystical. We were able to pick out the shape of the face in the rocks, which looked more comical than scary and at great risk of losing its nose in the next storm.

So, what has this chapter got to do with hills or eisteddfodau? I'm sure I can weave them in somewhere. Our knees weren't up to any hill walking this weekend and we felt we just about managed the steep walk past the castle into the town from our flat. But we did glance frequently towards Moel y Gest, between Porthmadog and Borth-y-gest, the closest hill to Cricieth that we yet hoped to conquer, but it was always covered in cloud so that was a convenient excuse. As for eisteddfodau, Cricieth has its own connections and these are proudly featured on a large poster board that we came across inside a bus shelter close to the memorial hall. The poster mimics the cover from the Beatles album *Sgt. Pepper's Lonely Hearts Club Band*, and has illustrations of 68 people or things that have a connection to Cricieth in some way. This includes winners of prizes at eisteddfodau over the years, such as Twm Morys and Gwyneth Glyn as already mentioned. William Richard Philip George, who was born in Cricieth is also included. His father William George was the younger brother of David Lloyd, the prime minister, and while his brother pursued his political career, had taken care of the family firm of solicitors until the age of 101. WRP George had continued with the family business in Porthmadog up until his death at the age of 94 and was solicitor to the Steddfod. In his spare time, he was a poet and in 1974, he won the crown for his poem **Tân** (fire) and was Archdruid of Wales from 1990 to 1993, taking the bardic name '**Ap Llysor**', which means son of solicitor. WRP's son Phillip, continued with the family's business which amalgamated with law company Gamlins in 2013 and continues to run successfully on the high street in Porthmadog. Phillip is often seen with his sister Elizabeth at events in Cricieth, including the Bob Delyn gig where he ran the raffle, and he is currently the director of the Cricieth Arts Association.

Eisteddfod Ramble 15
February and March 2023
Do the Little Things

A couple of days after arriving home from our weekend in Cricieth, I received a message from Llŷn friend Amanda, asking for my email address, so that she could put my name forward to enter the **Dysgwr y Flwyddyn** (Learner of the Year) competition at the Steddfod. This competition was introduced in the 1980s and is open to anyone who has learnt to speak Welsh and who uses it regularly in their life, either in work, the community or with their family. Amanda and another friend ('eBay Ann' as mentioned earlier) had mentioned this idea to me a while before, but I had said thank you but no thank you to both, and explained that I didn't want to take part as I would be much too nervous. Both felt that it would be especially meaningful to me because of my love of the area where it was to be held this year and they were right really. I felt flattered by them thinking I was an appropriate nomination but as I explained to them, I've always become anxious at exams or any situation where I feel judged in any way. I passed my driving test on my fourth attempt, even though I'd felt a confident driver for years before, because I used to shake and become too anxious to hear the instructions of the examiner. I won't tell you the tale of the shocked looking lollipop man crossing the children over the road during one of my tests, but will reassure you that no one was hurt. I declined Amanda's request once again and chatted to Jim about it. He said that he thought I could manage to enjoy the experience as I had done overall with the book launch, despite my anxieties. So, I got back to Amanda and agreed to do it 'for research purposes'. If I was accepted into the competition, I could experience what being a small part of the Steddfod felt like and would be able to write about it in this book.

I certainly did not expect to win and however wonderful it would be, the idea of winning would also fill me with dread as it would mean being in front of television cameras. I later referred to my copy of Testunau Llŷn ac Eifionydd 2023, to find the details about this competition and to discover that one of the judges, if I were to reach the final was to be Tudur Owen, the radio presenter and comedian. I have often listened to Tudur Owen in his show on Radio Cymru, where in between playing pop music, he banters with others in the studio. I have often jokingly referred to him as the fastest speaker in Wales and great for listening practice. I can now keep up a little better with his quick fired wit, than when I first heard him many years ago, but I hoped that if I did get to be interviewed by him, he would keep it at a slower pace. There's a very funny short video clip on Facebook from one of Tudur's stand up shows, dated August 2020 and called '**Cofio 'Steddfod Lerpwl?**' (Do you remember the Liverpool Eisteddfod?). In his Welsh scouse accent, he voices the responses of the local visitors to an imaginary eisteddfod held in Liverpool, including their bewilderment at parts of the ceremonies, especially the use of the sword.

In early February, the SSIW (Say Something in Welsh) team released some free lessons, aimed especially at rugby fans in preparation for the Six Nations Championships. It was called a mini-course for **Calon Lân**, which is an old Welsh hymn (mentioned earlier) and now often sung by fans at rugby matches. The course taught the first verse and the chorus in two half hour lessons. The day it was released was perfect as I had longish car journeys to make to and from the clinic where I was working that day. I'm not a rugby fan, but I loved the idea of being able to learn all of the words – I could already mutter my way through quite a bit of it so I had a bit of a head's start. But the SSIW magic worked once again and by the time I arrived home, I'd been able to sing along with Cerys Matthews in the car – I only ever sing in the car when no one is listening – reasons given earlier. Calon Lân also has an eisteddfod connection. In 2010, Wales based boys' choir Boys Aloud was formed and in 2012 they came third in the I.T.V. talent show Britain's Got Talent, singing Calon Lân at their audition then again in the finals. Later that year they performed at the opening concert of the Steddfod, along with Only Men Aloud and Only Kids Aloud, in the Vale of Glamorgan. I challenge you to watch the YouTube video of this powerful performance and not be moved to tears.

In the middle of February, there was news of a free day-long festival at The Lion Hotel in Treorci to mark the launch of the 2024 Steddfod, which was to be held in the county of Rhondda Cynon Taf, in South Wales. It seemed funny that preparations were being made for this before the 2023 had even taken place, but I was beginning to realise why this was and how much work goes into these annual events.

On a cold but bright afternoon at the end of February, we arrived at our caravan for a full week, our first for the season; I was blissfully happy. Along the journey and approaching our caravan site, occasional clumps of snowdrops were beginning to wilt and give way to daffodils blooming in readiness for St David's Day on the 1st March. I was delighted by the sight of the new lambs, frisking about in the fields close to the caravan; it was good to be back at **Fan o Hiraeth** – van/place of longing, which is the name of our caravan.

A trip to Pwllheli was our first outing, to stock up on local bread and eggs from one of our favourite bakeries Becws Islyn, then into Spar for Llaeth y Llan yoghurts and the delicious oaty bread from Glanrhyd Bakery, that we buy regularly. We both love bread, as you may have detected, and there are a few excellent bakeries in Llŷn. Only a few weeks after this visit, Becws Islyn were deservedly awarded Family Business of the Year award by the Welsh Federation of Small Businesses. I'd also read recently about Glanrhyd, which is in Llanaelhaearn and only a stone's throw from our caravan, and how the local community organisation **Antur** (mentioned earlier) were trying to save the place, which had been going for more than 100 years, with the hope of also reestablishing a shop there. I wished them every success. Close to the harbour, we stopped at the relatively new **Y Sied Laeth** (the milk shed), which is exactly that – a shed with a very clever machine where you can help yourself to locally produced delicious organic milk and milkshakes – on receipt of payment of course. Our next very important stop was at the book shop Llên Llŷn, to buy the local **papurau bro** (Welsh language local papers) and to pick up tickets I'd ordered for events in Llŷn this week, including a St David's Day concert. But our

Y Sied Laeth, Pwllheli

Karyn's Hairdresser shop, Pwllheli decorated for St David's Day

very first stop was Caffi Largo, close to the beach, for a panad, where we were greeted like old friends by the ladies who run this great little café. With one of my favourite Welsh songs playing in the background over the speakers, I had my first Welsh chat for the week with one of the very familiar looking members of staff who I later discovered was called Kim. I told her how happy I was to be back in the café and how I'd missed the place. I asked how business had been and it was good to hear that the café had continued to be busy over the winter. It is perhaps even more popular with locals than it is with visitors, which is part of its appeal to me. I spotted posters asking people to vote for Dylan Morris, a Pwllheli based pop singer, who was in the finals of the Cân i Gymru (song for Wales) competition which was to be televised live later that week on S4C. Dylan had risen to fame on social media during the Covid-19 pandemic. As we strolled around the streets of Pwllheli, we noticed some of the shop windows decorated with flags, dragons, and daffodils in preparation for St David's Day, but it was a shame to hear that there was to be no parade this year. It was good to see the wooden thermometer showing that the town was getting close to their target of £62,000 raised as their contribution to the Steddfod.

The day after, I drove back towards Caernarfon and stopped off at the beautiful seaside village of Dinas Dinlle to visit another café by the beach, Braf. This time, it was to join up with a learner's chat group organised by Ffion Ellis, who I'd met with before in the Caernarfon group and at my book launch. They were a great bunch of people and it was good to be amongst other learners. I was lucky to get the chance to chat for a while with Ffion and also another Welsh tutor Audra. I'm always trying to find ways to set myself challenges and keep developing my Welsh but this can be difficult when I'm back home with less opportunities to meet with first language folk.

That afternoon, Jim and I visited Plas Glyn y Weddw art gallery where this time we were able to see the latest art exhibition and try out the new café – we weren't disappointed. I read an information poster, that explained the background behind this unusually shaped café. Matt Sanderson is the artist who designed the building and he based the 11-metre-wide self-supporting structure on the shell or 'test' of a small green sea urchin, which he had discovered on nearby Llanbedrog beach. I love the Welsh for sea urchin – **draenog y môr**, which means sea hedgehog. He was also inspired by the colonies of acorn barnacles along the coastline of Llŷn and made the outer layer of the café out of 89,000 handmade stainless-steel versions of these. Now you'll have to go and have a look. But if you can't visit soon, check out an interesting YouTube film showing Matt and the staff of the gallery and café talking about its development – 80,000 *Barnacles Above the Sea*. On the table in the foyer of the gallery, I was excited to see four small free pocket guides encouraging people to learn some Welsh at home or on holiday, giving useful relevant vocabulary. These had been produced jointly by the Ecoamgueddfa and Nant Gwrtheyrn, organisations mentioned earlier. I have to admit that I then got rather too excited at spotting my book displayed on what I have always considered to be the 'special table' in the gallery. I try hard to be cool and calm when I spot my book, but I never quite manage it. This excitement returned later when I received a phone call from Cadi Dafydd, a reporter from the Welsh weekly magazine *Golwg*, asking could she interview me later in the week about my book and my experiences of walking and learning to speak Welsh. Jim teased about my new 'celebrity' status.

That night, I visited the local hair salon for a trim, something I'd never done before in Llŷn as I'm loyal to my hairdresser at home – sorry Karen if you happen to be reading this. I thought it would be a treat and an ideal opportunity for some Welsh chat as we all know how much ladies chat at the hairdressers. Kate, the hairdresser, who our Llŷn friend Amanda had recommended, was happy to chat in Welsh with me as she fought my thick head of hair, and her other friendly customer joined in with our conversations. I was happy with my tamed hair and came away with some interesting information – eisteddfod and non – eisteddfod related. Kate had asked where our caravan was situated and the other customer told me that she had lived on a farm close to the site. She asked did I know that the daughter of the site manager, was making this year's eisteddfod crown. I knew that Elin Mair Roberts, our site manager's daughter made jewellery and sold it throughout Wales, but didn't know she had been chosen to make this prestigious award. I later read in local papers that as with the chair, the details of the crown remain a closely guarded secret until nearer the event, but that it would also have a connection to Lôn Goed, the local wooded lane immortalised in song and poetry. The other piece of news that took me by surprise was regarding the café at Plas Carmel, near Aberdaron. I'd heard that Ffion and Coco, who had been running the place when we'd visited last year, were now moving on to do other things. Ffion had recently had a book published called *Cwlwm* (meaning knot or tie), which is still on my wish list. I'd glanced photos on social media of the new owners and had been struck by how the man had looked very like Bryn Fôn, the very popular and successful actor and singer. To my astonishment, Kate informed me that Bryn Fôn and his wife were now in charge of the café. I couldn't wait to tell friend Amanda, as she was a huge fan of Bryn, who is famed for many things including being the first to play live on Radio Cymru in 1977 and for his involvement in political protests around protecting the language. When I returned to the caravan, I told Jim what I'd heard and I quickly shared my new found knowledge with Amanda, but of course she already knew and typical of all Llŷn people, had taken the news in her stride and not become over excited as I had.

Recent petitions to make St David's Day or **Gŵyl Dewi Sant**, a bank holiday in the same way as St Patrick's Day in Ireland and St Andrew's Day in Scotland, were unsuccessful, but you get a sense of its importance to the people of Wales. It is celebrated on the anniversary of his death which occurred on the 1st March either the year 589 or 601. It is said that his final words were 'Be joyful, keep the faith, do the little things you have seen me do'. The words **'gwnewch y pethau bychain, '** which mean 'do the little things', are often heard incorporated into songs and poems and sometimes related to the learning of the language as an encouragement. The little thing we had thought of doing on this St David's Day in 2023, was to walk to the summit of Moel y Gest from Porthmadog, but the grey skies and drizzle had put us off. Instead, we visited

Porthmadog and browsed the shops. In Browsers Bookshop I was in awe when I spotted the author Angharad Tomos (mentioned earlier). We then managed to find the wooden sculpture of William Madocks's head, which was positioned at the town end of the Cob, and was much taller than I'd expected, with by now a large deep crack in the wood giving him a scarred face. William

William Madocks statue Porthmadog

Madocks, born in 1773, was the founder of Porthmadog and Tremadog – which mean Madock's port and Madock's town, and his greatest achievement was thought to have been the construction of the Cob, which is the sea wall. This contributed to the development of the Ffestiniog Railway which subsequently allowed the transportation of Welsh slate around the world. Good lad Bill!

I'd heard that to celebrate St David's Day, Portmeirion was free to visit all day, so as the sun began to peep out from the clouds, we decided this was our next stop. Portmeirion is an Italian style village, designed as a tourist attraction by Clough Williams-Ellis, who happens to have been the great uncle of the owner of our caravan site. It has certainly attracted many visitors over the years but thankfully today it wasn't as crowded as our most recent visit in 2020 soon after the main covid lockdown had been lifted, when it appeared that the whole of Wales had been released into the village. Our visit this time was much more leisurely and relaxed and we were able to admire the colourful quirky buildings and sculptures, without having to dodge lots of mask wearing people. On our way into the village, I glimpsed a suited man dashing out towards the car park and realised it was Tudur Owen, the comedian and radio presenter mentioned earlier, who would be one of the judges in the final of Dysgwr y Flwyddyn (learner of the year). At the 2019 Steddfod, Tudur was welcomed into the Gorsedd of the Bards and awarded the green robes for services to the arts. In the central part of the village, we spotted some camera crew and presumed they'd been filming Tudur for something on S4C. I joked with Jim, that I could ask Tudur what was going on if I did get to the final in the competition.

St David's Day wouldn't be complete without some music, especially a Welsh choir, which is exactly what we got at the evening concert arranged at Nant Gwrtheyrn. We were entertained by performances of singing and acting by local school children under the watchful eye of the conductor and keyboard player Siân, who I knew from Llanaelhaearn church. I enjoyed the adult soloists, which included Lleucu Gwawr and Elidyr Glyn. Lleucu brought the whole of the room to life when she sang the ever-popular Calon Lân and I was pleased to be able to join in quietly with the chorus and first verse, having recently mastered it with Say Something in Welsh. Elidyr is a singer songwriter and guitarist, and a member of the popular band **Bwncath** (meaning buzzard) and one of the songs he sang tonight won him first prize in 2019, in the S4C Cân i Gymru competition – **'Fel Hyn 'Da Ni Fod'** (this is how we should be). He has also won an award for music composition at the Steddfod in 2016. In the break, a familiar smiling face appeared close to our table. It was Sally, the Welsh learner who we'd met on the beach at the shanty evening last year. She congratulated me on my book and updated me on the project she had told me about where Angharad Tomos was helping her with research about her grandfather, the poet Robert 'Silyn' Roberts. Angharad had now written a book, about his life with his wife Mary, and this was to be launched very soon. My reading list is getting increasingly long. We bumped into Sally again a short while after this and she told me that she was in the local **Côr Gwerin** (folk choir), a choir that had been recently formed especially for this year's Steddfod. They were going to be performing with Pedair in one of the major evening performances there. I'd said we hoped to get to that concert and to be able to see her there.

Carnguwch men's choir filled the large hall with their amazing voices, under the leadership of Ann Hafod and accompanied on keyboard by Nia Wern from the café in Nefyn. The night ended with the national anthem of course, which again I felt proud to be able to contribute to – although mutely. It was a highly successful evening and the proceeds went towards the village of Pistyll's contribution to the Steddfod funds. The organisers of the evening announced that almost £2,000 pounds had been raised by this event and that over £300,000 had up to now been made throughout Llŷn and Eifionydd, which was a large chunk of the needed £400,000. As we dashed back to the car park in the drizzle, we came upon Myrddin ap Dafydd and his wife Llio. We all agreed what an enjoyable evening it had been and again rather over excitedly I shared that tomorrow I was going to be interviewed by a reporter from *Golwg* magazine about my book.

The following evening, having survived the Welsh interview for *Golwg*, thanks to the kindness and patience of the reporter Cadi Dafydd, I attended an interesting event which was being held to raise funds towards Pwllheli's Steddfod contribution. This was held in Plas Heli, home of Pwllheli sailing club, and consisted of a lecture by Gerwyn Williams about the poet and previous archdruid, Cynan with related musical interludes by local singer and harpist and one quarter of the band Pedair, Gwenan Gibbard. The lecture was in Welsh with an accompanying PowerPoint presentation which helped me to follow what was being said. I knew a little about Cynan already, but learnt some other interesting facts. One of the most interesting to me, being a fan of Welsh music, was regarding his poem Aberdaron. I'd heard a few versions of songs called Aberdaron, including Elidyr Glyn's only the night before, and a recent version by the Welsh/English folk band The Trials of Cato but hadn't realised that the lyrics were taken from Cynan's poem. Tonight, Gwenan Gibbard sang his poem beautifully, set to another tune which she played on the harp. I think I was the only non-Welsh person there but a group of three friendly local ladies – Gwyneth, Mair and Maggi, joined me at my table and soon involved me in their pre lecture chat. The evening ended with a photo shoot with Gerwyn, a bust of Cynan, and fellow poets Myrddin ap Dafydd, and Pwllheli born Guto Dafydd, who has twice won both the Crown and the Daniel Owen Prize at Steddfodau. Guto's book *Carafanio* was still on my 'to be read' shelf after buying it at Llanrwst Steddfod. A while after the lecture, I sent a message asking Gerwyn about a couple of things I'd not managed to grasp from the lecture. One was about an eisteddfod chair in Nefyn. Gerwyn very kindly replied that as well as his wins at the Steddfodau, in his earlier years Cynan had also won chairs at some local eisteddfodau and the one he won in Nefyn in 1914 at the age of 18, was the first one he'd won for writing poetry. He'd previously won chairs in children's local eisteddfodau in Pwllheli (1909 and 1910) and Bethesda (1913), but these had been for answering questions in an exam. Gerwyn also answered my queries about the bust. It had been made by John Meirion Morris in 2016 and was usually available to be seen in Pwllheli library in Neuadd Dwyfor – another trip needed soon. For any fluent Welsh speakers with an interest in Cynan, Gerwyn Williams has written the first full biography about him.

St David's Day Concert Nant Gwrtheyrn – Elidyr Glyn

Carnguwch choir and Nia on keyboard

Walk 15

Moel y Gest, Porthmadog
3rd March 2023
Sneezing All the Way

Eisteddfod rambles have taken over this book somewhat recently, but finally we had the right conditions – weather and health wise – to manage another hill walk. We'd been reading Des' book in the break and decided we'd give Moel y Gest a go, but to the lower of the two summits only, returning to Porthmadog. Des had described this hill as mountainous and the path down to Borth-y-gest as steep and rocky, which sounded a bit beyond our capabilities. I woke excited at the prospect of the walk but also with an annoying sniffle that felt like an allergy, accompanied by frequent violent sneezes. I hoped the fresh air would cure me and we set off in the car for Porthmadog on a cloudy but not too dull a day. We left the car close to a garage near the Travelodge, crossed over the A497 and headed for the public footpath sign that took us to the start of our journey. It was a perfect walking day, dry with a gentle breeze. I took Des' book in my pocket so we could follow his instructions. The smell of bacon butties wafted towards us from the transport

Moel y Gest from Cricieth

At the lower summit

Summit with Cnicht in the distance

cafés at the industrial area below. When I first became vegetarian over 30 years ago, I would have been tempted by this, but I no longer like the smell. Jim and I reminisced about a couple of bargain breaks we'd had in the Travelodge here, when the boys were little and money was tight. Our best deal had been a room for all four of us for £9 a night when we'd even taken our own breakfast cereals from home. But more often we would manage to stay in the caravans or chalets of the people of Llŷn which was much more enjoyable.

As Des had warned, the path quickly became steep but thankfully was clearly defined and dry with a carpet of fallen oak, beech and birch leaves, with plenty of beech nuts for extra crunchiness. We were too early to see the bluebells in bloom but could see leaves already forming a carpet beneath the trees along the wooded path. As we passed a large clearing we could see the remains of a slate quarry. We kept to the outer path amongst the bare trees which were unable to shield us from the noises of industry, traffic and an occasional train. We reached a three trunked silver birch, mentioned by Des as a landmark as we needed to turn left at this point. Jim double checked with his navigational gadget as there was no marker stone that Des had said was often there. This confirmed our route and we zigzagged steeply upwards along the increasingly rocky path. We took plenty of rests, propping on our walking poles but I still felt more out of breath than usual but realised my sneezing had finally stopped. Quite a lot of scrambling was needed to proceed along the rocky path but we

Looking across to Cricieth

eventually reached a 'Y' junction which after turning steeply right led us to a clearing. From here we got great views over Porthmadog and the cob dividing the Glaslyn Estuary, with Eryri and her array of hills and mountains that my peak finding app identified for me, including the famous and easily spotted Cnicht with its conical peak. It was a relief to have some flat ground to walk on for a short while and to rest. I commented on the lack of birds on today's walk, when a couple of crows flew over and squawked as if in response. We continued and soon after passing through a low broken wall, the path was steeper than ever. Annoyingly my sneezes returned as if in response to the exertion needed for this last stretch and my heart was pounding. I was really feeling my age. I've hardly mentioned Jim in this walk so far but he was most definitely there and I wouldn't have made it to the top without him. He helped me across awkward groups of rocks where I had to focus very hard on my foothold and amused me with his grumblings about the steepness of the journey, muttering that we weren't mountain goats.

The path finally emerged onto another grassy clearing from where we could now see Ceredigion Bay and Cricieth, including the castle. We propped for a little while to take photographs, eat lunch and enjoy the views, but most importantly to get our breath back and for me to blow my nose. We hadn't realised that just around the corner from this clearing was the smaller of the two summits – we'd arrived without fully realising it. As we wandered to the large rock at the summit, a couple appeared out of nowhere – Jim guessed they'd come up from one of the campsites on the other side. They were younger than us and much more agile and after obligingly taking a photo of the two of us, sprinted on towards the second and highest summit.

We made our way back down carefully and I sneezed almost continuously, which made me more tired than usual. There was less heart pounding on the way down but it felt harder on my knees and trickier to find safe footholds. The sun never quite made an appearance other than a peep or two between the grey clouds and when we were almost back out onto the main road, we heard the crying of a buzzard high above the trees.

Before we went on to Cricieth, which is where we'd decided to grab a **panad**/cuppa, we took a little excursion. I wanted to see the Porthmadog Gorsedd stones, which I knew were in a field alongside the A487. Jim parked up in a layby and I wearily wandered to a good spot for a photo but was also thrilled to see a pure white bird – a little egret from the heron family – just perched on one leg not far from the stones with Moel y Gest itself creating an attractive background.

Thankfully my sneezes eased as we had a cuppa in Tir a Môr café in Cricieth. The man who served us with our apple pie and panad chatted in English and asked about our day. He said that Moel y Gest was an easy hill, perhaps a twenty-minute walk? We smiled, but didn't tell him that it had taken us just over an hour and a half and that was just to the lowest summit.

By the time we arrived back at the caravan I was feeling full of a cold. I contacted friends to cancel some planned meet ups for our last two days of our holiday, including watching a drama with Amanda, and a walk with fellow Welsh learners from Nefyn, Chris and Dave. Tests suggested it wasn't covid, but I didn't want to take any chances of passing anything on. I managed to enjoy my weekend of isolation and Chris and Dave joined the Zoom Manchester Welsh Learners' Chat group which was scheduled for the Saturday morning. The weather was changing and getting much colder, with snow appearing on the summit of Yr Wyddfa so I enjoyed snuggling under a blanket and catching up with some reading. This included finishing *Llyfr Glas Nebo*, a book I'd highly recommend in Welsh for more advanced learners, or the English translation *The Blue Book of Nebo* if you don't speak Welsh. We both enjoyed watching Cân I Gymru on S4C. Gwyneth Glyn had been one of the judges who had decided on the eight finalists. It was then up to the viewers to vote on the night for their favourite song. The winning song was Patagonia sung by Dylan Morris, and written by Alistair James. I liked this lively song but Jim and I were rooting and voting for our favourite – **Tangnefedd** (peace), a gentle song by Eve Goodman and Sarah Zyborska. On our final day before taking my cold bug back home, we had a gentle but chilly walk along Nefyn beach, always excellent therapy for the body and mind.

Porthmadog Gorsedd stones and Moel y Gest

Eisteddfod Ramble 16
March – April 2023
Soap and a Devil

Towards the end of March, Tom and Simon took some time off work, meaning that the four of us could have a long weekend together at the caravan on my usual four days off work, then Tom stayed on to catch up with some old college friends who happen to have moved to Llŷn. We were lucky with the weather which mostly remained dry and reasonably warm for March. On our first day, while waiting for Tom to finish work and join us, Simon and I enjoyed a trip into Pwllheli with a browse around The Bookseller bookshop on Gaol Street. As we headed up the street, I was pleased to see the Steddfod '**Cronfa Pwllheli**' (Pwllheli fund) thermometer sign showing that the town's target of £62,000 had almost been reached. I was delighted to see my coastal walk book being sold in the bookshop and the shop owner asked me to sign the ones remaining on the table – I still feel rather pretentious when I do this, but I do like to have my books signed by the author even if they're unknowns like myself. I told him of my current plans and how I was writing about eisteddfodau. He joked that he'd enjoyed the Steddfod in Pwllheli in 1925, then pointed to an old faded poster, slightly chewed on the edges, displayed in the shop window which was an original one advertising the event.

The Steddfod has taken place in Pwllheli in 1875, 1925 and 1955. The majority of the books sold at this shop are in English, but I was drawn to the shelf of Welsh language books and found an interesting book in Welsh about the Gorsedd and eisteddfodau *A Fu Heddwch?* 'was there peace?' by Robyn Léwis, a rather difficult read for me yet, but with lots of pictures to help me out. A quick Google told me that Léwis had died in 2019, at almost 90, and had studied at Pwllheli Grammar School. He was a solicitor and at one time was vice president of Plaid Cymru. In 2002, using the name Robyn Llŷn, he was the first winner of the prose medal to become Archdruid. He was quite a colourful character I'd heard, and I remember a story appearing in local papers some years ago, about him refusing to pay for his shopping in Pwllheli Spar, when the person serving him at the till told him the total of his shopping in

English. Although for most things Welsh speakers use their own language for numbers, I have noticed that amounts of money are frequently said in English by many.

The following night, we gave the 'boys' (both in their twenties) some space and went off to a gig in Bangor. Tapestri, the band made up of two female singers (mentioned earlier) –were playing in the north again, this time at the Blue-Sky Café and supported by Eve Goodman. I'd pre ordered the Tapestri C.D., and the T-shirt which I wore to the gig. Eve spotted us as we arrived and kindly came over to chat. We congratulated her on having been in the final of Cân i Gymru along with Sarah, who is the northern half of Tapestri. Lowri and Sarah were busy setting up their gear but gave us a wave and commented on the T-shirt. I'm such a groupie! I told Eve that I'd seen on Facebook that she'd been performing in Dubai recently. She explained that the Welsh government has a base there because of their trade connections and they are keen for St David's Day to be celebrated. This was the second time she had been invited over and, on this occasion, she sang the Welsh National Anthem and Calon Lân with a Dubai young people's choir, the SPAA Singers, at the British Embassy. The gig tonight was a huge success with a packed-out taproom and great performances by all. My only regret of the evening was that after we'd bought the tickets, I'd found out that yet again another favourite singer Steve Eaves was playing the same night in the pub Tafarn y Plu in Llanystumdwy. Coincidentally Steve sings a song about a lady in the Blue-Sky Café – 'Y Ferch yn y Blue Sky Café'. If we'd had to choose, it would have been a very difficult decision to make.

Our last night at the caravan, was a memorable one, with Tom showing us the moon and galaxies through his telescope and managing to capture a stunning image of the whirlpool galaxy. Jim, Simon and myself set off back home the following morning leaving Tom at the caravan to enjoy the rest of the week meeting up with friends. On the journey back in the car, I reflected on our special weekend. It had been some time since just the four of us had spent time together in Llŷn – a memory for me to treasure. Sadly, my reverie was interrupted abruptly by some sad news when we were only a couple of miles from home. Jim's sister rang to let us know that their brother, John had died that morning. Jim is the youngest

Tom setting up his telescope on the decking

The night sky close to the caravan

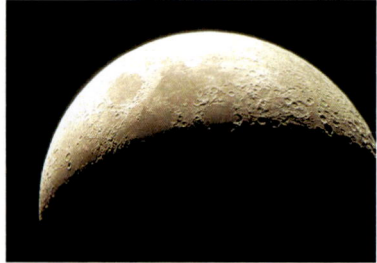

The moon

Whirlpool galaxy

of seven siblings and John was ten years his elder. They had spent a lot of time together over the years as they had worked together as sheet metal workers, including on the electrical boxes for the tunnel at Conwy as mentioned earlier.

We had already booked tickets to see the group Pedair at the end of March and Jim agreed that it would be good for him to have some distraction from the sad news of the loss of his brother, so we continued with our plans. We had the afternoon in Wrexham and visited Tŷ Pawb for the first time. Tŷ Pawb, means everyone's house and is a community space, which houses two galleries, a theatre, several meeting rooms, a bar and food court and market hall which is home to over 30 local independent businesses. We ordered a panad from one of the eating places and the friendly owner told us how busy it would be the following day as it was the fifth anniversary of the place and there were lots of art and music events taking place. I felt sorry that we would miss this but we hadn't planned to stay over. Wrexham is just less than an hour from our home near Manchester, so is easy to pop there for the day. The venue for the gig was just across the road from Tŷ Pawb at the community pub **Saith Seren** (seven stars) and this was my first visit there also. Saith Seren isn't just an ordinary pub, but advertises itself as a Welsh Centre and its aim is to provide a focus for Welsh speakers, learners and supporters of the language and culture. For some time, I'd been intending to pop there on a Thursday evening after

Cerys Hafana in Saith Seren

Saith Seren

Tŷ Pawb

work, as for several years now, with a break during the covid 19 pandemic, a Welsh learners' chat group, **Clwb Clebran** (chat club) has been meeting up there. Pedair were warming up as we arrived and Gwyneth Glyn welcomed us and asked had we seen the support artist Cerys Hafana before and praised her talent. I explained that I'd only ever seen her on the T.V., when she was filmed at the AmGen (alternative) Eisteddfod in 2021. This was during the covid pandemic, when she and other artists including Pedair and Eve Goodman performed at the National Library of Wales, Aberystwyth in the **'Tŷ Gwerin o Bell'** (folk tent from afar). In normal circumstances, the folk tent would be on the field (the Maes) with all the other tents at the Steddfod, of course. Saith Seren was soon filled with a large crowd of friendly folk, eager to hear the music.

Cerys Hafana wowed the audience with her beautiful high voice and playing of the triple harp, despite a string breaking early on in her performance. Pedair were excellent too of course and played songs that were now quite familiar to us from previous performances and from listening to their album. I'd noticed that the background to the stage was a huge Owain Glyndŵr flag, red and gold with the lion on each of the four panels. Today was **'Diwrnod Llythyr Pennal Owain Glyndŵr'** (The Day of Owain Glyndŵr's Pennal Letter). On the 31st March 1406, Owain Glyndŵr, the last Welsh Prince of Wales, sent a letter to Charles VI, King of France, outlining his ambitions for an independent Wales and asking for help for his campaign to stop the oppressive English rule at the time.

I'd also noticed some gold helium balloons making the number 40 and at the end of the gig we discovered that it was a special birthday for the youngest of the band – Meinir Gwilym, as we all joined in singing **Penblwydd Hapus** (Happy Birthday) to her as she blew out the candles of a cake presented to her. This was followed by Twm Morys reading a poem that he had composed for her. The evening came to an end with an up-to-date announcement that delighted the audience – the 2025 Steddfod was to be held in Wrexham!

Simon Chandler introducing the film at Home Cinema

On the 3rd April, Jim and I went into Manchester to Home, the Arts Centre, which amongst many other things, regularly offers viewings of independent films. The manager had contacted Simon Chandler, who organises the monthly Sgwrs a Pheint (chat and pint) group for first language and fluent Welsh speakers in the Manchester area. The group were invited to a special evening with a viewing of a new Welsh language film. The event was also advertised outside of the group and a large audience of mostly Welsh speakers attended, and the inclusion of subtitles meant that many were able to bring friends and relatives to enjoy the film.

Simon did a short speech at the beginning to introduce the film, **'Y Sŵn'** (meaning the sound) which told of an important moment in Welsh history and featured some of Wales's best actors including Sian Reese Williams, Mark Lewis Jones and Rhodri Evan. In 1979 Margaret Thatcher, came to power as prime minister with a manifesto promising to establish a Welsh language television channel. The film tells the story of her revoking that promise and of the protests that ensued including the threat of a hunger strike by Plaid Cymru's Gwynfor Evans which eventually led to the Conservative government doing a U-turn. S4C (**Sianel Pedwar Cymru** – Channel Four Wales) was eventually established in 1982. A short film was shown before this which was set on the peninsula in Nefyn and Morfa Nefyn. Very cleverly in just 10 minutes, it spread the message about the second homes crisis, coastal erosion along the north Wales coast and concern about the continuity of the Welsh language. Both films were very moving and the almost

100 strong audience clapped fiercely at the end. I was ready to stand and sing the Welsh National Anthem! Following both films there was opportunity to mingle in the bar, and for some Welsh chat with friends from the group and with some new faces. Members of the Sgwrs a Pheint group were thrilled to see that the director Lee Haven Jones had attended and some got to have a chat with him.

The traffic wasn't as bad as expected when we next travelled to the caravan on the night before Good Friday. Our Good Friday was spent mostly in Pwllheli and began as it often does for me with a visit to Llên Llŷn book and record shop, where I added to my C.D. collection and ended with our third visit of the day to Caffi Largo and a meet up with a friend. The friend was Peter, who I'd first met at the Sgwrs a Pheint group when it began a few years ago, and Jim and I had been chatting to him and his wife Lesley in the bar at Home in Manchester just a few days earlier. Peter originates from Pwllheli and often visits his brother there, and we had been trying to arrange a meet up in Caffi Largo for some time as it is also one of his favourite haunts. He teased that he knew we'd been in Llên Llŷn and explained that he'd asked Llifon, the owner, how my book was selling and was told that we'd been in the shop that morning. We got chatting about our mutual passion for Welsh language music and we told him of our recent Pedair and Tapestri gigs. Peter is a mine of information about the arts of Llŷn and has introduced me to some older Welsh artists, including Endaf Emlyn who was brought up in Pwllheli. I'm currently enjoying listening to his first album from 1972, Hiraeth, which is a combination of old folk tunes and original lyrical songs, said to have an American influence. In 1972, I would have mostly been listening to my pop favourites David Cassidy and the Sweet! Emlyn's second album, Salem, was recorded in 1974 at Sain studios, which is just about on the peninsula, close to Dinas Dinlle in Caernarfonshire. It is said to be the first Welsh language concept album, with songs inspired by the 1908 painting of the same name. The painting by Sydney Curnow Vosper, depicts a scene inside Capel Salem in Pentre Gwynfryn, Gwynedd (not on the peninsula) and is famous especially for the shawl of the traditionally dressed Welsh lady. Some say that the face of the devil is hidden amongst its folds. I've seen the original painting in Lady Lever Art Gallery in Port

Sunlight on the Wirral and could see the suggested face but whether this was deliberate by the artist or not we'll never know. Lever Brothers (William Hesketh and James Lever) were the manufacturers of Sunlight soap in the late 1800s. Prints of this painting were given to people who collected enough Sunlight soap bar tokens and were therefore seen in the homes of many throughout the UK. How on earth did I get onto the topic of devils and soap?

Peter had also told me of Endaf Emlyn's other talents. In the late 1980s, he wrote and directed a film called **'Stormydd Awst'** (August Storms), which was filmed mostly in Pwllheli (renamed Aberheli). Based in the 1950s, it tells of the arrival of television to a small community in north Wales and its influence on its people especially a teenage boy and his family. Peter can remember the excitement that the filming caused amongst the people of the town at the time, and Caffi Largo, then named 'Caffi Melyn' but renamed 'Rita's' for the film, which is situated close to the sea front, features quite heavily. Stormydd Awst can be found on YouTube in its entirety and is worth a watch even if you don't speak Welsh just to spot the locations. Another interesting piece of information that Peter shared this morning was that this year's Steddfod was the first to have a resident poet and Iestyn Tyne had this very important task. Iestyn is very familiar in Llŷn, because of his music and literary talents and his role will be to chronicle the festival through his poems, which will be available to see on the Steddfod website. He was brought up on a farm in Boduan, close to where the Steddfod was to be held, and as well as being a published poet, he has been a member of several musical groups. He is a very skilled fiddle player and Jim and I have seen him in previous years, performing live with a very young-looking folk band Patrobas as well as regularly accompanying the increasingly famous folk artist Gwilym Bowen Rhys. He was the first person to have won both main literary prizes in the Urdd National Eisteddfod, the Crown in 2016 and the Chair in 2019, and by the time the Steddfod takes place this year, he will be the ripe old age of 26.

Walk 16
Mynydd Rhiw and Clip y Gylfinir, Rhiw
9th April 2023
A Lone Rider and a Chocolate Treat

Easter Sunday was cloudy but dry and we both felt up to getting back to the hills. We packed an Easter egg in the rucksack to share at the summit. Well we had to didn't we? Our hill for today, Mynydd Rhiw, is easy to spot from miles around because of the tall radio mast not far from the summit and also because of its proximity to a small, but steep conical hill, curiously called **Clip y Gylfinir** (curlew's slope), with a radar station nestled at its foot. Neither hill is high, but the views are stunning all around this area and compensate for the presence of the tall metal structures and rather ugly looking concrete buildings. I later looked back on photos to find when we had visited with Tom and Simon and found it was in 2004 and 2014. How time flies. I admired the hedgerows on the drive to Rhiw, alive with the yellows of daffodils, primroses and gorse and the white blooms of the scurvy grass and blackthorn. As we crossed the small cattle grid leading to the car park, marked with a National Trust sign 'Mynydd Rhiw', a solitary horse and rider were disappearing beyond the low summit of that hill. As we stepped out of the car, we were both taken by surprise at the strength of the wind and it whipped my hair into my face. The views of distant mountains were fuzzy in the mist.

Clip y Gylfinir

Approaching Mynydd Rhiw

We decided to go with Des' recommendation of ascending Clip y Gylfinir before heading up Mynydd Rhiw; both hills being easily accessed from the same car park. We began the climb optimistically as although it is very steep, we could see it was a short walk to the summit. We puffed and panted up the grassy slope, bald apart from one blooming gorse bush, to about the halfway point and then realised that continuing onwards would require a scramble on hands and knees across large rocks – not something that either of us felt capable of especially in the strong wind. We satisfied ourselves with the views, which were stunning even from here – with the island Ynys Enlli visible across the roof tops of the radar station buildings, and in the other direction the wide sandy bay of Porth Neigwl and the sea shimmering in the rays of sunshine that were forcing their way through the clouds. After descending carefully, we headed along the wide, clear path towards Mynydd Rhiw summit, where a few sheep were grazing contentedly. Large areas of low gorse and heather, still very bare, created an interesting patchwork pattern between the dry grassy paths on the wide, gentle slopes.

We heard the loud song of skylarks as we strode out, but they were too high in the sky to make out. We greeted two other people returning from the summit and returned their English greeting, followed by a **bore da** from me – I like to sneak the Welsh in when I can. We soon reached the trig point after a clamber over a short rocky stretch. My knees can manage clambering but not scrambling. We joked about this being the perfect hill walk for us now at our age. The wind stopped us from lingering too long at the very summit and we were soon sheltered against the rocks where we devoured a whole easter egg between us. As always, the views didn't fail to impress and we admired the hills – some we'd already climbed including Garn Fadryn, Foel Felin Wynt and one of the three Yr Eifl hills, the quarried Garn Fôr, and others we hoped to attempt soon, including the other two Yr Eifl peaks. Jim likes a scenic view as much as me, but being an engineer by nature and previous trade, his attention was also often drawn to the radio and radar structures. Helped by the proximity of two white wind turbines, we managed to locate a favourite spot – Felin Uchaf (the area mentioned where the storytelling takes place in the roundhouses). As we looked down the gentle north eastern slopes of Mynydd Rhiw, we remembered that this was where following gorse burning in the 1950s, a Neolithic axe factory had been discovered. As we headed back the way we came, we reminisced about visits here with the boys when they were little, and us all rummaging together amongst the prickly gorse hoping to find remaining pieces of stone axes. We found nothing of course but the joy was in the search. A skylark flew low enough for us to spot it, which was a delight and we both agreed this had been a blustery but easy and pleasant walk, which we could manage again in the future.

Summit of Garn Fadryn with the radio and radar masts and other hills of Llŷn in the distance

Eisteddfod Ramble 17
19 April 2023
A Chapel Eisteddfod

On the evening of Easter Sunday, our Llŷn friends Amanda and Brian called to see us at the caravan, bearing some of Amanda's delicious baking. We caught up with how both our families were getting on including sharing our losses as Brian's father had also passed away not too long ago – a popular local farmer who carried on working on his Llannor farm into his 90s. He always had time for a friendly chat with us when we bumped into him in the shops or at Tyddyn Sachau garden centre café where he liked to have Sunday lunch with his wife. Amanda, who works as a teaching assistant in a primary school, told me how busy the children were with creating things towards the Steddfod. This included the making of short films, creative writing and helping with a project called **Gair Mewn Gwlân** (Word in Wool). This project had involved the knitting or crocheting of small squares by local volunteers, with the intention of them being used to create murals.

The children were being asked to add the final touches to the squares by adding words – names of local sites, such as bridges, caves, farms, houses, or paths. We had already seen one or two brightly painted wooden signs appearing in different parts of the peninsula identifying similar sites. Many of these had been created by a lady called Morwen Jones, mother of the Welsh tutor and artist Marian Brosschot, mentioned earlier, as she'd been posting images of them on a Facebook page that she'd started, named after her project Cofnod 2023. Cofnod means record or memo and this project's aim was similar to that of Gair Mewn Gwlân, that of recording and remembering these special names that are at risk of being forgotten by future generations. Not long after this visit, it was announced on the news that another area of Wales, the Brecon Beacons National Park, was going to be using its original Welsh name of **Bannau Brycheiniog**, as another contribution towards protecting Welsh place names. Brycheiniog (Brecon) took its name from the fifth century legendary king Brychan. Back to Amanda who told us that there was talk of changes to the Steddfod pavilion this year. She'd heard that there may even be more than one, which as far as I was aware had never been known before. The pavilion is seen as the most important structure at the event and as mentioned is home to the main events including the Gorsedd ceremonies. The structure of the pavilion has changed over the years, and records from the 1800s describe some as being tent like and some to have been made of wood but always built to hold huge audiences. But unfortunately, they were often damaged by strong winds and rain.

The first Steddfod pavilion I ever saw was the famous Pink Pavilion, when I visited the Denbigh Steddfod for the day in 2013. Yes, the whole structure was fuchsia pink, with six fairytale spires topped with Welsh flags and was the first thing that caught my eye as I parked on the field at the edge of the Maes. The Pink Pavilion was introduced in 2006 at Swansea and took over from its stripy green and yellow predecessor. This sturdy tent lasted for a decade and at each Steddfod, it took 30 workers four days to erect it, after which the seats, stage and set were then constructed. In 2015, a new pavilion was introduced – a rectangular modern looking building called 'Evolution'. I was looking forward to seeing what the pavilion or pavilions would be like this year and was hoping to get into one of them to watch the Gorsedd ceremonies.

Just less than two weeks after Amanda and Brian's visit, I attended **Eisteddfod Gadeiriol y Ffôr**, which was a local annual eisteddfod being held in Chapel Ebeneser in the village of Y Ffôr, which is only about five minutes from our caravan. Gadeiriol means chaired and this eisteddfod would involve the chairing or awarding of a chair to the main poetry competition winner. As mentioned earlier, I'd attended part of one of these in this same venue several years before, but this time, with my improved understanding of Welsh, I hoped I would be able to follow a little more of what was going on around the performances. I'd picked up a copy of the pamphlet that listed the competitions in Llên Llŷn book shop a

Eisteddfod y Ffôr

few weeks ago and had decided to attend the later session (**Hwyr**) only, as I'd remembered how many hours these could continue for. The earlier session started at midday and was recorded as **Prynhawn** on the programme, which just means afternoon. This was when the children and early teens were competing. I arrived just before the advertised starting time of 6pm for the Hwyr and after paying the small fee to the man at the door, I sat on an old solid hardwood pew at the back of the chapel. I quickly moved sideways onto a cushioned chair, when I recalled how long I may be sitting. I was surprised at how few people there were in the audience, mostly who appeared to be parents and children. I was also surprised that on the small stage at the end of the hall, there was already a performance going on. It was obviously a children's duet competition and I enjoyed listening to the different renditions, with piano accompaniment. It eventually dawned on me that I was witnessing the tail end of the Prynhawn/afternoon session and it had run over time. A judge came out to the front following the performances and before announcing the winners, gave a detailed account of the strengths and weaknesses of all the performances.

People then began to disperse and it was announced that the late session would start in about half an hour.

For about ten minutes, the audience consisted of me, then gradually people of all ages drifted in and filled up the pews and chairs. The session was opened with everyone standing and singing Calon Lân – another chance for me to practise the words. Bethan Jones-Parry, the announcer, invited the competitors out to the stage to do their bit, starting with the three men competing in the over 55s solo, who sang a Welsh hymn of their choice. The rest of the competitors were mostly from late teens to early twenties and the competitions included solos, recitations, cerdd dant (explained earlier) folk songs and piano solo. I realised that the pattern of the evening was for about two or three competitions to take place and for the judges to then step forwards to give their comments and announce the winner. One young lady, from Trawsfynydd, stood out especially. She had a very sweet voice which gained her several prizes, each consisting of small amounts of money, and it was quite amusing to see her dashing to her proud mother in the audience with her winnings then back again to the front after being called out for the next competition. One of my queries about local eisteddfodau was answered – could people from outside of the area compete? Trawsfynydd is in Gwynedd but not in Llŷn, so the answer is yes. Myrddin ap Dafydd, was to be one of the judges at this event and I noticed him arriving and discreetly taking a seat on one of the pews which were now filling up. Sitting just in front of me, I'd noticed Esyllt Maelor, the author and winner of the crown at last year's Steddfod, who was also acting as a judge this evening. She came out to the front and talked about the **Cystadleuaeth Tlws yr Ifanc** (the young person's trophy competition) which was a literary competition for 15 to 25-year-olds, where work is submitted prior to the eisteddfod enabling time for reading and judging. Esyllt spoke about how high the standard of the work had been and about the importance of encouraging young people to write. She announced the winner, who was a local young lady Efa Hodge, from Pontllyfni on the peninsula. The Prifardd Geraint Lloyd Owen presented Efa with her prize, an engraved slate trophy, which he explained had been created by a Pwllheli company Cerrig Granite and Slate. Geraint Lloyd Owen, often known by his bardic name Geraint Llifon, is a poet, winning the crown in the 2011 Steddfod and was Myrddin ap Dafydd's predecessor as Archdruid of the Gorsedd. He added more words of encouragement and praise to Efa and talked fondly of members of her family that he knew. He then congratulated and sang the praises of Esyllt, whose family he was also familiar with. **Byd bach** – small world as they say.

Myrddin ap Dafydd was then invited out to the front to announce the winners of the poetry competitions, again entries will have been submitted earlier in the year for reading and judging. The three different categories for poetry were **Englyn**, **Telyneg** and **Limrig**. Englyn as explained earlier is a four-line verse, with particular rules to be followed and the topic given to competitors for this competition was **Ffordd** (road or way). I'd not heard of Telyneg before and Myrddin joked that it may be easier to explain what Telyneg isn't than what it is, so I've no chance at explaining it. It isn't even included in the New Companion to the Literature of Wales. All I can tell you is the word Telyneg translates as lyric and that the topic assigned to this presumably lyrical poetry competition was **Troi**, which means turn. I can remember even as a child, enjoying the sound of a limerick (limrig), with its comical punch line and lively rhythm and especially enjoyed reading those by poet and comedian Spike Milligan. I think most people are familiar with them and they continue to be very popular in Wales. Shân Cothi, Welsh singer-songwriter, television, and radio presenter, has a regular slot on her Radio Cymru show where she reads out limericks sent to her on a given topic. Myrddin read several of the ones that had been submitted much to the delight of the audience. I caught some of the punchlines but not all – I find poetry in the Welsh language especially the most difficult to keep up with. The names of the winners were read out but it appeared that none of them were present at the event to collect their prize. Bethan Jones-Parry commented jovially on how lucky this local eisteddfod was to have such distinguished people present, with the archdruid himself, the prifardd Geraint and the prifardd Esyllt and she added not forgetting **y dyn ifanc hwn** (this young man) and pointed to the treasurer who had been handing out the ten or twenty-pound notes to the winners throughout the afternoon. I recognized him as Guto Dafydd, who is also a prifardd, having won the crown twice for his poetry in previous Steddfodau. I remembered him from the Llanrwst Steddfod of 2019 when he won the Daniel Owen Memorial Prize for his novel *Carafanio* (caravanning), which I have finally started to read and enjoy as I'm writing this chapter. You can guess why it appealed to me although it is about the exploits of a family in a touring caravan not a static.

By now the chapel was bursting at the seams and Geraint announced that the Cadeirio (chairing) would be taking place – the awarding of the prize for the main poetry competition. The subject of the poem was **Gadael** (meaning leaving). What then followed was what appeared to be an adapted version of the chairing ceremony to be seen at the Steddfod, one that was manageable in a small chapel rather than a large pavilion. Ten Y Ffôr primary school children in their bright red school sweatshirts then paraded into the chapel and lined up along the stage behind the wooden chair where the winner would be seated. A small model chair of a simple design, with an engraved plaque was placed on the seat of this chair – this was to be the prize. Geraint spoke highly of the children and explained that they had needed a couple of volunteers to help with the chairing ceremony. The organisers had then been overwhelmed by the eagerness and enthusiasm of all of these children who were willing to give up their time. A man with a trumpet joined the children at the front and with a dose of humour, blew the trumpet to announce the start of the occasion. The ffugenw (false name) was then announced and a young lady towards the back of the room stood up smiling. Two of the children went to meet her then escorted her to the front, as the pianist played and the audience clapped rhythmically until they reached the stage. I was then surprised to see the appearance of a sword as used in the Steddfod. Geraint took charge but was assisted by some of the children. The sword was unsheathed and replaced three times, with the question 'A oes heddwch?' (Is there peace?) and the response 'Heddwch' (peace). I noticed this was done very carefully and not above the head of the winner as would be done at the Steddfod – health and safety rules at work here.

The real name of the lady was announced – Elin Evans, originally of Morfa Nefyn. Geraint gave her history and explained that she was now working as a family doctor in Ruthin. He knew her family also. Each of the ten children then stood by the side of Elin one at a time and read out a celebratory poem that they'd written in school especially for the occasion. Some of the poems had humour and some were more poignant and I was very impressed by their writing skills. They would have been much more deserving of the Blue Peter badge with their poems than I had been all those years ago. A song was sung by the children at the end, that I was not familiar with but clearly the audience were as they all joined in with the repeated couplet at the end of each of the three verses. I discovered later that it was **Cân y Cadeirio** (chairing song) and was sung at chairing ceremonies at all eisteddfodau and spoke of greeting the king of bards and mentions some of the traditions of the ceremony, such as the horns being blown to the four corners of the world, the sword being unsheathed and peace being shouted by all. The tune was familiar to me and I found out that it was called **'Rhyfelgyrch Capten Morgan'** (Captain Morgan's March) but I realised that it reminded me a lot of the tune used by Bob Delyn a'r Ebillion for their comical Christmas song 'Dolig Del'. If you'd like to hear it, look on YouTube for 'Song for the Bard' and you'll find a young, robed Shan Cothi singing it at a Steddfod in about 2007, with English subtitles if you so wish. This was then followed by singing of the Welsh National Anthem, which I could join in with and then a few people began to disperse. I was surprised that the evening was ending so early as it was just after 9pm, and I remembered the last time it continued for many more hours. I'd been enjoying the whole event but my back and my knees were ready for moving not to mention my bladder. So, I headed out to the car park where I soon noticed that there was a car blocking the exit. I sat in the car and waited for others to come out of the chapel, but very few did. I presumed people were having a panad and socializing, so I returned to the door of the chapel where there were a few people whispering in the porch outside of the main door as if waiting to go in when they could do so without disturbing whatever was now going on inside.

I noticed typed sheets of paper on the table and as I looked more closely, a man pointed to halfway down the sheet and smiled. I realised he was showing me where the evening was up to. The cadeirio wasn't the final event of the night but only about halfway through! I whispered to the man about my predicament in the car park and he came to have a look. He knew who owned the car and he spied his moment to go into the chapel to let the lady know. She then came and moved her car, while I had a little chat with the kind man who was interested to know about my learning to speak Welsh. On returning to Jim and the caravan, I recounted my experience. I'd taken one of the sheets, which was of course the programme that I should have had and realised on reading it that there were a lot more interesting competitions still to come including choirs. I also realised I should have paid someone 30p for the sheet. Woops – I'll pop some money in a local charity box to make up for it when I next see one. I'm amazed and impressed at the stamina of the competitors and organisers of these local eisteddfodau – I'm sure this one must have continued beyond midnight by which time I'd have been asleep for more than an hour.

An outdoor panad at Plas Nanhoron

Bluebells at Plas Nanhoron

The following day, we visited Nanhoron Park and Gardens, which is situated close to Botwnnog beyond a lodge and some very grand looking iron gates. We have passed by this country estate many times and been curious about it, so our nosiness was finally satisfied when this open day was arranged to help raise funds for Botwnnog's contribution to the Steddfod. It was a very popular event and the sun came out to greet us all. The highlights for me were the woodlands which were carpeted with bluebells and the mature azalea and rhododendrons which always remind me of my dad as they were his favourite shrubs. A panad and cake was served through a hatch and enjoyed outdoors close to the large hall, (Plas) and I was reminded of the covid lockdowns when cafés had to serve customers this way. The bilingual guide we were given explained that Nanhoron Estate has belonged to the same family for more than 700 years, but that the layout of the mansion with its lawn and park running down to the lake had followed the 'classic eighteenth century plan'. I was half expecting Mr Darcy to appear at any minute. It was almost 3pm when we were having our cake and coffee and we'd remembered that at 3pm precisely there was to be an emergency alert test organised by the UK government sent to all UK mobile phones. This alert had been designed to notify people about potentially life-threatening disasters. We stood away from the crowd of people and watched the seconds counting down amused at what was about to happen, but all we heard were a few low ringing sounds, and life continued as normal. We found out later that a large percentage of alarms had not worked especially with one particular mobile network which Jim and I both used. At the time of writing this we're both still waiting.

That evening we spent time on the caravan decking watching the night sky, something we often enjoy doing. There had been sightings of the aurora borealis recently even from parts of Wales and other areas in the UK, and it was forecasted again tonight.

There was quite a lot of cloud northwards, but as our eyes got accustomed to the dark, we both agreed that something looked different about the quality of the clouds. To our naked eyes it all looked grey. Jim set up our 'proper' but rather old digital camera on the tripod – as opposed to our phone cameras which we tend to use for day-to-day photos. He played around with different settings and we could eventually see through the view finder that indeed there was something going on – the sky was purple. We managed to get a couple of rather blurry images but that night and the following day, some brilliant images appeared on Facebook of Aurora's visit to Llŷn.

Another very special event that was shown on a post on Facebook at the end of April, was the first performance of the Llŷn children's choir. A film clip from Heno, the evening T.V. Welsh news show on S4C, showed the 500 children from nine different primary schools, singing a brand new song, called **'Anthem Ysgolion Llŷn'** (Llŷn pupils' anthem) composed by Huw Griffith and Anni Llŷn. There were many comments in response to this post in Welsh and English and all agreed, even those that hadn't understood the meaning of the lyrics, that the children made a beautiful sound together. The lyrics were touching and as well as referring to various parts of the peninsula and the importance of their language, spoke of the children of Llŷn being the ones that put the sunshine and colour into the area.

A hint of aurora borealis from the caravan

Walk 17

Garn Ganol, Yr Eifl, Llithfaen
29th April 2023
The Big One

Our next visit to the caravan was a special one for us, as Tom and Simon were both able to join us and we planned to do a hill walk together. For years we had talked about 'doing the big one', meaning the highest hill on Llŷn, **Garn Ganol**, but for one reason or another we had never got around to it. Garn Ganol means central hill and is the middle peak of the range of hills called Yr Eifl – sometimes referred to by their mistakenly pronounced anglicised name The Rivals. Eifl rhymes with naval not rival. You'll by now be sick of hearing me mention Yr Eifl and the fact that they're my favourite hills, but up until a few years ago I thought they were my favourite mountains, and they are sometimes referred to as such in guide books. But even Garn Ganol standing at 564 metres, doesn't quite qualify for mountain status, but it certainly looks and feels mountainous. Des describes a triangular route, taking in all three summits, but Jim and I knew that would be too big a challenge for us and we were all happy to just focus on 'The Big One'. Jim and I had already managed as far as we could get up Garn Fôr, and we would save the third hill, Tre'r Ceiri for another day.

On the way to Garn Ganol

The morning of the planned walk wasn't quite what we'd expected. In the right conditions, Mynydd Carnguwch, Garn Ganol and Tre'r Ceiri appear very close through our bedroom window, but as we looked out this morning a heavy mist hid the three of them completely. We decided to wait a while and see how the weather progressed, and considered the idea of climbing Tre'r Ceiri instead if the mist lifted enough. We felt certain that the peak of Garn Ganol would remain in mist for the rest of the day. By early afternoon, the sky had begun to clear and we decided to set off to see what we could manage – by now we still couldn't see the summit of Garn Ganol, but the other two were beginning to clear.

As we arrived at the car park, above Nant Gwrtheyrn Language Centre, we were excited to see that although there was quite a lot of remaining cloud, the mist had totally lifted from the whole of the hill range, so Garn Ganol it was then!

From the car park, we followed the advice of Elain, our young Welsh friend, who we knew had walked to the summit several times. She'd suggested the easiest route for our old knees, and Tom and Simon were happy to go with that too. The main thing we had to remember was to stay to the right and to not follow the route taken by most walkers which takes you towards the pass (**bwlch**) between Garn Ganol and Garn Fôr. We began by taking the route that quickly links with an obvious straight path that follows the line of a dry stone wall. This straight path is part of a trail known as **Llwybr Gwyn Plas** (Gwyn Plas' path) and was created in memory of Gwyn Elis, a local historian, walking leader and a trustee of Nant Gwrtheyrn. The long straight wall is **Wal Mawr** (big wall), which was built in about 1815, by unemployed soldiers on their return from the battle of Waterloo. It was built to partition the land following a London Parliamentary Enclosure Act, which resulted in shared community common land being removed from local people by estate landowners. I remembered a walk with Jim along Llwybr Gwyn Plas, where we came across a derelict cottage, with a plaque explaining that it was a **'Tŷ Unnos'**, (one night house) called Cae'r Mynydd and had been the home of Robert William Hughes, who was transported to Botany Bay in Australia in 1813 following the Llithfaen riot. There was an ancient Welsh custom that if a person could build a house on common land in one night and have smoke coming from the chimney by daybreak

Tŷ Unnos, Llithfaen

then he would be the legal owner of the house and some of the land around it. Robert William Hughes was said to have been a ringleader in Llithfaen, who arranged protests against the officials who tried to evict people from these cottages. There are tales of him rounding people up to gatherings using a large sea shell as a megaphone. Now where was I?

Tom and Simon stopped intermittently and patiently waited for us to catch up. We also stopped intermittently to catch our breath. Two men were approaching the end of the path we were taking, and I checked with them that we were taking the correct one, asking if the summit was manageable from this side without scrambling on hands and knees. With what looked a mixture of amusement and sympathy they reassured me that this was the easiest of the routes and that it was steep but the rocks could be trod like steps to the summit. We thanked them and went on our way, but I still wondered if I'd make it, with my stiff knees, even with my walking pole and knee supports.

The skylarks sang high above us out of sight and lots of other small birds flitted past too quickly to identify. The heathland around us was very dry and humming occasionally with the sound of bees. We were all soon peeling off jackets as we warmed up along the slowly inclining path. Tom and Simon have always got on well together give or take a few skirmishes in childhood. They now work together and they speak the same language – often related to computer technology – a language that Jim and I are often bemused by. They chatted animatedly together ahead of us and I felt blissfully happy to be in my special place with the three people that mean the most to me in the world. The path was wide and obvious, as we approached Garn Ganol, and we could now see the path winding its way around the eastern side of the hill and the stone cairn at the summit. It looked a long way ahead. Jim and I waved to Tom and Simon who had made some headway by now and were sitting on a boulder amidst the dry bare heather, admiring the views. I propped on the seat of my walking pole, my heart pounding, and looked back with Jim at where we'd come from and the scenery beyond. The straight line of Wal Fawr, now looked like it had been drawn by a black marker pen along the landscape, and Garn Fadryn and the adjoining bays of Nefyn and Porthdinllaen dominated the views.

The path became narrower, rockier, and steeper as we made our way to Tom and Simon. Southwards we looked down at the craggy ridge Caergribin, and Mynydd Carnguwch the hill we refer to as Booby Hill, with Ceredigion Bay shimmering in the sunshine, and the mountains of Eryri beyond topped with white fluffy clouds. Low growing, lush green bilberry bushes were dotted amongst the boulders and heather, some bearing new red berries. Tom and Simon shouted down to us to warn us of how steep this part of the climb was and I was touched at their concern for their aging parents. It doesn't seem that long since we carried one or the other up some of the hills of Llŷn in a backpack. As Jim and I were trying to spot the location of our caravan site, a young lady ran by and upwards with her dog. I was beginning to feel rather old. We finally reached Tom and Simon and sat with them for a while

Bilberries

Views of the hills and bays of Llŷn and the line of Wal Mawr

on some nearby boulders, watching shadows of the clouds drifting across the fields below us.

Onwards for us all and the path became increasingly rocky but there were good footholds that were probably what the man had described as steps earlier. By now with my grumbling knees, I was wishing it was an escalator! We were all keeping an eye on the clouds which seemed to be drifting towards us and it made us put a spurt on. Tom and Simon reached the summit ahead of us and we could see them taking photos from the stone trig point, which has a curious metal adornment on the top. I'd seen images of this before – a large number four with the letters A and H attached to each side. I was rather disappointed to discover that this had no historical significance but the most likely explanation of it was that it was erected by a local blacksmith who wanted to declare his love for his partner by announcing 'A for (4) H'. So not even in Welsh – oh my! When I saw how rocky the cairn was at the top to reach the trig point, I was unsure I'd make it, but the 'steps' in the rocks (and Jim's outstretched hand as always) made it manageable. What a wonderful feeling to be at the highest point in Llŷn with my lovely family. I felt truly blessed. A young local couple soon joined us on the summit and I had a quick chat in Welsh with them and there was a mutual taking of photos. They had come from the other side via the bwlch path and agreed that it was trickier that way, with rocks that were more difficult to navigate. We all continued the journey downwards, with the clouds beginning to creep closer. The couple branched off towards the adjoining hill

Tre'r Ceiri, but we agreed to leave this for another occasion and returned the way we'd come. In no time at all Tom and Simon were back on the wide grassy paths as we plodded on slowly. We stood at one side to allow three younger walkers get past, then a small party of people approached us heading up the hill and laughed saying to us that maybe their timing hadn't been that good. We looked back and Garn Ganol was now almost hidden in mist. By the time we reached Tom and Simon at the car park, the whole area was in mist. On our way home to the caravan, I sent a picture to Amanda with the four of us on the summit and she replied with **'Llongyfarchiadau!'** which is a wonderful long Welsh word, which rolls off the tongue after quite a bit of practice and means... yes you guessed... congratulations.

Mist at the summit

Eisteddfod Ramble 18
April to May 2023
Losing the Plot

The day after our last hill walk, on a rather damp afternoon, I found myself at a familiar old well only a short drive from our caravan – Cybi's well, in Llangybi, as described earlier, due to its proximity to a previous hill walk. I'd spotted a poster earlier in the week advertising a poetry and music event inspired by a pilgrimage along the **Llwybr Cadfan** – The Cadfan Way. I was a little early but was still surprised to be the only one at the well, which is where the event was to be held. A trendy looking young man in a colourful scarf and knee-high boots appeared from amidst the nearby trees. He greeted me in a friendly manner in Welsh and I could see he also looked a little puzzled about where he should be. As I often do, much to my regret, I made an assumption, this time based on his clothing, and asked if he was one of the poets for the event. Then as he turned towards me, his dog collar gave me a clue to his identity. He smiled and explained that he'd come from Bangor. I wasn't satisfied to leave it at that and asked did he work in the church at Bangor, then quickly recalled that there was a cathedral in Bangor, so apologized and continued **'sori, mwy na eglwys?'** (Sorry more than a church?) as I'd forgotten the word for cathedral. He smiled and said that yes he was from the **'eglwys gadeiriol'** (cathedral). Oh no, what had I done again, had I just offended the Bishop of Bangor? Was it an offence to assume a man of the cloth was a poet? He could be both, as was R.S. Thomas and many others. Have I mentioned that my maiden name was Tonge? No, it wasn't spelt Tongue, but maybe it should have been. He suggested we head to the church across from the well and I followed him carefully over the slippery stone steps into the graveyard.

Path to Ffynnon Gybi

There was a group of people gathered at the church and I recognised some of them, including poets Siân Northey and Twm Morys, and Siân, the keyboard player from Llanaelhaearn church. I soon did an about turn and headed back to the gateway of the well as they were now ready to start the event. I was surprised to see singer

Dewi Pws entertaining at the well

Dewi Pws Morris approaching the gate from amongst the trees, with his banjo strapped to his back. He asked was this the way to the well and followed me through the gate. We were soon joined by other audience members and performers. I chatted to Sian a little and then with a friendly local young lady, who was involved with the organisation of the event and she explained a little more to me about the background of it. It was part of a Welsh language literary project, following the pilgrimage route of St Cadfan and had begun in 2022 to celebrate 1500 years since he left his church in Tywyn to set up a Christian settlement on the island Ynys Enlli, off the tip of the peninsula. Events had already taken part at other churches or holy places along what would have been his route, beginning in Tywyn. Following today's event, the pilgrimage was to continue along the peninsula, including activities to take place at the Steddfod in Boduan in August, and reaching the end of its journey with a retreat on Ynys Enlli at the end of August.

Poets Siôn Aled Owen, Siân Northey and Gareth Evans Jones read out poems written especially for the occasion with themes of saints and sacred wells, and Twm Morys read out a poetic history of this holy area which is connected to Cybi, the sixth century saint. Later research told me that Siôn had a passion for theology and endangered languages, had won the Steddfod Crown in his youth for his poetry and was now preaching in Welsh and English with several denominations. Siân Northey has won the chair and the crown at local eisteddfodau for her poetry. She is known to me as one of the voices of the Welsh podcast *Colli'r Plot* mentioned earlier in the book. Gareth has twice won the Steddfod Drama Medal and is currently a lecturer in Religious Studies at Bangor University. I find poetry the most difficult to understand in Welsh and felt frustrated with myself that I'd not grasped a lot of the detail of the poems, but bilingual cards given out to the small audience after the event helped me later. Dewi Pws has been a long-standing supporter of the adult and youth eisteddfodau, often helping with entertainment and fundraising. He is known for his comedic style and today he sang a couple of lively songs, accompanied by his banjo, including 'Lleucu Llwyd' which has a well-known catchy chorus that the audience were able to join in with. This was then followed by a short prayer and sermon by the trendy young man from Bangor Cathedral, who I later found out was Revd Siôn Rhys Evans, who was the Sub-Dean and not the Bishop.

Everyone returned to the church for hot drinks and **bara brith** or Welsh cakes and I chatted to one of the regular members of the congregation. He pointed out things of interest inside the church to me, including a wall mounted monument, carved with an eagle on a wreath, dedicated to John Clough Williams-Ellis who had been a clergyman and poet – another example of one not excluding the other. He died in 1913 and it has been said that he was possibly the first Welshman to climb one of the highest mountains in the Alps. The monument was thought to have been designed by his son, Clough Williams-Ellis; the architect famous for creating Portmeirion. In February, I'd been contacted by Jean Napier an author and photographer who had worked with the publishers Gwasg Carreg Gwalch for many years. I was already familiar with her book about Ynys Enlli, which I had read and enjoyed. We agreed we would like to meet up some time but hadn't yet managed this. I have also yet to buy and read her most recent book *The Cadfan Way*, which was published in 2022 and looks a very interesting celebration of this pilgrim's route with her stunning photographs lavishly illustrating it throughout. On my way out of the church to head back to the caravan, I had to squeeze past Siân Northey, so I used the opportunity to tell her how much I enjoyed her podcasts. She said that she was very pleased that they were accessible to learners.

Just less than two weeks after this event, I was sitting extremely nervously at our small dining table in the caravan, with my iPad, waiting to be invited into a Zoom meeting. Ten days before this, I'd received an email congratulating me for being accepted into the **Steddfod Dysgwr y Flwyddyn** (Learner of the Year) Competition and explaining that the next step was an interview with three judges over Zoom video, who would then select the four finalists who would go forwards to be judged again at the Steddfod in August.

Ready for my interview for Dysgwr y Flwyddyn

I felt proud to be accepted but also felt nervous at the idea of the interview, and then of having to appear in front of T.V. cameras if I did get through, not that I was expecting this to happen. Three smiling and kind looking faces eventually appeared on my screen and introduced themselves. I'd been cheeky and asked the person who had sent the email if the judges were the same ones who would be judging at the Steddfod and was told that two of them were, but that Tudur Owen would only be at the final.

I'd read in the catalogue of competitions 'Testun', that the other two judges would be Geraint Price and Liz Saville Roberts. Geraint's name is familiar to me as he often shares information about his courses on the Facebook page for the Manchester Welsh Learner's Group that I organise; he's a Welsh tutor in Gwent. Liz, who is a politician and mentioned earlier in the book also felt a little familiar to me as she is often seen at events around Llŷn. The third judge today was Hannah Thomas, who led the interview and explained that she was from the National Centre For Learning Welsh. I could feel myself trembling, however much they tried to put me at ease and my response to Hannah's first question '**Sut dych chi Jean?**' (How are you Jean), was '**Dw i'n jyst trio cofio anadlu**', which means I'm just trying to remember to breathe. My memory of my responses to the four questions put to me is rather vague, but I recall finding the background sounds of bleating sheep and the man from Pwllheli Gas changing our gas bottle reassuring in a strange sort of way. I was asked about how learning Welsh had changed my life, how I used my Welsh when not in Wales, what had been the main thing that had helped me to learn the language and what advice I would give to other learners. I can remember rambling on about my love of Welsh culture especially the music and about using Welsh with other learners and fluent speakers in the groups I attended in Manchester. I also talked about the course I used to learn to speak Welsh, 'Say Something in Welsh', but how also the people of Llŷn had been an amazing help with their patience and encouragement over the years. I told them about meeting up with similar chat groups when at the caravan whenever possible including the one held in Caernarfon at the bookshop Palas Print and the ones that are organised by Martyn Croydon and held in various local venues. My self-appraisal following the interview was that I'd spoken too quickly and too much and had been overly repetitive at times, which is my tendency when nervous. I also felt that I may have come across as rather forward which I really hadn't intended. I had mentioned to Geraint that I recognised him from Facebook and then had shown them my coastal walk book and gave it as an example of my use of Welsh when not in Wales. I rambled on, as I do, about how despite it being in English I had communicated at all times in Welsh with my publisher when discussing the editing and then at my book launch interview. I couldn't resist adding that my publisher just happened to be Myrddin ap Dafydd. Oh dear, did that sound like I was eisteddfod name dropping to gain points – I hadn't consciously done this but who knows what my unconscious was up to. I had already gone and mentioned Martyn Croydon, who was a previous winner of Dysgwr y Flwyddyn and was the organiser of Maes D (learner's area) this year and now I'd mentioned the archdruid himself. As the interview was coming to an end Hannah asked if I was intending going to the Steddfod and I said **'yn bendant'** (definitely) and proceeded to point out that I was wearing my locally designed Steddfod T-shirt. Oh no, I felt I'd gone too far again even though they all admired it and smiled kindly at me. I really can't help myself. I was told that I'd hear the following week if I was one of the four. They wished me well and we said our goodbyes. Jim knew just what I needed and gave me a big hug as soon as I came off the video then rushed me off to Caffi Largo in Pwllheli for lunch to recover from the adrenalin rush!

Walk 18: Mynydd Cefnamwlch – Eastern Summit, Penllech

13th May 2023

A Hare and a Tyre

The sun was shining making the views out to sea extra stunning as we drove along the B4417 to the layby parking spot. The hedgerows were bright with blossoming yellow gorse, and bluebells. We were following Des' advice and ignoring the walk to the main western summit, which he describes as 'unremitting toil through dense brambles, high bracken and hidden boulders' – a perfect recipe for me to fall and break something. The lower eastern summit was the one for us which Des reassured could be 'easily followed on a track and a grassy path'. The layby was on the right-hand side of the B4417 heading south towards Aberdaron from Tudweiliog, close to the village of Penllech. After crossing the road, we walked on for about 100 metres, until we spotted the wide, dry track leading to farms and the hill. We had driven past this low hill many times on our way to Aberdaron, not realising there was a path to the summit – this was new territory for us which I always find quite exciting.

The lane to Mynydd Cefnamwlch

Bluebells near Parc-bod-Badrig

The dirt track was steeper than I'd expected but this meant that we were soon able to get a good view across fields of grazing sheep, with the hill Anelog, the sea and Ynys Enlli in the misty distance. We passed a couple of farmhouses on our right and a tractor was ploughing in one of the fields with gulls following enjoying finds from the disturbed ground. Cow parsley and bluebells lined the track and spilled into the adjoining fields.

We reached the farmhouse Parc-bod-Badrig and took the left dirt track which rose above the farm and led into the woodland which consisted of a mix of coniferous and deciduous trees. We soon agreed that we had been missing a treat on this walk, with birds singing from high up in the tall conifers. We passed a group of deciduous trees in an area carpeted with blue bells, with a car tyre strung to one of the trees acting as a swing, presumably for children from the farm. I thought what a blissful place this would be for any child to spend their time playing and daydreaming, and I wondered what memories had been made here.

The track had been even and quite easy to walk along until we took the left fork which continued upwards between an avenue of conifers along a rougher, uneven grassy path. There were lots of fallen branches to step over, and we paused for a while to catch our breath. Foxgloves were growing in the shade of the trees, with no sign of buds yet, but there were still plenty of bluebells for us and the bees to admire. We suddenly realised the track was heading downwards and that we had missed a turn off, so we backtracked until we found an almost overgrown path heading upwards to the right. Just as I stopped to admire a clump of white blossoming three cornered garlic, Jim whispered 'Jean, look'. There ahead of us was a beautiful hare, sitting upright as if alert and aware of our proximity. I felt privileged to see it as we have only occasionally had a glimpse of a hare on the peninsula. I managed to capture a blurred photo with my phone camera before it ran off into the bracken and out of sight. The path sloped gently to the right and we could see that we were almost at the summit which was marked by a short, wide conifer.

The views had opened again, although the sea was covered in mist, and we were now able to see some of the hills we had recently climbed. South westerly was Mynydd Rhiw with the conical Clip Gylfinir close by, and north easterly across the fields was Garn Fadryn and Yr Eifl. We could make out the headland at Porth Neigwl and recalled a story we'd read in the news about a week ago about a static caravan for sale there. The caravan had been used for over 30 years but was being sold with its surrounding secluded site (field) beside the coast path with a guide price of £150,00. It was expected to be snapped up by a surfing enthusiast as Porth Neigwl (sometimes referred to as Hell's Mouth) is known as the best surfing beach in Gwynedd. With all the news recently of the erosion of the cliffs around the peninsula I'd like to see the insurance quote for this caravan!

The walk back down the track felt easy and we were soon back in the car and on our way to our lunch stop, which was the newly opened café at Felin Uchaf only a few miles away. As I've mentioned before Felin Uchaf has to be seen to be appreciated and Caffi Felin is the latest venture there. The café is

Caffi Felin

Becws Islyn

located inside the CLAS (Centre for Living Arts and Science), which is a stunning naturally curved timber-framed and straw bale building, crafted by volunteers from all over the world using locally sourced materials. We were greeted by a friendly bunch of young people, who I presumed were volunteers and we thought we could hear English, Welsh, Scottish and Irish accents amongst them. We enjoyed a very tasty salad which included ingredients from the organic garden, accompanied by delicious home baked bread and posh organic lemonades. We then continued to the coast – to nearby Aberdaron, another of our favourite haunts. After a walk along the beach, we sampled the delights at the recently extended café at Becws Islyn bakery. Sitting on the rooftop area, next to the thatched roof, we shared a sweet sticky millionaire's slice with our coffees. We felt that was a good balance after our very healthy lunch.

The tree topped summit

Eisteddfod Ramble 19
May 2023

Ironing? What's That?

On the night of the previous hill walk, I had booked a ticket for a gig at Yr Heiwr, the community pub in Nefyn. I was to meet friends Chris and Dave there – Yr Heiwr is their local as they live in Mynydd Nefyn. I was finally in the right place at the right time to see singer songwriter Steve Eaves perform with his band members who he calls **'Rhai Pobl'** (some people). I've enjoyed his music for many years but he doesn't perform publicly very often – this was the third time I'd seen him, having missed a couple of opportunities already this year which I've grumbled about already. He's been writing and recording albums for about 40 years with a mixture of rock, jazz, blues and folk and also holds two doctorates, both related to Welsh language and culture. Steve's eisteddfod connection is through his daughter author Manon Steffan Ros, who I've already talked about. She has won drama medals and the prose medal at previous Steddfodau. I've finally read and thoroughly enjoyed her novel for young adults, *Llyfr Glas Nebo*, which I described earlier. Soon after this I bought the English version of this very special book – *The Blue Book of Nebo*. I was fascinated with her rewriting of the story, and how to make it accessible to non-Welsh speakers, she had changed details about the main characters and their proficiency in Welsh. I will say no more – no spoilers. But I found both books very moving and thought provoking, well worth a read and I'm pleased to be able to share the English version with my non-Welsh speaking friends, who hear me rambling on about this wonderful Welsh author. About a month after this, Manon

Steve Eaves a Rhai Pobl in Yr Heliwr

With Steve

won the UK's most prestigious children's books award, the Yoyo Carnegie Medal, for the English version, and this was the first time a translated book had ever won this prize.

Back to the pub which was packed out and as lively as it had been at the Geraint Lovgreen gig, and I noticed there were some fellow musicians in the audience who I'd seen performing recently with Bob Delyn, including Edwin 'Chwarae fo powb', Humphreys (mentioned earlier), and his wife Einir. Despite the noisiness of the customers in between songs, you could sense the respect of the audience for this much-loved singer, and people were shushed if they got too loud, especially when Steve was speaking and introducing his songs. In the intervals, I chatted to Chris and Dave and another familiar person Marian Brosschot, mentioned earlier. Chris informed me that the book of Welsh short stories by and for learners (one of which Chris had written) was finally going to be published soon and was to be launched at the Steddfod. She was going to be involved with this and I said that I would definitely try to come along. I chatted to Marian and said how much I was enjoying the YouTube videos she was producing for learners and that I regularly shared these on the Facebook page that I manage for Manchester Welsh learners. She explained that there were a group of them producing videos now in a new series called Easy Welsh, which is part of an international video project aiming at supporting people to learn languages through authentic street interviews and at the same time showing the street culture of participating countries. Marian had produced one of these which had been filmed in Caernarfon recently.

I did my groupie bit at the end of the gig, which I'd thoroughly enjoyed, and asked Steve to sign my C.D. and also a poem he'd written in one of my favourite Welsh poetry books *Cerddi Llŷn ac Eifionydd* (Poems of Llŷn and Eifionydd). The poem was a rather cheeky, comical one telling of what the local young people used to get up to at Butlins Holiday Park in the past. I'll leave that to your imagination. Steve was happy to oblige and said he hadn't realised that his poem was in this book. He asked my name to add to his message on the C.D., and when I said how much I'd enjoyed the gig, he said he preferred playing to small audiences. I told him that I'd been rather late in discovering his music and the first time I'd seen him was in about 2012 in Bethesda. He then looked at me and asked '**Dych chi wedi sgwennu llyfr?**' Have you written a book? I was taken aback and said yes I had but how did he know. He replied that he wasn't sure and asked if I'd ever spoken to his author daughter Manon. I said that I hadn't but that I enjoyed her books very much and that I had spoken a couple of times to his other daughter, singer Lleuwen, as I'd seen her numerous times at small local gigs and she had begun to recognise me and have a little chat sometimes. I have to confess to being flattered by his comment and it was soon on a message to Llŷn friend Amanda, with a photo of me and Steve taken by one of the band members. Amanda soon sent a jokey reply '**Wyt ti'n dechrau dod yn wyneb enwog yn y sîn Gymraeg Mrs B!**' (You're beginning to become a famous face in the Welsh scene Mrs B!) I'm not so sure about that.

Two days after the gig, when we had arrived back home, I received a sensitively written email, letting me know that I wasn't in the final four who would be going forward to compete in the Steddfod for learner of the year. It let me down gently by stating that there had been a lot of entries and that the standard had been particularly high this year. My feelings were a mixture of disappointment and relief. Of course, I would have loved to have been acknowledged in this way, but I now no longer had to worry about being in front of TV cameras and could relax and enjoy the Steddfod in August. I sent messages to friends and family who knew I'd given it a go. Amanda was disappointed on my behalf and my brother Ste's response was 'congratulations and commiserations' as he fully understood my ambivalence about the whole thing.

On the 19th May, Sain recording studios digitally released a new song by Twm Morys and Gwyneth Glyn, which was soon downloaded to my phone and listened to. **Cymru'n Un** (Wales is One) is a song celebrating the beauty of the area and offering a welcome to the Steddfod 'where there'll be a place for every harmonious soul' the chorus tells us... **hyfryd** (lovely).

My Welsh evening back home at Market 362 shop

That evening, I had an event on close to home. Just before Christmas, a recently opened craft shop in my home village, Market 362, started to stock my books. I was thrilled to hear that they were selling well, as I'd felt they may be unlikely to sell outside of Wales. The shop owner is a lovely Irish lady, Bernadette, who with the support of her lifelong friend Grainne has created a wonderful addition to the community. I love visiting and chatting to the ladies, especially finding out about their Gaelic culture and language. Bernadette had begun to offer workshops and events in her shop and asked could I do a mini book launch. I agreed as I especially liked the idea of being able to share a little about the Welsh language and culture with people in the north west of England, who made up a large percentage of visitors to Llŷn. I was rather nervous, but the small audience who were mostly familiar with Llŷn were friendly and full of questions and comments about the area and the language and culture. I even got requests to return to do some taster sessions in Welsh, which I hoped to offer soon. I received some lovely feedback after the session and hope that this wasn't just because of the tasty Llŷn baked bara brith and Welsh cakes that I'd provided.

I was on the mailing list to receive regular updates about the Steddfod and also kept an eye on social media and in both of the peninsula monthly Welsh language local newspapers – *Llanw Llŷn* for Llŷn, and *Y Ffynnon* for Eifionydd. I now have a subscription for digital copies of *Y Ffynnon* which means I don't need to wait until we're at the caravan to be able to buy it. On the 22nd May there were three announcements – there were only 75 days to go until the start of the big event, tickets to get onto the grounds (Maes) were now on sale and the names of people who were to be welcomed as new members of the Gorsedd had been published. I had also read that the Steddfod caravan site was now full, but that there were still some spaces for tents. In true festival style, many visitors to the Steddfod camp for the whole week. I felt lucky that we were able to 'glamp' at our caravan only a few miles away. I had already decided that I wanted to attend each of the eight days and Jim was keen to come with me to some of them. But we held off ordering the tickets as we were waiting for the schedule to be released as we especially wanted to know which singers were performing in the folk tent, to know which days Jim would choose. On the Steddfod website I read the list of names and descriptions of people who would now be entitled to wear the blue robes (and to become Honorary Druids for their services to the nation), or the green robes for their contribution to the arts. The only name that I recognised immediately was Edwin Humphreys on the 'Green Robes List', the musician who had been in the audience of the Steve Eave gig only days before. I discovered that he had played with more Welsh bands than any other musician and can be heard on over a hundred albums. I was full of admiration to learn that he had also been a mental health nurse and had used music therapeutically with his patients.

On our next visit to the caravan, I picked up the May edition of *Llanw Llŷn* from one of the local shops and discovered some more interesting bits of Steddfod related trivia. On the front cover was a picture of a lady and little girl cutting a ribbon to officially open a new bridge. They were councilor Anwen Davies and Magi Griffiths, a pupil from Pentreuchaf school. Magi had won a competition to name a new bridge with her suggestion of **'Pont Bodefail'**, which was a clever combination of the names of the two villages on either side of the bridge – Boduan (the site of this year's Steddfod) and Efailnewydd. The bridge is a replacement for Pont Bodfel, a 19th century bridge which is a Grade 2 listed structure and carried the A497 road over the river Afon Rhyd-hir until it partially collapsed in 2019 following heavy storms. An emergency temporary bridge was installed parallel to the original one with traffic controls, until it was eventually decided that a new replacement bridge was needed. The clock had been ticking as this new bridge was vital for the transporting of thousands of people on the final part of their journey to the Steddfod, but they had completed it in time much to the relief of the officials I can imagine.

I was amused by a short article further into the paper, which was calling for the help of ironers. They were needed to iron the robes for the members of the Gorsedd. I had never considered this idea before and had presumed that each person was responsible for their own robes. I loved how it reassured that this task was a lot of fun and didn't require 'noble' ironing skills, merely for people to turn up with an iron and ironing board. Also, they were asking for people to help members of the Gorsedd to put on their robes on the Wednesday and Friday of the week of the Steddfod, the days when the main Gorsedd ceremonies take place. My ironing skills these days are much less than noble. Jim deals with our laundry mostly these days since he retired and ironing has been a rare event in our house since the boys stopped wearing school uniforms. We have mastered the technique of shaking clothes before hanging them to dry and most things look fine. The eisteddfodau depend quite heavily on volunteers and I was keen to volunteer for something during the week but I decided that this was not the one for me.

Walk 19

Tre'r Ceiri, Yr Eifl, Llithfaen
28th May 2023
A Walk and a Half

We were getting to the stage of feeling that we'd completed most of the hill walks in Llŷn that were within our capability. But there was one important one remaining. Tre'r Ceiri is the second highest of the wonderful hill range Yr Eifl and is famous for having what is often reported to be the best example of an iron age hillfort in Europe. We had wondered whether to wait until Tom and Simon were available to meet up again and climb it together but we decided to go ahead with it today and then just repeat it with them if the opportunity arose.

We confidently strode off along the B4417 away from the car which we'd left at the lay-by between Llanaelhaearn and Llithfaen, and staying on the same side of the road continued in the direction of Llithfaen for about a hundred metres until we reached the stone steps. This was very familiar territory to us as we often passed this way en route to Nefyn and other favourite parts of Llŷn, and had taken this straightforward route to the summit in the past, the hill

Tre'r Ceiri from Llanaelhaearn

Setting off from the layby on our first attempt

being not far from the road. Memories came flooding back of doing this same walk with Tom and Simon when they were much younger. On looking back at photos later, I was reminded it was in the summer of 2005 when Tom was ten and Simon five. I had remembered that we had gone for a swim and mess about in the sea at Nefyn to cool off afterwards. In 2015, Jim and I had also walked to the summit with our Llŷn friends Amanda, Brian, Elain and Owain, whilst holidaying in their static caravan, a couple of years before we bought our own. Today was cloudy but we hoped the weather forecast could be trusted which promised bright sunshine shortly. We'd plastered ourselves with suncream in case.

The steps and wooden fingerpost directed us onto the field sloping steadily upwards to the foot of the hill. We both stopped still to listen to something that had caught our attention. I beamed as I realised it was the sound of a cuckoo coming from somewhere near the summit. As far as I can remember this was the first time in Llŷn, that we'd heard the cuckoo, or **gog** to give it one of its Welsh names. What a great start to our walk. We stopped at the metal gate at the top of the steps to read the bilingual information board, giving some of the history of this very special site. We were told that the dry-stone ramparts enclosing the fort still survived to near their original height of 3.5 metres in parts. The fort is 2.5 hectares (one hectare equals about 10,000 square metres) and contained the remains of over 150 huts. It suggested that the fort was constructed in the late iron age and was in use until the 4th century AD. Excavations have produced finds including Roman pottery, and a gold-plated bronze brooch probably made during the middle of the first century AD, now in the care of the National Museum of Wales, Cardiff.

We continued across the field with the dry-stone wall to our right and Tre'r Ceiri looming ahead. Jim pointed out some rather fresh-looking cow pats – oh dear. Always the optimist, I suggested that they had most likely just been passing through – the cows not the pats – and the farmer may have moved them to another field by now. We heard the cuckoo several more times as we continued, its call coming from different parts of the hill, but not one sighting. I was satisfied to have heard it at least. Through a second small gate, the field was a little less steep, allowing us to stride out a little but we soon came to a sudden stop. A dry-stone wall with large gaps in it appeared ahead of us, with several serious looking black cows peering over the top towards us and with no fence between them and us. We disappointedly did an about turn and agreed on plan B by the time we reached the car. We would walk the longer way, from Nant Gwrtheyrn car park where we had started for the other two Yr Eifl hills, Garn Ganol and Garn Fôr. I've added the QR codes for the start of both walks and Des describes the two of them very well in his book.

From the car park, we headed across the grass towards the long straight stone wall Wal Mawr, described earlier, passing the slate engraved plaque fixed to a large rock, which explained its history in Welsh. We came across three larger slate plaques, which identified various landmarks including the distant hills, villages and bays. Each also had two lines of verse by a local poet, relating to the views. My favourite was by J Glyn Davies and read **'Felly Llŷn ar derfyn dydd. Lle i enaid gael llonydd'** 'Such is Llŷn at the

Garn Fôr and Garn Ganol with Tre'r Ceiri still hidden from view

end of the day. A place for the soul to find peace'. Davies also wrote the famous shanty Fflat Huw Puw, which I mentioned earlier.

We soon realised that we were diverting away from Garn Ganol, which is adjacent to Tre'r Ceiri, although Tre'r Ceiri was still out of view for now. We'd taken the wrong path but this was soon rectified by cutting across the low growing dry heather and gorse, until we met the path we should have taken. The cuckoo was silent now or had flown elsewhere. We could see the path on Garn Ganol that we had taken recently and were both impressed with ourselves that we'd ever managed it. We took the right-hand fork veering a little away from Garn Ganol now and heading towards a distinctive outcrop of rock known as Caer Gribin, sometimes referred to as the fourth 'false peak' of Yr Eifl.

There was still no sign of any sunshine and the wind was quite chilly. Jim said that we should have rubbed on Deep Heat instead of suncream. I asked did he mean to keep us warm or to ease our creaky joints and he said both. Views of the sea and distant hills were hazy but stunning nevertheless. The path, now lined with bright green ferns, became quite rocky and uneven but not too tricky if we took care. We headed towards a metal kissing gate, which didn't appear to have a purpose up here but still it was a good landmark to guide us on our way. Just beyond this was another information board, which reassured us we were heading the right direction as it had more details about Tre'r Ceiri as well as showing an aerial plan of the whole of Yr Eifl. It mentioned the English translation of its name 'Town of the Giants'. **Ceiri** is thought to have been a form of the word **cewri** which is plural of **cawr** (giant). The board also showed a chough and as if on cue, one flew over, looking as if it was enjoying itself, playing about in the wind and making its lovely chee-ow sound.

We continued on the stony path and the summit of Tre'r Ceiri finally appeared on the horizon. Clumps of thick grasses and rushes were dotted about the nearby landscape and white candy floss looking cotton grass blew around in the breeze. As we approached the foot of Tre'r Ceiri, our surrounding area became damp and slightly boggy in parts and we remembered Des mentioning in his book about strategically placed rocks to help walkers navigate. Large areas of almost fluorescent lime green low growing bilberry bushes, grew in between the rocks on the face of

Tre'r Ceiri. The path got steeper towards the summit and we soon reached the path that we would have come along from the other starting point. A group of about six people had come from that way – obviously not cowardly like us when faced by cows. The last few metres taking us to one of the gateways to the fort was almost a scramble but with the help of my stick and Jim's guiding hand, I made it without having to resort to going on hands and knees. Large areas of rocks became recognisable as the remains of circular stone huts and we stepped inside of one of them, its 'floor' filled with bilberry bushes. I joked with Jim about guessing what they had for dinner each day in Tre'r Ceiri – bilberry stew, bilberry crumble, bilberry soup... We wondered what else they would have eaten – presumably they would have bred animals – sheep or goats to get milk and meat. I wonder if there were any iron age vegans or vegetarians. That would have been tricky. One last stretch to reach the summit now. The group of young people – well they were all below 50 and that now seems young to us – were on their way down and we greeted them as we crossed paths. A large heap of stones marks the summit and I told Jim to go ahead as I was unsure if I'd manage to negotiate this steep rocky clamber. But as he scrambled up, I explored around the back and found an easier, winding route that took me almost to the very top, taking Jim by surprise. We didn't linger too long as it was very windy at the top but what an amazing feeling to be standing inside what was home to a village of people so many hundreds of years ago. If you have an interest in history and only climb one hill in Llŷn, this is definitely the one to do. Not forgetting as always, the stunning sea and mountain views all around.

Skylarks serenaded us from on high on our way back and we were finally treated to a viewing as one of them flew a little lower for us to admire it. As J Glyn Davies put it so well 'Such is Llŷn at the end of the day. A place for the soul to find peace'.

The day after this walk, we visited Llanaelhaearn village which boasts one of the best views of Tre'r Ceiri. We wanted to see what the members of the Antur had been up to, as we'd heard that there had been developments and that the area behind the Antur building had been landscaped. It was well worth a visit. A new boardwalk had been erected next to the allotments, creating a short walk which will eventually join the existing public footpath

The Antur shelter Llanaelhaearn

that runs through the village. Saplings had been planted on either side of the boardwalk to create a future mini woodland and a wooden shelter with a bench was in place part way along with carvings of creatures that looked as if they'd stepped out of the Mabinogi. I tried out the bench which offers stunning unbroken views of Tre'r Ceiri across the fields. We spotted Lynda and I said how proud she should be of all her hard work and she told us that the community shop ' Pantri Beti' would be opening in early June. I said we would definitely be calling in to support it especially with the temptation of the honey which was soon to be produced from the Antur hives. The shop and the honey (**Mêl Beti**) is named after Beti Hughes, one of the founding members of the Antur.

Entering the gateway of the fort

Eisteddfod Ramble 20
June and July 2023
Preparations

In addition to all of the day time competitions and events going on throughout the week at the Steddfod, there are always special evening shows, concerts or dramas held in the pavilion. Additional tickets need to be purchased for these and on the 5th June, the 2023 schedule was announced. This year, I was surprised to see that there were no dramas but four different concerts over five nights. The first concert was **Y Curiad** (The Beat), which featured the band Pedair and **Côr Gwerin** yr **Eisteddfod** (The Eisteddfod Folk Choir), and other special guests. This choir had been made up of local interested people and I'd seen notices about practice sessions being held in various halls, including in Caernarfon, where their first practice attracted more than 200 people. The next concert was the **Cymanfa Ganu** (singing assembly), which I learnt was a traditional singing festival, held each year at the Steddfod (and often held in many Welsh towns and villages), and consists of congregational hymn singing. Cracharela was the name of the third and fourth concert of the week – a cabaret show. The final concert was **Gig y Pafiliwn** and featured some big names in the Welsh language pop scene such as the rapper Mr Phormula. I'll let you guess which one Jim and I were keen to go to. But we had to wait until the 16th June, the date when the tickets were to go on sale and also another landmark in the lead up to the opening of the Steddfod – only 50 days to go.

On our next short visit to the caravan, hill walks were off the cards, as the garden needed tidying and the decking needed painting. It's not all fun in Llŷn. Well, it mostly is really. I was excused from the painting on the Saturday and went into Caernarfon to meet up with the Welsh learners in Palas Print bookshop again. It was a beautiful day and we all sat out in the garden under the awning and Sel from the shop, took our orders for hot drinks as always. I heard some interesting bits of Steddfod information, including the fact that tutors Bethan and Meira, who I was chatting to for some of my time there, were part of the Steddfod Folk Choir. I said that I was hoping to get a ticket to see

Near Boduan

the show and they encouraged me to be ready as soon as the booking line opened. All of the concerts were expected to be popular and because there were two smaller pavilions this year instead of the one huge one, it would mean less seats for all of these large events. Meira also told me about some fabric art she was involved in doing as part of a large piece of work being produced by her local Merched y Wawr group. There was going to be so many interesting events and exhibitions on the Maes, I was beginning to wonder how I was going to see everything I wanted to see. Bethan asked would I be volunteering at the Steddfod this time. I said that I'd hoped to, but that although this sounded rather selfish, I was holding back from committing myself to a particular day yet as I didn't want to miss any of my favourite singers, especially in the folk tent. The schedule for the week hadn't yet been published and I wasn't sure when this would happen.

On Sunday, Jim and I had a trip to Pwllheli to get some DIY bits for our jobs at the caravan and we were both taken by surprise and simultaneously said '**Helo**' as we spotted a very familiar face, forgetting that of course she wouldn't know us. It was Gwenan Gibbard, one of the four members of Pedair. I apologised for our over familiarity and explained that we were big fans of Pedair. She was very gracious and thanked us. I told her that we were hoping to get tickets for their concert at the Steddfod and she reinforced the idea of booking early to ensure a place. On the way back to the caravan, we called into Tyddyn Sachau garden centre to buy some plants for our tiny caravan garden, ideally drought resistant ones as it had now been dry for so long and this weekend was an especially hot one. We bumped into Martyn Croydon, the Welsh tutor and previous learner of the year as mentioned earlier. He was with his wife Eluned (previously a tutor) and two lovely young children and it was lovely to chat with them. I told Martyn and Eluned about my nerve-wracking experience at my learner of the year interview and they were both very encouraging, saying that they were surprised I hadn't been selected. Martyn explained that 40 people had been nominated for the competition and 30 had got through to be interviewed so I had reached a semifinal. He had heard that the panel had picked nine people that they had wished they could put forward but had to whittle these down to four. He said that he felt sure that I would have been one of the nine. I said I wasn't so sure and told him what my opening comment had been. I mentioned my dilemma about wanting to volunteer, ideally in the learner's areas **Maes D**. He said that he was pretty sure the schedule of events was to be published soon, so I'd be able to plan when I could be available. We talked about there being two pavilions and how this would of course mean less seats available for some of the big events held there. Martyn said that he'd heard that one of the pavilions held about 1000 people and the second about 500 or 600. We chatted about the recent news about a Welsh bilingual rapper who had pulled out of performing at the Steddfod because the Welsh language policy had pointed out that he used too much English in his songs. We had similar views, that although this may seem petty to some, it could set a precedent and it is the fact that the Steddfod is a totally Welsh language event that makes it so special. There are plenty of other festivals – inside and outside of Wales, where bilingual and English songs can be performed alongside Welsh language ones.

That evening our Llŷn friends Amanda and Brian called round to see us and we caught up with family news. Amanda talked about something I'd been reading about lately on social media – '**Harddu Llŷn ac Eifionydd**', which means beautifying Llŷn and Eifionydd. The 30th June had been suggested as a day of tidying up of villages ready to be decorated with banners, buntings and whatever the local people chose to produce, to welcome visitors passing by on their way to the Steddfod Maes at Boduan. Community meetings were going to be taking place throughout the area at the beginning of July, where people could share their creative talents and ideas for this. Amanda explained that they were being asked to decorate the small primary school where she works, even though it isn't on a route likely to be taken by anyone heading to Boduan. I'm sure the children will all have fun creating, but can imagine it being an exhausting time for staff as they approach the end of the school year.

On the 12th June, the four finalists for the Dysgwr y Flwyddyn (learner of the year) competition were identified. Short biographies were published on the Steddfod website of the two young men and two young women, and all sounded like deserving winners, all living in Wales and working through the medium of Welsh. I looked forward to hearing more about them and seeing them in the pavilion in August when the winner would be announced.

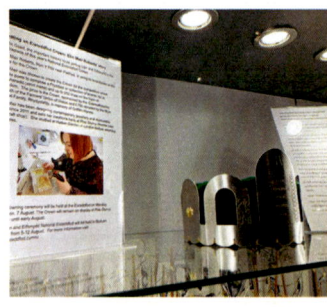

The Eisteddfod Crown and Chair at Plas Glyn y Weddw

The day after this, we chatted to Glyn, the site manager at our caravan site and he proudly told us that the Steddfod crown that his daughter had made was going to be on display at Plas Glyn y Weddw art gallery from that evening, alongside the Steddfod chair. He'd heard that there were fifty contenders for the crown but only six for the chair. After returning home, I watched the Welsh evening news programme on S4C called **Heno** (tonight), which showed the unveiling of them both in the gallery. A film clip was shown of Elin Mair, a trained silversmith, in her workshop at Yr Iard in Caernarfon, where she creates and sells her jewellery. Elin showed her paper template that she had started with for the shape of the crown and explained that she had made a prototype in copper first and then the final one in silver. She pointed out the engravings of trees and dry-stone walls on the side of the crown which represented Lôn Goed, the famous tree lined lane in Eifionydd. It was explained that one of the requirements of the crown is for it to be adjustable ensuring that it fits the winner's head. The winner would be the one judged to have written the best **Pryddest** (collection of free style poems). Elin would be making the adjustments once she had the measurements of the winning poet's head. Engraved on the front of this beautiful crown was the three lined symbol, the Nod Cyfrin (as spoken of earlier) and the space in the centre of the crown was filled with emerald green velvet. Back to Plas Glyn y Weddw and it was time for the chair to be unveiled. Myrddin ap Dafydd had this honour and he and Michael Strain (Chairman of the Work's Committee for the Steddfod) were asked by the reporter what they thought, before showing some film footage of the creator of the chair. They couldn't be anything but impressed by the stunning hand carved chair and Myrddin mentioned that he had regularly seen the tree, from where the wood had been sourced, lying on Lôn Goed, since it was felled by storm Darwin in 2014. The film showed Stephen Faherty, and it was explained that he was the first person to create an eisteddfod chair carved from a single piece of wood. A chunky piece of Irish slate, made up the right arm of the chair and was engraved with the Steddfod details and another piece of slate on the upper part of the seat bore the Nod Cyfrin. I thought how the winner of the chair (the one judged to have created the best poem in cynghanedd form) would need to be rather slim as this prize wasn't adjustable.

A few days later during a family weekend at the caravan to celebrate Tom's birthday, we were able to see the chair and the crown 'live'. The chair remained in the main art gallery space but the crown was now in the cabinet in the shop accompanying Elin's delicate handcrafted silver jewellery which she has on sale there. I now noticed a tiny gold coloured daffodil fixed to each side of the crown, identical to ones featured on some of her jewellery. I felt sure that she would have a boost in sales now as a result of her commission. On this same weekend, the four of us made a visit to Porthor beach and café and on our return, we called in at the nearby Plas Carmel, near Anelog. We were greeted in the car park by a friendly young man who explained that the café was to reopen the following weekend. I asked if the Black Shed – **Sied Du** – was open for us to have a look around and he kindly unlocked it for us. As you may recall this plain looking black corrugated shed was being made into an exhibition centre and I'd read online that it was now open. There were various interesting displays, especially about the people of this locality but the one I'd like to share with you featured a simple candle in an old fashioned brass candle holder. The title of the display was '**Eisteddfod Hyd y Gannwyll**'. The title defines the nature of the event as it means 'length of the candle eisteddfod'. It explained that these local eisteddfodau were held in the barn in nearby Tŷ Lôn Farm, Rhosirwaun, at the end of the nineteenth century and that the eisteddfod lasted as long as the candle burned. Later that week, I saw a notice on Facebook with a picture of the young man welcoming people to the newly reopened Caffi Siop Plas that he would now be running. I wondered what had happened to Bryn Fôn.

On the 16th June, after much queuing online, I was thrilled to have managed to book two seats for us for the Curiad show with Pedair. Amanda sent a message to me later that day and asked how I'd got on with booking the concert as she knew how keen I was. I told her of my success and she said that she was really pleased for us as she'd heard it had sold out within twenty minutes of the box office opening! I'd already read comments on social media from disappointed people who had been unable to get a seat who pointed out that there being only one performance of the show, and this in a much smaller pavilion than usual, meant too few seats for the demand. Steddfod officials were reassuring them that there would be repeat performances in local venues later in the year. My excitement was dampened somewhat as I felt sad for those who had missed out.

At the end of June, the four of us enjoyed a warm week by the sea in Aldeburgh Suffolk, a place none of us had been before. Jim was celebrating a big birthday that week – 70 – and wanted to escape from any fuss. As we were negotiating the extortionately priced M6 toll near Birmingham, over in the town of Aberdâr, Rhondda Cynon Taf, in south-east Wales, the proclamation ceremony for the 2024 Steddfod was taking place. It was hard to believe that a year had gone by since I'd managed to worm my way into the Llŷn and Eifionydd proclamation ceremony in Porthmadog and now preparations were underway for the following year's Steddfod. I was excited to read that the new Archdruid for 2024 to 2027 had been announced, and it was

Mererid Hopwood, an acclaimed author and poet. This was only the second time that a woman had held this role, with the poet Christine James being the first in 2013 to 2016. The article I read, also stated that the Chairing Ceremony at this year's Steddfod would be Myrddin ap Dafydd's final ceremony after holding the position since 2018. His time had been extended because of the Covid-19 pandemic and I wondered how it would feel for him, after five years, to be letting go of that responsibility after what I imagine must have been a different experience to what he had envisaged.

On the first of July along our journey home from Aldeburgh, I read of interesting developments taking place across Llŷn for the 'Harddu' weekend. Pictures were appearing on the Facebook pages of various villages, showing brightly painted Steddfod signs and the official banners adorning the lanes ready to welcome passing visitors in August. I looked forward to admiring these and the many other creative efforts on our next Llŷn visit.

The following day, some exciting, long-awaited news appeared on the Gwasg Carreg Gwalch Facebook page. My fluent Welsh learner friend Simon Chandler had written a novel in Welsh and it had finally been released into the shops – what an achievement. I sent him a message of Llongyfarchiadau and told him that a visit to Llên Llŷn bookshop in Pwllheli would be top of my agenda on our next visit. I would have to put some other Welsh books on hold and hurry along with *Carafanio* now. I was finding this book by Guto Dafydd, a funny yet touching tale, written from a dad's viewpoint, describing a couple coping with their two young children on an enforced and extended mobile caravan trip. As a learner, it was a tricky read for me, but after a while I'd become acquainted with the style of the author and managed to get the gist, enough to keep going without reaching for my translation app too often. Simon's book was called **Llygad Dieithryn** (eye of a stranger) and the blurb said it was about a young girl from Germany, who discovers a letter in Welsh, sent to her great, great grandfather by a Welsh friend. In addition to being an excellent Welsh speaker, Simon can also speak fluent German and I remembered him telling me that the novel would be drawing on his knowledge of Germany but would also be partly taking place at the 2019 Steddfod. I was rather envious to hear that there was also going to be an audio book of his story and that this was to be read by Mererid Hopwood, the newly nominated Archdruid! Simon had already told me that his book was to have two launches on the Monday at the Steddfod. There were also to be two Gorsedd ceremonies that day, so I could already envisage myself racing back and to between the pavilion and the tents that day...

During another long weekend at the caravan in early July, we had wondered about a visit to the isle of Enlli (Bardsey) to walk up the mynydd but my knees and the weather were against us. Our son Tom was also at the caravan that weekend and had also hoped to visit Enlli with a friend but boats to the island were cancelled due to the strong winds. It was at this point that I decided not to include Mynydd Enlli in my book even if we manage to get there this year. As you can see this book is already long enough and Enlli could take up another whole book... well there's an idea! So, as we leave the hills behind, the remainder of this book will include any further bits of Steddfod trivia that come my way, descriptions of further Llŷn and Eifionydd Steddfod preparations and finally reporting on my experience of the big event itself.

During this weekend, Jim and I strolled around Pwllheli and admired the Steddfod themed decorated shop fronts and walls. I stopped off at Llên Llŷn to buy Simon Chandler's book, taking photos of it displayed in the window and on the 'special' table to show him. As I was peering at the door of the art gallery shop Tonnau, checking the notices of events taped to the glass panels, who emerged from the shop but the archdruid himself. Myrddin ap Dafydd is the owner of Tonnau. We had a quick chat and he asked had I seen the chair and crown in Plas Glyn y Weddw yet and I told him that we had and that today I'd bought Simon's book which had been published by his publishing company. He commented on what an excellent Welsh speaker Simon was and I agreed. He hurried off on his way and said what a busy time it was now with the Steddfod being only a month away. Further along the high street, in a second-hand shop window, my eyes were drawn to a colourful framed pictorial map of Enlli, dated 1991 and signed by an E Meirion Roberts. I couldn't resist and bought it for the caravan and soon after it was adorning Tom's bedroom wall – a small compensation for not being able to visit yet. I was curious about the artist and after doing some research, I managed to buy an out-of-print book – **'Darlun o Arlunydd'** (picture of an artist), edited by Robert Owen and John Gruffydd Jones. This was heavily illustrated with images of his beautiful maps, including the Enlli one, and of his other pictures, all crammed with his interpretations of people and geographical features connected with the areas they depicted. Many of the people were caricatured, showing his sense of humour, and the added labels, poems, and phrases in Welsh, demonstrated his excellent calligraphy skills. Several of his pieces of work were posters done as tributes to eisteddfodau of the 1980s and 1990s. In his younger days Roberts worked as a commercial artist and illustrated books for children and adults. His detailed maps and posters were created after his retirement, when he is said to have concentrated on supporting good causes including the Urdd and the Steddfodau. So, I'm guessing that the prints like the one I bought (which was number 788 of 1000) were sold in aid of Steddfod funds. I also realised that it was his illustrations on two commemorative plates that I bought from a charity shop some time ago, that had been produced for the Llŷn and Eifionydd 1982 Youth/Urdd National Eisteddfod. I like to get these out when I offer friends Amanda and Brian Welsh cakes and bara brith when they call by at the caravan. It always fills Amanda with amused horror to see the extent of my geekiness for all things Llŷn.

Over the next couple of days, we passed through some of the villages and towns of Llŷn and saw some of the efforts of the residents. The village of Efailnewydd had a large red Steddfod sign and red dragon made from painted tyres, sited on either side of the rugby club gateway. Hay bales in fields had huge official Steddfod advertising signs on their edges and as we approached Nefyn there were brightly painted 'Croeso' signs along the route. In the centre of Nefyn there was a board with painted caricatured features of the town, including the church, the white painted beach cottages and three herrings (Nefyn's symbol), with the words **'Nefyn, angor gadarn cyn hwylio'r don'**. (Nefyn, a firm anchor before setting sail), which I later discovered is the motto for the town's primary school. The style of painting was immediately recognisable as that of Carys Bryn, whose new gallery 'LleArt' we had visited not long ago. Later that weekend we called into her gallery again and there were several other similar painted boards, propped on the fence outside, waiting to take pride of place in

Village boards at LleArt

other villages such as Abererch and Lwyndyrys. Carys had also offered workshops to local school children enabling them to create boards for their areas. We had already spotted her Pwllheli one displayed on the wall at the top of Stryd Moch along with the thermometer which was now indicating that the town had reached their fund-raising target. I was thrilled to see that Carys was by now also selling my book in LleArt, along with others published by Gwasg Carreg Gwalch.

We later drove past the Steddfod site at Boduan and could see the pavilions were now in the early stages of being erected. Boduan hill gave an impressive backdrop to the Maes and I wondered if they would be putting a Hollywood style 'Boduan' sign on the slopes as we had seen done on the slope at Gwydir Forest in Llanrwst in 2019. I was keen to visit Criccieth, where there is constantly a display of art around the town, as I knew from social media that there had been another surge of creativity going on in the lead up to the Steddfod. There was a brightly painted blue bench near to the John Ystymllun bench outside of the library, painted by local Welsh learners and decorated with Steddfod symbols. An archway in front of the memorial hall had been created and this was decorated with a large fabric dragon and multicoloured woolen pom poms created by the locals. More pom poms and colourful fingerpost signs brightened up the town square and the four postboxes of Criccieth had new knitted or crocheted Steddfod themed toppers. These featured cute dragons, an archdruid hat and my favourite was topped with several Gorsedd members, each with a different coloured robe – white, blue and green, a trumpeter with his corn gwlad and two flower girls. Having recently relearned how to crochet, I could appreciate the work that must have gone into these. My creative contribution to the Steddfod was a new set of caravan cushion covers in the Welsh flag colours – red, green, and white. These won't be seen by people on their journey to the event of course, but with the yarn remnants I did make myself a bag that I intended using during Steddfod week.

By the middle of July, programmes for some of the sites at the Steddfod were being released on the website, including the main outdoor stage (**Llwyfan**), the folk tent (**Tŷ Gwerin**), the Literature Tent (**Babell Lên**) and the learner's area (**Maes D**). I was starting to form a mental timetable of where I'd want to be each day. I could already see I would have to miss some favourite musicians as some of their performances coincided with the large pavilion ceremonies, or with other favourites performing in a different tent – it was going to be hard to choose and prioritise. Jim decided to come with me every other day and his day tickets were booked. Although he hasn't learnt a lot of Welsh, he understands how important it is to me and is always supportive. He enjoys a lot of Welsh folk music and was keen to accompany me to the folk tent especially, but also said that he didn't want to prevent me from being totally immersed in Welsh on the Maes. I was more than happy with the compromise as I love his company, even after more than 30 years together. I began to wonder if competitors who had submitted compositions would by now know if they had been successful or not. How exciting for someone to know they had won

Cricieth Eisteddfod bench

the chair or the crown, and what a difficult secret it was for them to have to keep until August. Submission dates varied depending on the competition but by April they should all have been received. The majority of competitions happen live on the various stages, and performers find out on the day if they are winners. I hoped to get a taste of as many different areas and events on the Maes.

I was disappointed around this time, when my Steddfod email update told me that the closing date for volunteering in Maes D had passed. I had held on too long, waiting for the timetable. But that same day I received an email from **Cymdeithas yr Iaith** (Welsh Language Society) which made up for it – they were also asking for volunteers for their stands. I'm a member of this organisation, which has campaigned since the 1960s through non-violent means for the rights of the people of Wales to use Welsh in all aspects of their lives. I replied to the email, volunteering to help out on the Wednesday morning, explaining that I was a learner but that I could manage a decent-ish conversation with folk. They accepted me almost immediately and said they were more than happy to have learners with them. My timetable was getting filled for the week and I was getting increasingly excited. We would be making one more weekend visit to the caravan towards the end of July then our next visit to Llŷn would be Steddfod week. I'd booked a week off work of course, but I was now wondering if I should have also taken the week after off to recover.

A trip to Llên Llŷn bookshop was my first errand when we returned at the end of the month. School children had created a colourful Steddfod sign for the shop which was lovely to see, but my main reason for the visit was to buy a hard copy of the **Steddfod Rhaglen** (programme) which had just been made available to buy, and this month's local Welsh language paper *Llanw Llŷn*. Martyn Croydon produces a page for learners in each issue of *Llanw Llŷn*, encouraging students from his classes to contribute an article. In this issue he mentioned three Steddfod awards for learners that had been created by artistic Welsh learners. One of these was a small chair which was to be awarded to the winner of the best poem submitted by a learner on the theme of **glannau** – shores. I have to at this point reveal that I'd a go at this competition but hadn't won as the winners had by now been informed, but I was looking forward to reading the judges' comments in the book that is released and sold on the Maes towards the end of Steddfod week – **Cyfansoddiadau a Beirniadaethau** 2023 (compositions and judgements 2023). The attractive wooden chair – **Y Gadair** – had been made by Berno Brosschot, who is a well-known character on the peninsula, father of Marian Brosschot, the tutor and artist, and husband of Morwen Jones, who had been creating the wooden place name signs. He came to Wales from Holland about forty years ago and learned to speak Welsh and is known to many as the man who sells bikes, but before this he made a living from making wooden furniture for locals. Another Welsh learner and artist Katy Mai Webster, from Yorkshire, had created a beautiful prize made of wood and ceramic, the **Tlws Rhyddiaith** (prose award), to be awarded to the learner who submitted the best piece of prose on the subject of **Ennill** (win). The third learner artist was familiar to me as I'd met her a couple of times at learners' chat groups organised by Martyn and had visited one of her art exhibitions at her home in Trefor several years ago. Andi Chell had been given the honour of making the award for Dysgwr y Flwyddyn (learner of the year) and had created a stunning framed needle felt landscape picture.

Most of the Steddfod events were by now published online, but timetables for some of the smaller tents, were only to be found in the **Rhaglen**, which was an A4 tome full of other interesting facts about performers etc. There was even a list in the back, divulging the **cyfanswm** – total amount – of money that each area had contributed and the names of the contributors. The total for the whole of Llŷn and Eifionydd was almost half a million pounds. I could now complete my task of creating a personalised timetable for the week for myself and Jim, which I started that afternoon, not as easy as it sounds. I wanted to try and fit in all five of the Gorsedd ceremonies, at least one of Simon Chandler's book launches, a meetup with friend Amanda (she'd messaged with a suggested time), listening to friend Chris's story being read in Maes D and eBay Ann competing in a choir competition, volunteering for Cymdeithas yr Iaith and then fill any gaps with as many performances by favourite singers, poets and speakers as possible. Jim was coming with me on non-ceremony days and I made sure these days were mostly musical ones. I wanted to try and experience as many of the different venues as possible, but I couldn't help prioritising favourite musicians. Oh yes, then we also wanted to browse all of the interesting stands and stalls on the Maes. For the purpose of being able to tell you about it in this book, I'd even intended experiencing at least five minutes of **Maes B**, the late-night music festival aimed at young people, which is held from Wednesday to Saturday. After checking the Rhaglen and discovering that the earliest performance on either of the two stages began at 10.40pm and the latest at 1.50am, I decided you didn't need to hear about it. I'd want to be in bed with a warm drink by 10.40pm. Anyway, I've heard that if you're over 25 you'd feel out of place there and I'm a little over that. Talking of age, I mentioned to Jim that the latest gig on my timetable was Steve Eaves in the Tŷ Gwerin at 9pm and he jokingly said that he should act his age and be home by then. I think he's a similar age to Jim. I'd recently finished reading Simon Chandler's book and had thoroughly enjoyed it –he included a lot of detail from the Llanrwst Steddfod and it had made me even more excited about this year's event. While trying to sort out the timetable I recalled an expression from his book, when he'd said that with regards singers, bands and literary events especially, the Maes was like an all you can eat buffet! By tea time I was exhausted with all the figuring out for our buffet – I needed a gig to recover and as usual there was one lined up.

Gwilym Bowen Rhys, local folk singer and a familiar face to us, having attended many of his gigs over the last ten years or more, was performing at Yr Ysgwrn, Trawsfynydd, previously the home of Hedd Wyn the poet who died in WW1 as mentioned earlier. He was also introducing La Tropa Son, a three-man band from Colombia. Another attraction for this visit was the chance to see an exhibition about the book The Lost Words, and the Welsh version **Geiriau Diflanedig**, before the gig started. The display showed some of the artist Jackie Morris's original beautiful nature paintings used in the books, including ones of magpies and conkers. Alongside were some of the words that accompany the pictures in both books, the English ones written by Robert Macfarlane and the Welsh ones by the future Archdruid Mererid Hopwood. I have one of each of these two huge books, the English copy at home and the Welsh one at the caravan. They're books of imagination but also of caution and the words are said to be 'spells' to conjure back flora and fauna that have been forgotten by our world. They are beautiful books to browse and despite my generally restless nature, I have at times found myself lost for hours in an almost meditative state whilst reading the spells and admiring the pictures in these books. And as if it couldn't get any better, a group of folk musicians got together and formed 'The Spell Songs' ensemble to complement the Lost Words book and they have now produced two albums of related songs. Of course, what I'd now like to see (or rather hear) is a Welsh language version album.

As we waited for the gig to start with a panad, Gwilym and the band were setting up their gear at the other end of the café area. Gwilym spotted us and came over with a big smile. I joked and reassured him that we weren't stalking him, as we'd seen him only a week earlier but nearer to home in Bury, when we'd been in the small audience at The Met with other Manchester based Welsh learners and first language Welsh speakers. He laughed and pretended to be scared of us, then chatted about the band he was introducing and then asked if we'd be at the Steddfod. I told him of our plans and that he and his band with his sisters (Plu) were definitely on our timetable. There was a fifth person with the performers and I realised that this was another familiar face. I remembered him as the storyteller from the event at Plas Glyn Y Weddw in January, Meic Llewellyn. He also came over for a chat and we told him that we remembered him. He explained his connection with the band – his son had been living in Columbia and had been friends with one of the band so he had introduced Gwilym to them and they had all performed together in Columbia. This was the band's chance to now experience performing in Wales. Gwilym's performance was to his usual high standard and he left the band to do their bit while he headed off to a local pub for a second gig. He is in high demand these days. La Tropa Son were great and played instrumental and vocal sets. They named their different string instruments, similar to a small guitar in looks, that gave that distinctive south American sound but I can't pretend to remember what they were called. They're worth looking out for and hopefully they'll return to Wales in the future. After the gig, we chatted further with Meic, who told us that he'd written a book of Welsh folk stories for children and that it was to be illustrated by

Near Llanystymdwy

Tess Urbanska, my favourite Welsh artist and published by Lolfa. I said I'd definitely be looking out for this when it was launched. I shared with him about my coastal path book, and he kindly bought a copy from the shop at Yr Ysgwrn for his son who he said enjoyed walking.

The following day was as predicted, wet with heavy rain most of the day. We decided to do a road trip around parts of the peninsula. Jim agreed to drive, while I took photos of more of the bright signs and displays that were popping up in the area. There were lots more Croeso signs in gateways of farms and in front of school and models of Gorsedd members on village greens. More Hollywood style Eisteddfod signs had appeared – some in the middle of fields and one had now appeared on the Maes, which we peered at over the security fencing. Most, if not all of the buildings and tents were now erected and they all looked white so far. There was no pink pavilion this year, but it was now confirmed that there was a **pafiliwn mawr** (large pavilion) and **pafiliwn bach** (small pavilion), and that the large pavilion would be where all the main ceremonies would be taking place. When the rain eased off, we had a walk around Cricieth and spotted the seaside style cut out board, where you could peep through and become either the winner of the chair, the archdruid or as was my choice (well I had to didn't I?), the presenter of the Blodeuged (flowers).

During the fortnight at home leading up to Steddfod week, I finalised our timetable for each day on the Maes. Ecoamgueddfa Llŷn announced some interesting events, including book launches to be held at their stall. Their LIVE (Llŷn IVeragh Eco-museums) project was reaching the end of their funded three years and they wanted to demonstrate what the area had to offer for tourists.

Ecoamgueddfa had produced some more of their handy leaflets but this time with Steddfod related words to help visitors to have a go on the Maes. The Steddfod resident poet Iestyn Tyne had provided the text for these.

Just before it was time to head back to the caravan ready for the big week, I received a letter telling me that my recent mammogram and examination had shown that I was still clear of breast cancer for the fifth year and so I was now discharged. Perfect timing! Apart from unpleasant, but manageable side effects from the medication, my cancer journey had been smooth compared to what many go through and I hadn't lost a lot of sleep over it. I did have to lose a breast though, but I took this in my stride as I knew it reduced the risk of reoccurrence. I like humour, as you may have noticed, and often use it as a coping mechanism. When I was presented with my false breast – I'd decided against a reconstruction as I'd have to keep still for too long – I decided I needed to give it a name. So naturally it had to be a Welsh name. Bronwen seemed the obvious choice – **bron** meaning breast and **wen** meaning white or pure – so pure breast. I also have one to go swimming with that just tucks into my swimming costume and it didn't take much thinking for me to come up with the name **Brondŵr** – **dŵr** meaning water.

Near Nefyn

Eisteddfod Ramble 21
Saturday 5th August to Saturday 11th August 2023
Llŷn and Eifionydd Eisteddfod

An app with a map and a full programme for the week was released just a couple of days before the Steddfod began and I discovered even more events I wanted to somehow squeeze in. There were also gigs taking place at various other venues in Llŷn in the evenings, such as the Nanhoron Hotel in Nefyn, but I decided there was more than enough for me to keep my feet firmly on the Maes. Here is a list of the different areas on the Steddfod grounds (Maes) that I will be mentioning and their meanings:

Maes – literally field or area but used to mean the whole show ground, which this year was just outside the village of Boduan covering several fields.
Maes B – the name of the site and the night time festival for teenagers and young adults. This was held across the road from the main festival and opened on Tuesday night.
Maes D – D being for **Dysgwyr** (learners), this area had a tent which hosted various music and literary performances, and two other tents where tutors had organised events of interest to learners especially. Martyn Croydon did a sterling job of coordinating most of this and we regularly said hello to him during the week.
Tŷ Gwerin – literally folk house, the large tent where folk music gigs and competitions are held.
Encore – a smaller tent used for classical and alternative music events.
Caffi Maes B – a mini **Maes B** in a tent on the main Maes, mostly featuring musical artists that would appeal to younger people.
Y Babell Lên – the literature tent, which hosted regular talks by authors.
Pafilwn Bach – small pavilion, where many different music, dance, drama and recital competitions were held on the stage and where choirs were able to practise before going into the large pavilion.
Pafiliwn Mawr – large pavilion, with a large stage, where all of the main indoor ceremonies took place, as well as the evening concerts

and any competitions involving larger groups of people such as choirs. The two pavilions (both plain looking white constructions this year) were linked together by a **Neuadd Ymgynnull** (competitors' lounge) where people could relax and get changed before appearing in front of the audience.

Llwyfan y Maes – the huge outdoor stage, where bands and choirs performed to people as they enjoyed food from the various surrounding food stalls.

Y Lle Celf – The art place, which hosted displays of work by competing artists.

Artisan – A large tent, housing various craft workers who were selling their products, including Janglerins, the silver jewellery company of Elin Mair Roberts who had made this year's crown.

Pentref Plant – the children's village, an entertainment area, from where we regularly heard lots of strange noises (vocal and instrumental), and sounds of excited young children, as we passed to get to the other tents.

Pentref Gwyddoniaeth a Thechnoleg – Science and technology village, which had various stands mostly aimed at children, encouraging exploration and discovery of various related topics.

Pentref Bwyd – food village, with a varied array of food stalls.

In the middle of all of these tents and areas were rows of hundreds of trade stands, selling or promoting their products or organisations, many of which hosted their own mini events throughout the week. One of the largest of these was the one for Ecoamgueddfa, the organisation explained earlier. This stand became one of my most regular haunts on the Maes, coming a close second favourite to the Tŷ Gwerin and the book stands. Each day interesting events were listed on the billboard outside, which challenged my existing 'plan' for the week.

Well, where on earth do I start with describing this amazing week. I've decided that the only way is to take you with me on the emotional rollercoaster that I experienced throughout the week, and describe to you the numerous events that stirred up so many different feelings in me.

But first a mention about the week's weather. After a relatively dry spell, the heavens opened throughout the night before the Steddfod, so wellies and raincoat were needed for the first day. But luckily the weather improved as the week went on and I only saw one car having to be towed out of a very muddy patch of car park on our way onto the Maes on the first evening. Anyway, less about the weather and let's get going. Are you ready for the ride – fasten your seatbelt...

Moments of joy
I'd been telling friends and family that the Maes was little over three miles from our caravan, but after nine return journeys I discovered that was only as the crow flies. By road the journey was about nine miles. I'm not complaining, as it was along the most regular route we took from Y Ffôr to Boduan via Rhos Fawr where I first experienced that sense of joy. I had my Welsh favourite playlist playing in the car on the Saturday morning – day one – and along the whole of my journey, I was moved to tears by all the banners, buntings, models, and signs of welcome (Croeso) along the route. It was an amazing nine-mile showcase of the efforts of the residents and school children, reflecting their pride in their villages and their language. Many of the signs had parts of a song lyric or poem related to the area, or a funny phrase made popular on a TV sketch such as **'Gwybod y Ffordd i Nefyn?'** (Do you know the way to Nefyn?). By the time I reached the Maes and could see the bright pink main entrance tent (which seemed like a nod to the pink pavilion of the past), I was almost euphoric!

As I drove across the field to my spot in the car park as directed by the cheerful volunteers, I was thrilled to see the large white Hollywood style 'Boduan' sign, not on the slopes of Garn Boduan, but on a closer hill Moelypenmaen. This is one of the hills we hadn't attempted as Des had advised it didn't have public access. I had a long wait in the queue to collect my wristband but enjoyed the opportunity to people watch and to chat with others including Val, a fellow learner, who I was to bump into again many times during the week. I've never seen so many Welsh authors, poets, and musicians in the space of an hour! As it was the first Saturday in the month, the Manchester learners' group would be meeting over Zoom. I had sent a message to the group saying that, if possible, I would try and join from the Maes. By the time I'd got through the turnstile and ran across the already muddy ground to the first shelter I could find, there were only ten minutes of the session remaining. I repeatedly tried to connect to the Wi-Fi, but all I could see on my iPad was my own face looking back at me, with dripping hair and a red nose from the cold rain. I found out later from the group that they had been watching my failed attempts with amused sympathy. However, this didn't dampen my joyous mood and the weather gradually improved during the day.

My next priority was a loo, and then a coffee which I enjoyed while drying off in my reserved seat in the large pavilion. My feelings of joy continued as I watched the opening event. This was a choir competition, with six large choirs competing, amongst whom I spotted many familiar faces from Llŷn. This was followed by the brief, official opening ceremony, which included Gwenan Gibbard on the harp and a lady singing cerdd dant, with some more familiar faces amongst the officials, including Liz Saville Roberts (one of my recent interviewers), and the author and winner of last year's crown Esyllt Maelor. What better start could there be to the Steddfod and what an amazing amount of Welsh culture I had just been fed within my first two hours of being on the Maes.

On the evening of this first Saturday, Jim joined me in the large pavilion to watch Curiad, the show I had been so lucky to get tickets for. There was a touch of sadness before the show, as a tribute was read out to Dr Llŷr Roberts, who had died in June, aged only 45. The tribute mentioned that as well as being an associate lecturer of the Coleg Cymraeg, he was well known by all involved in organising of the Steddfod, as he was secretary of the board of trustees, council and court. Even though I wasn't familiar with Llyr, I was moved by the tribute and sensed the strong feelings of loss and sadness amongst many others in the pavilion.

The show then provided a huge contrast to this sadness, with an amazingly joyful, memorable experience from beginning to end – a wonderful celebration of Llŷn and Eifionydd.

I'd forgotten that our seats were on the

Curiad – the show

Côr Eifionydd

front row and at times almost felt we were on stage with Pedair and the over 200 strong backing choir. Their incredible sound was complemented by other performers I've mentioned already, including Twm Morys, Gwilym Bowen Rhys and Edwin and Einir Humphreys. There was also some clog dancing from Tudur Phillips, including a demonstration of his skills at extinguishing candles with his jump heel clicks, something which recently got him into the Guiness World Records for managing 55 in one minute!

Some of my most joyous moments during the week on the Maes were my encounters with people. Each day I spotted a myriad of familiar faces, such as people from the Say Something in Welsh (SSIW) community (the online course that taught me to speak Welsh) including other learners and the founders Aran and Catrin Jones, other learners who had attended the Manchester groups over the years, tutors and members of groups for learners in Llŷn, people from Llanaelhaearn church congregation and other friends and acquaintances I'd met over the years from the area. The majority of these people were Welsh of course, but there were also people from other parts of the UK and Europe, but the thing we all had in common was a love for the Welsh language and that was the language in which we mostly communicated. On the days Jim wasn't with me, I rarely spoke a word of English until I got back to the caravan. I also met lots of new and interesting people and by the end of the week I was saying hello to almost twice as many as at the beginning.

It was during some of these encounters that I picked up interesting snippets of information, such as finding out who had won some of the competitions in the pavilion as these are often not announced until later. On numerous occasions, I bumped into Sally, who I'd met at the Porth Dinllaen Steddfod fundraising shanty evening so many months earlier. I discovered that she was a friend of Val, who I'd queued with on that first rainy morning. I congratulated her on the choir's amazing performance in Curiad as she was a member, and she shared her joy about this and about being in the winning choir (Côr Eifionydd) at the competition I'd witnessed on my first day.

Because of my love of music and especially of modern Welsh folk music, there were moments of joy every day for me as I was privileged to be able to watch and listen to some of my favourite performers and also to experience some singers and bands that were new to me. Here's my week's Steddfod 'playlist' arranged in venue order, with a bit of description if they've not already had a mention or if they're not described later in the book:

Tŷ Gwerin: Angharad Jenkins and Patrick Rimes (both fiddlers and half of the folk band Calan, launching their new album, Amrwd), Plu (Gwilym Bowen Rhys and his two sisters creating beautiful harmonies together), Tacla (a lively gypsy jazz band, with a surprise appearance – for me at least – of the Breton double bass player), The Trials of Cato, Steve Eaves a'r Band, Gareth Bonello, Tant (new to me, a young all female folk band, who I noticed were being proudly watched from the audience by the Plaid Cymru Leader Rhun ap Iowerth, who I believe is father to one of the band members), Siân James (one quarter of Pedair), Meinir Gwilym (supported by Gwennan Gibbard, together making half of Pedair), Gwyneth Glyn (quarter of Pedair) with Twm Morys (launching their new album).

Maes D: Cynefin, Cerys Hafana, N'famady Kouyate (new to me and an absolute joy to listen to, bringing smiles and lots of energy to the audience, with his lively performance. He originates from Guinea, is now based in Cardiff and is learning to speak and sing in Welsh. He accompanied himself on the balafon – a traditional wooden xylophone), and Gwenan Gibbard (supported by Gwilym Bowen Rhys, musically and practically – I saw him struggling across the Maes carrying her huge harp to the tent).

Caffi Maes B – Lily Beau, Glain Rhys and Ani Glas. I was possibly the oldest person in the audience at each of these gigs, but I didn't care and just soaked up the lively and happy atmosphere created by these three young talented female singers.

Llwyfan y Maes – Plu (again), the local all-male choir Côr Meibion Carnguwch (with Nia Wern/Humphreys on the keyboard as mentioned earlier) and the band Pys Melyn. The drummer in Pys Melyn, is Owain the son of our Llŷn friends Amanda and Brian. We felt proud to see him on the huge outdoor stage with his indie band who are becoming increasingly popular in the young Welsh music scene.

Ecoamgueddfa – another local, but this time all-female choir, based in Pwllheli – Côr yr Heli, led by Gwenan Gibbard – these Pedair people get around don't they?

I don't consider myself to be to be too materialistic and I'm not a keen shopper... unless there are books involved and then I am filled with joy. There were several book stands on the Maes including the ones run by Gwasg Carreg Gwalch based in Llanrwst (my own publishers), Cyngor Llyfrau Cymru (Books Council of Wales) and Ceredigion based publishers Y Lolfa. I was overjoyed to see my own book for sale on some of the stands and also excited to make some new purchases. As I can get rather carried away and as we don't have a money tree, I decided to try and limit myself to one book a day, which would mean eight books in total. You'll find out as we go on if I managed to keep to my target as I'll let you know what I bought, but not in the order of buying, as this chapter jumps about between days as you'll have already realised.

One final joyous moment I would like to mention was when the 2023 **Gwobr Albwm Cymraeg y Flwyddyn**/Welsh Language Album of the Year was announced in the Pafilwn Mawr on the Friday. I had hoped to watch this live from inside the pavilion, but I was trying to squeeze too many other things in. I compromised by watching it on the large screen just outside of the building, enabling me to dash off to Encore to watch singer Lleuwen. Pedair's album Mae 'Na Olau, had been one of the nine on the shortlist, as well as albums by a couple of other artists I enjoy listening to – Cerys Hafana and Kizzy Crawford. But Jim and I were rooting for Pedair as we are huge fans of the band and of the four members as individual performers, and have been following their progress from the start. I stared intently at the screen amongst a small gathering of others awaiting the announcement and as

Pedair's album was named as the winner, I totally forgot where I was and cheered and raised my arms. I hadn't been the only one thankfully, but I quickly dashed off feeling rather self-conscious but joyful.

Moments of anguish
After all of that joy, I'm afraid the rollercoaster is heading quickly downhill. There weren't many feelings of negativity during the week but to feel joy we also have to experience pain I suppose.

At the end of my first day on the Maes, I was feeling tired but content and slowly worked my way back to the turnstiles. The muddy ground was beginning to dry and I noticed things I'd missed on my wet hurried arrival that morning, such as the large board with a print of the painting by Sioned Williams used for the logo on the Steddfod T-shirt that I was proudly wearing again that day. I also felt moved to see an art poster in memory of Dyfrig Evans, the actor and singer who had died not long before last year's Steddfod. I soon found myself back in the field where I'd left the car, or so I thought. I'd remembered thinking I was quite close to the entrance with arriving early and I was looking forward to sitting and enjoying the drive back to the caravan soon. The plan was that I would be grabbing a quick meal with Jim, before returning with him to watch **Curiad**, the evening show. In my excitement, I'd forgotten to make a mental note of my exact car park spot, something I'm often known to do, especially in large supermarket car parks. After pacing up and down between the rows of cars in the uneven field several times, focusing especially on all the red cars, I realised the car wasn't there. My legs felt ready for dropping off and I rang Jim so I could vent. I knew there was nothing he could do, but in fact he did just what I needed which was to contain my panic and suggest I look in another field. I told Jim that I was

Gareth Bale and Dyfrig Evans posters

Sioned Williams Poster

certain I'd left it in this field and so the only possibility was that it had been stolen. As I strode halfheartedly to the next field, I spotted a solitary tree that I'd taken note of that morning as it was close to where I'd left the car and of course there it still was. As you can imagine I made a careful note of where I'd left the car each day for the rest of the week.

Another difficult time for me was when I was volunteering on the Cymdeithas yr Iaith (Welsh language society) stand on the Wednesday morning. Carole and Bethan gave me a friendly welcome and it was a great opportunity to practise my Welsh with them, the customers and Tony, another volunteer, but I was just hopeless at promotion. I was asked to hand out flyers advertising that afternoon's rally highlighting the second home situation in Wales. Tony confidently marched off amongst the crowds of people with a wad of flyers and soon returned empty handed. I stayed near the opening of the stand and smiled meekly at people handing one to them if they looked friendly and came near enough to me. I do feel strongly about this issue but I'm just not a good campaigner. I felt like I'd let them down in a way, and as if I'd gained more from this experience than I'd been able to offer. I was cheered by a visit from Greg, a fellow learner I'd met on Zoom meetings, who popped by for a chat. Then my confidence was boosted when I managed to complete my one and only sale of a Cymdeithas yr Iaith T-shirt, using the bank card reader, especially when I realised that my customer was Catrin Mara, an actress that I recognised from the soap opera **Rownd a Rownd**.

My reserved seat in the large pavilion caused me some anguish, especially when there were popular events going on. There was no separate door for reserved seat ticket holders, so I had to join the long queue for the three indoor Gorsedd ceremonies and the Cerdd Dant choir competition which all drew large audiences. I was happy to queue until I heard the man or lady at the door shouting **'sori, llawn'** (sorry full) and saw the doors beginning to close. This happened each time, and each time, my heart pounding,

I had to either run to the front of the remaining queue or to a different entrance and show my reserved seat ticket, sometimes being responded to by a look of disbelief or uncertainty from the person on the door. Once inside the pavilion, there was then usually someone sitting in my seat and I had to awkwardly apologise and explain the situation, feeling mean at their having to move.

From Wednesday onwards, the Maes got noticeably busier, with an influx of younger faces, which we presumed was because Maes B was now open. The tents were getting full to bursting and towards the end of the week Tŷ Gwerin even had a crowd control barrier outside of it. Sadly, I or we, had to miss some of our favourite bands as we just couldn't get into the tent, especially if they were performing in the evening or if we were last minute arriving at the tent, because of rushing over from another event elsewhere. I felt sad at having to miss a performance by Pedair, who unsurprisingly drew a huge audience. I then had to tell myself I was being greedy as we had seen them live at other venues as well as at the Curiad show... and we had planned to get tickets to see them at the end of August in Aberdaron. I said to Jim that I thought for future Steddfodau instead of a Tŷ Gwerin there should be a Pafiliwn Gwerin.

One last moment of anguish involved the friend I refer to as 'eBay Ann'. She had told me that her cerdd dant choir, Trillyn, had reached the final, and she would be performing 'on the stage' at about 7 o'clock after some practice sessions. Ann had been on the Maes for two days but we had still not managed to find each other as our messages to each other were delayed due to poor Wi-Fi connection, so I was determined to at least watch her in the competition. I checked the App and could see they would be practicing in the small pavilion at 6pm, so immediately after the chairing ceremony in the large pavilion I dashed over to the smaller one next door, arriving at about 6.30pm. I wondered if I'd missed them. There were very few people in the audience which surprised me, but I sat and enjoyed listening to the choirs who came onto the stage to practice and thought that I'd at least see her in the actual competition, which I presumed would be happening soon on this same stage. It suddenly dawned on me that the choirs I was listening to were not singing cerdd dant style. I asked another member of the audience who informed me that the cerdd dant choir competition was about to start in about 10 minutes in the large pavilion! So, I raced off to join the queue outside of the large pavilion and I've already grumbled about that experience. Three choirs had reached the final and one of these was the local Côr Heli (who I later found out won first prize) so I knew that Ann was in one of the other two choirs as she is not from Llŷn. I watched every member of the other two choirs carefully as they joined and left the stage and couldn't recognise any as being Ann. I'd remembered she'd said this year she was in the second row, but she's not very tall and I just couldn't make her out at all. Despite my distraction, I enjoyed the excellent performances by all three choirs. We later emailed one another and Ann said that Côr Trillyn came second. We laughed about her elusiveness, but at least I was able to say that I'd heard her even if I hadn't seen her.

Moments of spontaneity
Even though I had my timetable organised for the week, which got changed frequently when I discovered other events, some of the most memorable and enjoyable moments for me were when we were taken by surprise.

On a Jim and I day, we happened upon Gwyneth Glyn and Twm Morys sitting in the carriage of a Ffestiniog Railway train, singing the title track of their new album, **Tocyn Unffordd i Lawenydd** (one way ticket to happiness). We joined the small audience who had gathered round and it felt like a special treat.

Merched y Wawr in song

On another day, I walked past the large Merched y Wawr stand just in time to catch a beautiful rendition of 'Calon Lân' by a large group of the ladies. A tip for any Welsh learners visiting an eisteddfod is to head over to the Merched y Wawr tent. Not only do you get a panad and a Welsh cake in return for a donation, you are given one of the warmest welcomes you'll find on the Maes. I believe it was the

Nefyn branch of the Merched y Wawr who were organising the teas this year. I've found over the years that the majority of the ladies are my age or over, friendly and keen to have a conversation with a Welsh learner. Don't be put off if you're not female – men are also allowed in – I even spotted the archdruid himself in there one day as I passed by. They also had some stunning fabric pictures on display which were entries for their own art competition.

Not far from this stand was **Y Babell Heddwch** (the peace tent), and it was here that I enjoyed an unexpected performance of Meinir Gwilym singing one of her most famous songs **'Dim Byd a Nunlle'** (nothing and nowhere). She was surrounded by a small group of people who like me had happened to come upon her and I smiled at the difference between this audience and the one only the night before in the Tŷ Gwerin, when she'd sung this same song as her finale. The previous night's audience, fueled by plenty of drink from the bar, the **Syched** 'thirst' tent, next door, almost shouted the tent down as they sang along with the chorus. The audience this day were I'm sure just as appreciative but let Meinir manage all of the lyrics herself.

On Jim's first full day on the Maes with me, we were passing the **Samariaid**/Samaritans stand and I recognised the lady fronting it as Fiona Collins, who organises online Welsh storytelling sessions that I've attended a few times. She is now also a member of the Gorsedd after having won Dysgwr y Flwyddyn a few years ago. We had a little chat and we were about to go on our way, when Myrddin ap Dafydd appeared and Fiona pointed at the display board which announced that on their stand today it was **'Diwrnod y Beirdd'** (day of the poets). At 11am Myrddin was scheduled to provide a poetry session to support Samariaid. As we were the only ones at the stand at the time, Fiona asked could she film myself and Jim listening to Myrddin reading his poem. The touching poem was called **Mainc** (bench) and was a tribute to two Llŷn people who had erected a stone bench close to the hill Tre'r Ceiri, as a memorial to a local man when he died during the covid – 19 lockdown. The poem talked of their thoughtfulness in finding a different way of remembering a lost loved one in this time when churches were locked and other ways weren't possible. I felt privileged to have been part of this event. Fiona asked if we knew Myrddin and he explained about my book. Fiona told us that she had been asked by him to write some short folk stories for learners and soon after, I visited one of the book stands and bought **Ceffylau** (horses) – **Book One**. This book and her other published by Gwasg Carreg Gwalch, **Y Môr** (the sea), Fiona warned me, are aimed at beginners but I still bought a copy as I enjoy an easy read sometimes.

Later that same day, we were heading past Llwyfan y Maes, in search of a coffee and were just in time to see the wonderful Côr Meibion Carnguwch performing two songs, with the familiar Nia Wern at keyboard and Ann Hafod conducting. The second of these songs was a powerful rendition of the famous song **'Tân yn Llŷn'**, (fire in Llŷn) which received a huge cheer, I think from almost everyone within ear shot of the stage. This song was originally composed and sung by the group Plethyn in 1990 and its title was a familiar theme on the Maes this year for a good reason. There is a lot written about the history behind this song, including a mention in my coastal path book, but I'll give a brief background here. In 1936, despite strong protest, the UK government established an RAF bombing school and air base at the site of Penyberth, an old farmhouse in the village of Penrhos, which had been the home to a generation of poets. On the 8th September of that year, three members of Plaid Cymru, Saunders Lewis (dramatist), Lewis Valentine (poet and preacher) and D.J. Williams (novelist) decided to take action, setting fire to the new building then immediately turning themselves in to the police. They were sentenced to nine months imprisonment but on release were greeted as heroes by a rally of 15,000 people in Caernarfon. This event is seen as significant in the history of Welsh politics and the song is often used as a reminder of how today, the Welsh culture and language continues to be under threat for example by the second homes situation. I have heard it said that the 'Tân yn Llŷn' is now a symbol for the fire in the belly of the Welsh people who are concerned about this ongoing threat.

Myrddin ap Dafydd's poetry reading

Moments of speechlessness

Yes, I do have moments when I'm lost for words, believe it or not. I'm naturally rather a shy person despite my tendency to ramble, and these moments mostly often occur when I'm taken by surprise or when I'm feeling in awe of something or someone. Amongst the myriad of familiar faces on the Maes, were many what I consider to be famous ones, especially singers and musicians that I admire or people I recognised off the television. As the week went on, I got used to regular sightings of various Welsh celebrities including the actor Idris Morris Jones, who I know as the wacky Jac y Jwc from the children's S4C programme and Ken from Rownd a Rownd – he was everywhere... even in choirs! I didn't even flinch when I spotted Mark Drakeford, First Minister of Wales, strolling along the Maes with his entourage. And we got used to spotting Gwilym Bowen Rhys hurrying across the Maes to his next performance, often giving us a 'haia' and a smile on his way past. But there were some moments that took me off guard and left me gobsmacked as we say up north, or **cegrwth** as they say in Welsh.

On one of my alone days, I was walking across the Pentref Bwyd, with a mouthful of a delicious savoury pancake as I was making my way to the large pavilion to watch a ceremony. I looked up and there was Lleuwen Steffan, one of my all-time favourite singers, with her family including dad Steve Eaves (another hero of mine as you know), heading directly towards me. She greeted me with a hug and a 'helo Jean' and then asked how my book was doing. After gulping down a large piece of unchewed pancake, I managed to reply and said that it was lovely to see her back on the music scene after a break. My speechlessness was mostly about her remembering my name and knowing about my book, but the pancake contributed.

At the end of the spontaneous performance, by Twm Morys and Gyneth Glyn on the train, they walked by and Gwyneth greeted us as she has done many times before, but then left us both

Mark Drakeford and entourage

speechless saying that it had been lovely to see us at the **Curiad** show. We had almost felt on stage with the performers with our front row seat, but I'd not thought of the performers seeing us!

Even though we were used to seeing Gwilym Bowen Rhys frequently throughout the week, we were both still surprised when we saw him in the audience at the Cerys Hafana gig in the Maes D tent, especially when he leaned over to say that he also had spotted us in the front row at the show on Saturday night. We're going to have to start wearing dark glasses!

Another face that made me cegrwth on the numerous times I spotted it, was that of Angharad Tomos, the author already mentioned. I think it's because I consider her to be rather an icon because of my awareness of her efforts as a Welsh language activist. She was chairwoman of Cymdeithas yr Iaith during the campaigns for a Welsh Language Act from 1982 to 1984. This act was finally passed in 1993, putting Welsh on an equal footing with English in relation to business and justice. Before this, as an 18-year-old student, in 1977, Angharad, with three other protestors, broke into a Lancashire transmitting station and turned the television off for a few seconds across the north-west of England to highlight the need for a Welsh language television channel. Strange to think that this had happened at the top of Winter Hill, which is not too far from my home and is a place where I had regularly walked from around this period of time onwards, yet had been oblivious to its significance to the people of Wales until recently.

Moments of relaxation

As the week progressed, the weather improved, and it became quite hot especially by the afternoons. I enjoyed the energy of the Maes but there were times when we would suddenly both feel overheated, overtired and in need of somewhere away from the crowds. Glasu, the local producers of delicious ice-cream that we frequently buy from their shop and café in Pwllheli, had several stands on the Maes which were a great help when the queues weren't too long. But sometimes we just needed somewhere peaceful to sit.

I have to admit that I didn't often head to the **Pentref Gwyddoniaeth a Thechnoleg** as Science was never my strong point. Sons Tom and Simon are both great with science and technology – both gained a degree in related subjects – but they've inherited that from Jim, not me. On my third day on the Maes, after a morning packed with events, I was wandering around wearily when I found myself close to the science and technology area, where I made an interesting discovery. A teepee style tent was tucked just inside the entrance called **Pabell Pawb** (everyone's tent). I saw the billboard outside advertising a session called **'Gwrandwch ac Ymlaciwch'** (listen and relax), which I liked the sound of, so I settled down on one of the deckchairs inside and took the opportunity to eat my sandwich while waiting for it to start. To my delight it was a literature session with poets Siân Northey (mentioned earlier) and Annes Glyn, reading their poems and micro fiction, whilst being accompanied by improvised gentle music provided by Gethin Tomos on keyboard. I hadn't understood every word they said but had found this a thoroughly enjoyable and relaxing experience. They had a tiny audience but mentioned that they would be doing another session later in the week. I made a note of when and was determined to return. **Book 2** and **Book 3** were therefore by Annes Glyn – a poetry collection **Hel Hadau Gwawn** (collection of gossamer seeds) and Siân Northey – her first adult novel **Yn y Tŷ Hwn** (in this house), which I took with me to the second session for them to sign after sitting with their larger audience this time. I relaxed and enjoyed the words and music just as much as I had the first time, and even gained some advice about coffee and the menopause due to arriving a bit early and catching the end of the previous event. The tent was in the science area after all. What was the advice did you say? To only ever drink decaffeinated coffee and only then if it has been decaffeinated using the Swiss water method. Another reason to continue buying Dwyfor coffee.

On Thursday, a Jim day, we both returned to this tent for a similarly refreshing experience, to escape the heat and a light

Relaxing in Pabell Pawb

Annes Glyn, Siân Northey and Gethin Tomos in Pabell Pawb

rain shower. As we both slumped down on the deckchairs, a lady commented that we both looked totally relaxed and asked if she could take our photo. This time it was three young female musicians who helped us to relax with their session of gentle classical music performed on fiddle, cello and keyboard.

A lot of the bands and singers we watched were lively and if I'd been blessed with the ability to dance and was less inhibited, I'd have gone for it, but head nodding and foot tapping were about the closest I got. But there are some Welsh language singers that I enjoy listening to for their gentle voices and two of my favourites were performing during the week. Owen Shiers, sings under the name of **Cynefin** (simple translation is habitat, but like the word **hiraeth** it needs a poet or musician to convey its meaning well), and is from the Clettwr valley, west Wales. Owen sang songs from his album **Dilyn Afon** (following a river), which is the result of his three years of research and work. Listening to him singing his gentle arrangements of old folk songs from Ceredigion, I was able to leave the hustle and bustle of the Maes for a while and imagine some of the tales that unfolded in his songs, such as **Y Deryn Du** (the blackbird), the feathered cupid.

Gareth Bonello from Cardiff often sings under the name 'The Gentle Good' which seems to describe the style of his songs and the man himself who has an air of serenity about him. I've admired his music for a while and never having seen him live before, had recently been disappointed at not being able to see him at a Manchester gig. This solo session of gentle folk songs with acoustic guitar accompaniment, made up for that loss and Jim and I enjoyed a perfectly relaxed hour in the shade of the Tŷ Gwerin.

Moments of interest
There are plenty of opportunities at the Steddfod to have your hunger for knowledge fed and I managed to take advantage of a

few of these. I remembered Rhys Mwyn visiting a learners' chat group I had joined one Saturday morning in Gwalia café, Pwllheli. His mission had been to introduce Welsh language music to those not familiar with it, and he'd explained that he had once sung and played bass in the Welsh rock/punk band **Anhrefn**. Rhys now presents a Radio show on Radio Cymru and uncharacteristically for me, I'd recently responded to a Facebook request he'd made for people to send him selfies with a mural of punk rock singer Pete Shelley. This happened to have been painted in my local town of Leigh, Greater Manchester, so I'd felt obliged. Pete had been in the band Buzzcocks, was close in age to my eldest brother Ste, and had attended the same grammar school, also in Leigh. I spotted Rhys frequently on the Maes throughout the week, especially amongst the audiences of various bands. Rhys also happens to be an archaeologist and regularly offers guided walks of historical interest in the Gwynedd area. On my first day on the Maes, I enjoyed his talk in Maes D, '**Bryngaerau Llŷn**' (hillforts of Llŷn), where he shared his vast knowledge on this subject, including on the fort we'd recently seen on Tre'r Ceiri, but I'd felt frustrated at myself for missing some important details due to not always knowing the meaning of some of the more complex Welsh words. Luckily, he was selling some of his books and for once I chose one in English. The *Real Gwynedd* was therefore **Book 4** and I'm looking forward to discovering more interesting facts about Llŷn and about the ancient fort on Tre'r Ceiri, where our final hill walk had been. As Rhys signed it for me, he was surprised when I shared that I'd been the Pete Shelley selfie person and how I'd listened to his radio show when he'd mentioned my message.

The large Ecoamgueddfa stand was one of my regular haunts during the week as it hosted a large variety of interesting events, because of its involvement with some of the main cultural sites in Llŷn. It should have won a prize for presentation as one half of it felt like a cosy

Rhys Mwyn in Maes D

Gair Mewn Gwlân in the Ecoamgueddfa stand

cottage sitting room with a Welsh dresser, mock fireplace and easy chairs and the other half had a wooden stage where all the events took place. Lining the walls on each side of the stage were knitted or crocheted squares with names of features in Llŷn such as beaches, wells and woodlands embroidered onto them. These had been created by children from various schools in Llŷn as part of the project '**Gair Mewn Gwlân**' (word in wool), that Amanda had mentioned being involved with many months ago.

Because of trying to squeeze too much in, I only caught a small part of an interesting talk at the Ecoamgeueddfa stand, accompanying the launch of a new book '**Ciplŷn**'. This bilingual book (**Book 5**), as well as being filled with stunning photographs, explains the Ecoamgueddfa ethos and includes interviews with 14 different Llŷn ladies, as they share their experiences and feelings about their **milltir sgwâr** (localilty). I recognized two of the ladies on the stage who are featured in the book – Liz Saville Roberts (mentioned earlier, ever to be known as my interviewer) and Mared Llywelyn, who I've noticed involved in various projects in Llŷn including dramas and at Plas Carmel where she is currently the Education and Volunteering Officer. There are others of the fourteen that you may even feel are familiar to you by now as I've mentioned them rather a lot already including Meinir Pierce Jones and Nia Humphreys, both from Nefyn.

One talk I was determined not to miss in the Ecoamgueddfa stand was 'Milltir Sgwâr *Capten*' which related to Meinir Pierce Jones's book *Capten*. A map to accompany the book had been produced by Tom Workman, with details of the places mentioned in the text, both fictional and factual. Meinir and Tom explained how this had been created and a copy of the map was available to buy from the stand. This has now been added to our Welsh art gallery, otherwise known as the walls of our caravan.

Singer Lleuwen had announced on Facebook that she would be in the Encore tent, starting about 45 minutes before the chairing ceremony was to commence in the large pavilion. I was gutted that I wouldn't be able to see the whole of her show as I had not seen her perform live for several years. But I'd promised myself to see all of the Gorsedd ceremonies this year. The cheers and extended clapping from the audience demonstrated how thrilled they all were to see Lleuwen on the stage again. I was surprised to see musician Anghgarad Jenkins with her on the stage and soon realized that this was mostly a talk and not a gig and that she was interviewing Lleuwen. The talk was fascinating and was about Lleuwen's latest project for which she had been researching the sound archives at St Fagans National Museum of History. The name of her project is **Emynau Llafar Gwlad a Phregethau Rhyfeddol** (folk hymns and wonderful sermons) and for this she had taken copies of some ancient recordings of voices of Welsh preachers and of hymns (many that had never been published in hymn books) then blended the two together. The examples that were played sounded extraordinary and sent shivers down my spine. Unfortunately, I had to discreetly creep out of the tent after about half an hour and dash across to the queue outside the large pavilion. I may never know if I missed a mini gig at the end of the interview.

This year was the first time I'd dared to venture inside Y Babell Lên, which seems strange considering my love of all things literature, but I'd previously felt that any events going on in there would have been beyond my Welsh language and intellectual abilities. But I was pleasantly surprised and enjoyed three interesting events in there during the week.

The first of these events was an interview with photographer Emyr Young and poet Twm Morys about their book '**Prifeirdd Cymru, Llŷn ac Eifionydd**' (Wales' chief poets, Llŷn and Eifionydd) which was a **Barddas** publication and one of several to be produced. Barddas (bardism), is the name of the quarterly poetry magazine, produced by **Cymdeithas Cerdd Dafod** (Welsh strict metre poetry society) and edited by Twm Morys. Esyllt Maelor, one of the three poets featured in the book was also present and talked of her experience of having been photographed by Emyr and interviewed by Twm. She spoke of her usual dislike for being photographed, but how she was rather pleased with the result and that Twm's humour had helped her to relax. Following the talk, I headed over to the Barddas stand, to buy a copy (**Book 6**) and found that the other two poets featured in this book were Guto Dafydd (who wrote my *Carafanio* book) and Alan Llwyd (much to be revealed soon!).

Jim accompanied me to my second visit to Y Babell Lên and made use of the translation service, while we listened to an interesting presentation about Penyberth and the Tân yn Llŷn event. There were readings of a selection of literature that had been inspired by the burning of the bombing school. I was surprised to discover that the demolished cottage Penyberth and land surrounding it had belonged to the family of Helen Williams Ellis, who we have known since about 2 P.C. (pre caravan), when we stayed in two of her cottages. I have stayed in touch with Helen since and she is always enthusiastic about my learning Welsh. Helen and her sister contributed to the presentation. Gwilym Bowen Rhys appeared towards the end of the event and stunned everyone with his passionate rendition of the song Tân yn Llŷn – I thought his guitar was going to set on fire!

My last visit to Y Babell Lên was also with Jim on the final day of the Steddfod. It was the closing event for this venue, and for us, although we didn't realise it at the time. It was a performance of the podcast Colli'r Plot and was being recorded simultaneously. It was interesting to see all of the authors live on the stage rather than just hearing them on my car radio on the way to work. As well as discussing the books they'd read recently, they also talked about their experiences on the Maes and Siân Northey mentioned how much she'd enjoyed the **'Gwrandwch ac Ymlaciwch'** (listen and relax) sessions.

I'm no artist myself, but have always admired and had an interest in the art work of others, so I popped into Lle Celf several times during the week. Some of the art displayed left me feeling rather bemused as it does in any art gallery, but there was a lot that really grabbed my interest. One of these was a painting depicting Lewis, Valentine and Williams (or **'Y Tri** /The Three') as they're often known, who were responsible for the 'Tân yn Llŷn'. The fiery red background gave an extra dramatic effect to the painting. On a later visit, some drama had joined the painting, with three actors dressed as Y Tri, wearing life like masks. Standing close to the painting they demonstrated peacefully with their signs which read **'Gweithred yw Heddwch'** (peace is action) and **'Stiwardiaeth yn gofyn am Gamau Gweithredu'** (stewardship requires action). Y Tri could be seen regularly on the Maes throughout the week and were a striking reminder to people of the ongoing support needed to ensure the future of the Welsh language and culture. One of my other favourite pieces of art work, was a display of the wooden painted place name signs of Morwen Jones as part of her project Cofnod 2023, as explained earlier. It was a great opportunity to see them close up and, in the weeks, following the Steddfod, the signs were sited in their rightful places, as reminders to locals and visitors of the old names for the parts of their surrounding landscape. Seeing Morwen's work reminded me that Gwasg Carreg Gwalch had published a small book of her work **'Darn Bach o Dir'** (small piece of land), with photos showing her signs in their locations and poems accompanying them. So off to their book stand I headed (**Book 7**). There I spotted another book that I had seen advertised a while ago and 'needed' – **Mae Bywyd Yma** (this life), with poems by Guto Dafydd about different parts of Llŷn and accompanying photos by Dafydd Nant – **Book 8**. Let's see if I kept to my limit!

Moments of laughter

My first Steddfod moment of laughter was on my initial journey to the Maes, when I spotted a sign amongst the many others welcoming people to the area. This one wasn't a poem or a 'Croeso' but a statement – **'Dewi Pws Sant Pen Llŷn'** – Dewi Pws saint of Llŷn. If you recall Dewi 'Pws' Morris is the comedic banjo playing singer and poet. Two days later, he was performing outdoors in his white robes, as part of the first of the two **Cylch yr Orsedd** (the Gorsedd circle) ceremonies, where new members were welcomed into the Gorsedd with the **'Cyhoeddi Urddau'r Orsedd Eisteddfod'** – announcement of the order of the Gorsedd. The winners of the main awards in the 2022 Steddfod, including learner of the year Joe Healy, and poets and writers Llŷr Gwyn Lewis, Menir Pierce Jones, Esyllt Maelor and Sioned Erin Hughes appeared in their new white robes to have their headdresses presented and be received into the Gorsedd. Dewi was welcomed into the Gorsedd in 2010, when he had recently been appointed the children's poet laureate for Wales.

There were several fountains on the Maes, where Jim and I filled up our water bottles regularly, and there was one that from day one gave you a shower if you stood too close to it, due to the speed of dispensing. On the nice hot days, this was quite pleasant but not so much on the grey showery days. But I have to say that without fail, each time it happened to us or when we spotted it happening to some other poor unsuspecting thirsty person it made us both laugh.

Maggi Noggi is known and loved throughout Wales as the outrageous drag queen, who often appears on S4C and is frequently seen at eisteddfodau. This year was no exception and as Jim and I were strolling towards the pavilions we spotted her in her sequined pink dress speeding across the Maes on a disability scooter, shouting out as if she had lost control and creating a lot of hilarity amongst those whose attention she'd caught. The cameras were following her around the Maes and filming her antics for a special TV show. Maggi is the alter ego to Kristoffer Hughes, who works as a mortuary technician and is Chief of the Ynys Môn Druid Order. A couple of days following this, he was welcomed into the Gorsedd, at the second and final Cylch yr Orsedd ceremony, where he wore his green robes. As he was presented with his headdress, his contributions to Wales were announced and included his work as a grief and bereavement officer, which he has offered in Welsh, which brought comfort to a lot of Welsh speaking families. I heard a story later that Maggi Noggi had said that one day she hoped to be accepted into the Gorsedd but that she would want pink robes.

At this same ceremony the popular musician Edwin Humphreys received his welcome amidst cheers from the audience. As he stood in line, waiting to be presented to the archdruid, who was standing on the **maen llog** (large flat artificial stone stage), he performed to the delighted crowd, showing off his bare knees and the Crocs shoes he was wearing under his green robes. The Gorsedd members, in

Maggi Noggi

their long robes and headdresses who made up most of the seated audience within the circle of artificial Gorsedd stones, created a sea of blue, green and white. It was a blustery day and the wind frequently whipped their headdresses high up into the air, which added to the humour. There were more howls of laughter when Edwin's Gorsedd name (of his choosing) was announced… **'Arglwydd Snedli'**. Arglwydd means lord and I'd read online that this had been his nickname from fellow performers for many years but I was unsure what Snedli meant. So I contacted Edwin himself to find out for this book. He sent a friendly return message telling me that Snedli was a play on his own name, with 'Ed' at its centre, but he said as for explaining the Lord bit, he would need to explain that in person as it was rather complicated.

On the Friday, Jim and I bumped into our Llŷn friends Brian and Amanda. Brian is more of a Welsh Show person, being a farmer, but had come along to watch Amanda's friend Glesni take part in the comedy Stomp Werin competition in the Tŷ Gwerin. Glesni was already well known in these competitions and held 'champion' status. In 2019 at the Llanrwst Steddfod, she competed and won with her hilarious performance as the character Mena Menapôs and she sang of the sufferings experienced by women of a certain age. Amanda had written the lyrics, and this year had done the same for Glesni's two new alter egos, Mena having been left behind. This time she was a cyclist (wearing Brian's lycra cycling gear) and a policeman in uniform. This year, as well as performances in cerdd dant style such as Glesni's, some of the contestants performed comical clog dancing sketches. This event wasn't for children or anyone of a delicate constitution with the lyrics sung by some of the contestants containing a stream of sexual inuendos! Glesni (with the help of Amanda's lyrics) had the voting audience in hysterics and won once again, keeping hold of her champion title. I was surprised to discover at a later stage that Gruffudd Eifion who had been

Glesni in the Stomp Gwerin

Glesni's (and Amanada's) rival in the final was a Prifardd (chief poet) and winner of the chair in 2018. I told Amanda that therefore she should now be entitled to be a Gorsedd member. If you do a search on YouTube, you may be lucky enough to find videos of some of Glesni's performances.

Moments of admiration
On Jim's first full day on the Maes, Sunday, we headed to Maes D for **'Stori'r Dydd'** (story of the day). Each day a short story was being read from 'Byd Bach', the book of eight short stories aimed at learners, edited by Esyllt Maelor and written by herself and six different learners. (**Book 9** – although it was actually the first book I bought) – yes I did go over my target of eight books! It wasn't possible for me to listen to them all, but I ensured today's session was in my schedule as our friend Chris's story **'Mynd am Dro'** (going for a walk) was being read. The tutor Audra, who I'd met earlier in the year was reading the story and Chris answered questions put to her at the end. I was full of admiration for the whole project, but especially so for Chris today after hearing her entertaining and funny story and her witty answers to the questions put to her. We had a quick chat with Chris afterwards and my admiration increased as she told me that she would also be helping to dress the Gorsedd for the ceremonies during the week.

One event I had been looking forward to for a while, was the launch on the Maes of Manchester friend Simon Chandler's Welsh language novel *Llygad Dieithryn*. By now I had thoroughly enjoyed reading his book and was full of admiration for his huge achievement at writing a novel in a language other than his mother tongue. On Monday, I proudly watched him being interviewed in Maes D by editor Nia Roberts. Passages from his book were read out by his friend Daniela Schlick, who I also have a lot of admiration for. Daniela's first language is German, but in 2017 she won Dysgwr y Flwyddyn and is currently using Welsh daily in her position as project coordinator with Mentrau Iaith Cymru, whose role is to create opportunities for people to use Welsh every day within their communities. I bumped into Daniela regularly during the week and we had lots of interesting chats, sometimes when she was working on her stand. I had a quick chat with Simon after the launch and with some of his interested audience, including

Manchester friend Peter, and Aran from say Something in Welsh. But that was the last I saw of him that week, as he soon had to dash off to another important event – his son's wedding.

A lot of my jaw dropping admiration happened from row CH , seat 38 in the pavilion, whilst watching the three Gorsedd ceremonies on the large stage in front of me – once I'd fought to get my seat that is! The two outdoor Cylch yr Orsedd ceremonies were impressive enough to watch and I was full of admiration for all of the organisers and participants of these, especially the newly welcomed members as their contributions to Wales were acknowledged. But I would highly recommend you watch at least one of the three Gorsedd ceremonies held inside the pavilion, to experience the feeling of awe and wonder as I did, when the spotlight searches the audience for the winner, and the celebration is then acted out before your eyes on the stage, with music, dance and plenty of pomp. I have explained the format and the role of the participants in each of these ceremonies already but I will give a little of the detail of this week's ceremonies and reveal the winners of course.

Cylch yr Orsedd Ceremony

Monday afternoon was the **Seremoni Coroni'r Bardd a Chroesawu'r Cynrychiolwyr Celtaidd** – the crowning of the bard ceremony and welcoming of bards from other Celtic nations. I was full of admiration when I spotted Emrys from Llanaelhaearn church (and father to Catrin from SSIW). I'm sure he won't mind me saying that he's getting on in age now, but there he was on stage with the rest of the current Gorsedd members, proudly donning his green robes.

I found out later in the week that there were other people that I knew who were on stage with the Gorsedd audience, but I had not been able to recognise them at the time when in their gowns. This included three in white robes as they had previously been Learner of the Year – Fiona Collins, Daniela Schlick and Martyn

Croydon, although I had almost run into Martyn parading in his robes when I was dashing from one of the outdoor ceremonies to another event across the Maes. Then there was long-time acquaintance Jonathan Simcock, who I had a few chats with during the week, in his well-deserved blue robes for his contribution to the Welsh culture. I have met with Jonathan many times during my years of learning to speak Welsh and he has mine and many others' admiration and respect for his work in spreading the word and supporting other Welsh learners. He used to live in Derby where he ran groups for learners and even established a local Welsh paper, which he has managed to badger me into writing a couple of articles for over the years. He has finally fulfilled his dream of living in Wales and I can see on social media that he continues to be regularly involved in events for learners.

Back to the crowning. It was announced that there had been 42 entrants for the competition, the remit of which was to write a poem, not in cynghanedd form, and of not more than 250 lines on the subject of '**rhyddid**' (freedom). As the judge explained how they came to decide on the winner of the crown, he delighted the audience with his remark that Wales may have lost the crown earlier this year (referring to the position of the Prince of Wales) but that today's crowning was the most important one. The winner was Rhys Iowerth, who used the ffugenw Gregor, from Caernarfon, a youngster at only 40 and already a prifardd, having won the chair in 2011. You could feel the pride on the stage and in the audience that a local had won this prestigious prize and it was exciting to see Elin Mair's crown finally being placed on the winner's head. During the dance of the flowers, I noticed that one of the children was a boy. I felt full of admiration for him being the only boy amongst the dancers and following the ceremony, he was interviewed on S4C and praised for his talent and bravery.

Wednesday afternoon was the **Seremoni'r Priflenor Rhyddiaith** – ceremony of the winner of the prose medal. For this the contestants had to present a piece of prose of less than 40,000 words on the subject of '**Porth**' (port/gateway). The winner was Meleri Wyn James from Aberystwyth, using the ffugenw Fi a Ti. Meleri is a children's author and by amazing coincidence, the event following this ceremony in the pavilion was a children's musical show '**Na Nel**' based on one of her stories. I noticed in this ceremony that instead of the dance of the flowers, there were teenage dancers – male and female – performing a lively clog dance mostly in line on the stage, that reminded me a little of the famous Irish Riverdance show. As the ceremony ended, I spotted a familiar face in the audience not far from me – a lady I used to chat to at coffee mornings held at the parish church in Pwllheli. We had a quick chat and as I had noticed her husband had sung harmonies to accompany the National Anthem at the end of the event, I praised him for his singing.

Friday afternoon was the big one – **Seremoni'r Cadeirio** – the chairing ceremony. Contestants had to present a poem or collection of poems in cynghanedd style, up to 250 lines and on the topic of 'Llif' (flow). Before the judges discussed the contestants, there was an important job to be done by Myrddin ap Dafydd. He officially introduced and welcomed Mererid Hopwood as the new Archdruid. Mererid then praised Myrddin for all he had done whilst being in this post for over four years. She teasingly said that she was sure he was now due a well-earned rest. There was a bit of a shock when the judges' opinions of this years' contestants were revealed. It was stated that there had been only four entrants and the standard hadn't been as high as was expected. There was a wave of disappointed gasps from the audience, who like I wondered if this meant that this year the chair would not be presented. This has happened a few times in the past, the most recent being in 2013. The tension was soon relieved when it was stated that they had decided there was a worthy winner amongst the four and Myrddin ap Dafydd was asked to perform his last ever Steddfod act as archdruid and announce who this was. The ffugenw was **Llanw a Thrai** (tide and ebb) and when the searchlight stopped on the winner in the audience, I recognised

Mererid Hopwood's speech

him as prolific poet Alan Llwyd. He had already won the crown and chair twice (each time together in the same Steddfod) so this was his third time in winning the chair. There used to be a rule of 'twice only' for the winning of the chair and he is the first person to win a third since the relaxation of this rule. Alan was born in Dolgellau, but has spent a lot of his life in Llŷn and Myrddin welcomed him back to the area as he took his place seated on the beautiful Lôn Goed chair.

I felt rather sad at the end of this ceremony as I thought it was my last time in here – not knowing I'd be racing back in later that day to try and see Ann in the Cerdd Dant Choir competition! I also had to say goodbye to my neighbours – the lovely couple who I'd sat next to at each ceremony. They were a similar age to me and the lady had originated from Bethesda but they had lived in London for many years. We shared a mutual admiration for each other as she said tearfully that she was touched that I had learnt to speak her language and I told her how I admired her for managing to keep her language after living away for so long with so little opportunity to use it.

Another pavilion ceremony, but not a Gorsedd one, that filled me with admiration and was a not to be missed event for me was the announcement of Dysgwr y Flwyddyn (learner of the year). The four finalists would have had their further interviews by now and they were waiting on the front row with the audience, while on stage were the three judges, some other Welsh Learner officials including Martyn Croydon, and Michael Strain the Chairman of the Steddfod Work's Committee, who was making the announcements. It was strange to see two of my three interviewers – Liz Saville Roberts and Geraint Price, sitting alongside Tudur Owen the judge I never met. It was a short simple ceremony and the winner was quickly announced as Alison Cairns, originally from Scotland, but now living on a farm on Ynys Môn, with her partner and their seven children. As well as shepherding the children, Alison is also an experienced sheep shearer. Amazingly, she had learnt to speak Welsh without any formal lessons. Alison was presented with her prize (framed needlefelt picture) on the stage and the other three learners soon joined her to receive their follow up prizes. On my way out of the pavilion I came upon Andi Chell, who had made the award. She was chatting with some other learners that I had also met in the past so I had a quick catch up and congratulated Andi on her clever handiwork.

Moments of appreciation
One of the many attractions that drew me to the Ecoamgueddfa stand was a lovely lady called Eleri, who Jim and I have met many times over the years in Llŷn, as she often works as a translator at talks and presentations. From quite early on in learning to speak Welsh, I've preferred to try and manage without an interpreter and instead to try and get the gist of talks we've listened to, and as time went on of course, I've been able to understand more. Jim has frequently used the headsets and we have both been amazed at Eleri's ability to listen and then quickly translate for her audience. This week she was the interpreter for Ecoamgueddfa so she was often standing in the wings waiting to be needed. While doing this she regularly spared a few minutes to have a chat with me and I've noticed over the years that she seems to naturally adjust her conversation to pitch it at just the right level, something that I really appreciate.

Eleri the translator

Throughout the week, I regularly bumped into tutors who I have come to know from being allowed to gate crash their chat group sessions in various parts of Llŷn, despite not being able to attend any of their formal classes with living a distance away. I've always appreciated the warm welcome they've given to me and the same applied to this week, when they all took the time to speak to me even though they were busy either promoting their classes or just enjoying some family time. It was lovely to bump into Ffion Medi Ellis, who I'd met in Caernarfon and she shared with me that I was unlikely to see her at further chat groups as she was moving out of the area. I bumped into Bethan Glyn several times and was also able to congratulate her on one of these occasions, on winning The National Centre for Learning Welsh tutor award 'Tlws y Tiwtor', which had been presented to her in Maes D during the week. And as for Martyn Croydon, there he was each day, with his tie and a smile and a warm greeting for everyone who visited Maes D, including me.

Llŷn friend Amanda is always a busy lady, but we made time to meet up halfway through the week on the day that she was going to be volunteering on the primary schools stand. We met Amanda in 2010, when we first stayed in their caravan before I learnt to speak Welsh. Although we regularly send written messages in Welsh, we have continued to speak English with each other. I think this is partly because often Jim is present and we do not want to exclude him, but I think it's also because we can even give Tudur Owen a run for his money when we get together with regards the speed and amount of our chat. But when Amanda asked was I free for a meet up, I dared to ask 'in Welsh?' and she agreed. I was shocked at how I felt when we started – I was more nervous at speaking Welsh with Amanda than I was with complete strangers. But I survived and I appreciated Amanda's time and patience and her slowing down (a little) to help me to keep pace.

One large group of people that deserve a lot of appreciation were the numerous volunteers that made the Steddfod happen. They were to be seen everywhere, with their hi vis jackets, directing people to their parking spaces or rare vacant seats in the Tŷ Gwerin, helping on stands, dressing Gorsedd members and fulfilling many other behind the scenes tasks that none of us visitors were even aware of. I recognised quite a few of them as fellow Say Something in Welshers including Mel, who had been a regular member of the Manchester Learner Group. I got to chat with Mel a few times during the week, including when leaving the pavilion for the final time after the Cerdd Dant choir competition. She was guarding the door and she told me what a great, but exhausting week she'd had.

Martyn Croydon and other tutors in Maes D

I can't finish without mentioning the loos. Of

course, by the end of the week all three areas of portaloos smelt like... well toilets, but I'm full of appreciation for the people who worked so hard to ensure they were kept as clean as possible and I have to say on each of my many visits there was always paper and soap, something many ordinary public loos don't manage to achieve. Even the man who proudly directed all the ladies to particular toilets that 'haven't been used by men', despite lacking in political correctness, put his heart and soul into the job.

Sorry that you follow on from toilets Jim, if you're reading this, but I must mention how much I appreciate you. Jim understands more Welsh than he gives himself credit for and can say quite a few phrases now, but has struggled with his attempts at lessons even with SSIW. But he has always supported me fully in my learning of the language and in my general geekiness of all things Welsh, accompanying me to numerous events, including during this Steddfod week.

Moments of pride

Every time I spotted my coastal walk book on the shelves of book stands, I was filled with pride and sometimes disbelief. And yes, sometimes I had to straighten a copy if it was out of place on the shelf. Early in the week, I felt humbled and proud at the same time, during one of my Maes D visits, when I was approached by a smiling stranger called Simon, who explained that he was also a learner and that he had read my book and enjoyed it. I felt similarly when on a couple of occasions, friends found me on the Maes with a copy of it and asked me to sign it for them.

As I left the large pavilion following the chairing ceremony, I was surprised at being approached by some young lads with boxes of thick paperback books, shouting out '**Cyfansoddiadau a Beirniadau!**' (compositions and adjudications). These can only be sold once the winner of the chair has been announced, as they record the results of all of the week's competitions and the judges' comments, so these really were hot off the press. I could remember reading the story of the publishing company Gwasg Carreg Gwalch and Myrddin ap Dafydd recounting how this had been one of his jobs as a lad when he was helping his family's bookshop. I wonder if at that age he'd ever dreamt that he would be the archdruid. This was my final book and I'd gone over my limit as it was **Book 10**. I

My book on the Gwasg Carreg Gwalch stand

was excited to read one part of it, so whilst sitting in the small pavilion waiting for the Cerdd Dant choir practice to begin – but as you know it never did – I flicked through the pages until I came to the section for learners' competitions. As I've mentioned, in April I'd written and submitted a Welsh poem for the **Cystadleuaeth y Gadair** (chair competition for learners). This was an open poetry competition, with no rules about length or style, on the theme of **'glannau'** (shores) and the prize was a model chair. Unlike my learner author friend Simon Chandler, I've not mastered cynghanedd, so I had a try at using a different form – **englyn milwr** (soldier's verse). The rule for this type of poetry is that there are three seven syllable lines which rhyme on the last syllable. I wrote four stanzas of three lines each, describing impressions of the seaside, with each stanza focusing on a different sense. I knew that I hadn't won before I attended the Steddfod as winners were informed a few weeks before, but I was interested to read the judge's comments. Prifardd Ifor ap Glyn, was the judge and I felt proud to be in the book and pleased with his opinion of my poem, but I'd made a silly error in one of the verses. I'd intended describing the feel of kicking the sand on my last line, but instead of saying **cicio'r gronynnau** (kicking the grains), I said **cicio'r gronyn** (kicking the grain). Oh dear, I must have been too focused on getting the correct number of syllables – **gronynnau** would have made it too many. Fifteen 'poets' had entered the competition and on reading the poems, Ifor divided us into three classes, using appropriate titles – **'Trai'** (ebb) for the lowest, **'Llanw'** (tide) for the middle and **'Penllanw'** (high tide) for the highest. He commented that I had sent 'four undisputed englyn milwr' and recited one of the verses where I wrote of the sound of waves and the cry of curlews and seagulls. He felt my descriptions and use of this form of poetry was 'overall effective', but that my last line created 'a rather unfortunate picture'. His final comment was that I was a poet who understands the importance of subtlety and that but for my slip I would have been in the highest class. Praise indeed there from the prifardd, but for now I hold onto my Blue Peter badge as my only award for poetry. What ffugenw (false name) did I give, I hear you ask... Bronwen of course!

Entering the Maes

When looking back across the whole week and a day, I have to say how proud I felt of Llŷn and Eifionydd. Is it right to feel proud of somewhere where I don't even live and where I have no blood connection at all? I'm not sure, but I do, because through falling in love with this most beautiful part of the world and her people and through learning the language and consequently about the culture, I feel that at least a part of me belongs here and belonged at the Llŷn and Eifionydd Steddfod. I have Say Something in Welsh (SSIW) and all the people responsible for its existence to thank for having this beautiful language now. I'm still learning and will continue to make plenty of mistakes, but what an amazing feeling it was to be able to speak to whoever I bumped into on the Maes in Welsh and to be able to proudly join in with the singing of **Calon Lân** and **Hen Wlad Fy Nhadau**.

Missed moments

On the final Saturday, as Jim and I emerged from the darkness of the Babell Lên onto the Maes, it was about 5 o'clock. We'd intended staying until the end of the day, to watch the finale, a 'Tân yn Llŷn' music and poetry event with a fire installation and fireworks, which was to take place on the Maes at about 10 o'clock. Between 5pm and 10pm, we'd planned to settle down in the Tŷ Gwerin to watch various performers including favourites Bob Delyn a'r

Ebillion and Gwilym Bowen Rhys. But as we arrived Bob Delyn had started and the Tŷ Gwerin was bulging, and we could see there was no chance of a seat. We were both feeling tired and hungry and knew as we looked at each other that, however much we wanted to stay, we needed to go home. The following day, I enjoyed an afternoon walk in Clynnog Fawr with minister Rosie and some other learners and locals including to my astonishment Angharad Tomos! I overcame my sense of awe and was able to have an interesting chat with her. On my return, poor Jim was reclining on the caravan seating area with a positive covid test displayed on the table. Four days later after returning home, I also tested positive. Please say I didn't give Angharad Tomos covid! The latest strain, 'Eris', was on the rise and where better to get a grip than on a festival field. We soon heard that we weren't alone, but it hadn't spoiled it for us and the 2023 Steddfod in Boduan will be an experience we will both always remember.

Despite being there for each day of the Steddfod, I only saw a fraction of what was on offer. There were many things that I wished I'd been able to see, but over the next couple of weeks, I was able to watch some of them on catch up TV, as well as laugh at bits that Jim wanted to show me that he'd been finding on his 'days off', including when the cameras had caught me in the audience of the pavilion as I stood and clapped for the winners as they passed close by my aisle seat.

Last day – weary but happy

P.S. One Final Eisteddfod and Hill Ramble

In the following two weeks, as we and the peninsula recovered from the excitement of Steddfod week, the locals were told that they needed to remove the decorations and signs of welcome unless they had permission from the council to allow them to remain. When we next visited, after testing negative for covid, I was pleased to see that there were still plenty remaining and managed to visit a couple that I'd not managed to see as yet apart from on Facebook. One of my favourites was the mock Steddfod chair with a built-in crown, sited near Mynydd Mawr, Uwchmynydd and overlooking Ynys Enlli. We paid a visit, in the early evening perfectly timed to then head down into Aberdaron to watch Pedair in St Hywyn's Church. It felt like a mini revisit to the Steddfod, but was the only time you'll see me being chaired and crowned.

Pedair in Aberdaron

I can't finish this book, without mentioning that about a month after the Steddfod, we visited the beautiful village of Beddgelert to listen to two authors speaking of their experiences as travel writers. One was Jean Napier, who I'd been hoping to meet up with, since she got in touch and introduced herself to me, and the other was none other than Des Marshall, the writer of the hill book that we used to navigate our way up the hills! What an honour to meet them and I was intrigued by their accounts of the adventures they had both had. Des, who originates from Cumbria and I'm sure won't mind my saying is around his eighth decade, has written over

Des Marshall and Jean Napier in Beddgelert

thirty books mostly sharing his intrepid adventures in the hills and mountains of his spiritual home Eryri – and he called it that even though he doesn't speak Welsh. Jean, who is in her seventies, originates from London and is now living near Aberdyfi. She put us to shame with our fear of cows and grumbles about old knees, when she described dealing with white water rapids and a hippo approaching with large teeth and a gaping mouth! I finally bought a signed copy of Jean's book *The Cadfan Way* and I'd taken our well-thumbed *Walking the Llŷn Hills* which Des happily signed. I was able to thank him for the guidance that his book had provided for our own small adventure.

Uwchmynydd Eisteddfod Chair and crown

The Hills are Alive with The Sound of Music

I had to get that line in somewhere, and during the Llŷn and Eifionydd National Eisteddfod they most certainly were. By the way, I watched the movie *The Sound of Music* in two consecutive years as a young child in the 1960s – both times in Colwyn Bay which isn't too far from Llŷn! Visiting eisteddfodau and walking the Llŷn hills may have seemed an odd combination for a book, but our experiences showed that they can both enhance your awareness of the Welsh language and culture in such an exciting and enjoyable way.

Whether or not you're a learner and/or a visitor as I am, I hope that this book will inspire you to immerse yourself in Welshness at an eisteddfod if you haven't already, or to explore the beautiful hills of Llŷn, from where, if you listen carefully music really often can be heard.

Mum and Dad in Colwyn Bay, 1966.
Mum wearing one of her Welsh tapestry jackets.

Epilogue

This book was completed in 2023, but before going to press in 2024, there had been sad news of the loss of four local people who I mention directly or whose work I mention:

Berwyn Jones (April 2024), the artist who amongt many other things, designed the "iron man" statue overlooking Llanbedrog bay, which will continue to bring joy to locals and visitors for many more years.

Oldrich Asenbryl (May 2024), who created wonderful pottery and brought a smile to the faces of many (including mine) with his charm and wit.

Emrys Williams (June 2024), who did so much for the village of Llanaelhaearn and the Lloyd George museum, and who insisted I give the course "Say Something in Welsh" a try – diolch yn fawr iawn Emrys, I did!

Dewi "Pws" Morris (August 2024), the singer and actor who contributed a lot of his time to eisteddfodau, and who brought laughter and happiness to many with his humour and kindness.

All four will be remembered for their important contributions to Llŷn.

On a brighter note in May 2024, the names of those who were to be honoured by the Gorsedd at the Rhondda Cynon Taf National Eisteddfod in August were announced. I was thrilled to discover that Manchester friend Simon Chandler was included on the list of those being honoured with the green robes. Llongyfarchiadau Simon! Congratulations Simon – very well deserved!

Glossary

Glossary of Welsh Words Used to Describe Places or Features

afon – river
bach/fach – small
banc – bank
bryn – hill
bwlch – pass
cae – field
capel/gapel – chapel
carn/garn – a cairn (burial mound) and often used as part of the name of a hill with a cairn on the summit such as Garn Ganol
carreg – rock
castell – castle
cei – quay
clawd/cloddiau – bank/s or hedge/s
coed/goed – tree
comin – common
dôl/ddôl – meadow
eglwys – church
Eryri – Snowdonia
ffordd – road
ffynnon – well
glas – blue
hen – old
isaf – lower
llan – parish
llwybr – path
llyn – lake (notice there is no accent as in Llŷn)
maes – ground/field or square of a town
mawr/fawr – large
melin/felin – mill
moel/foel – hill with a bare summit
môr – sea
mynydd – mountain, but sometimes used for larger hills
nant – valley
oriel – gallery
pen/ben – head
pentref – village
plas – hall
pont/bont – bridge
porth/borth – harbour or gateway
stryd – street

traeth – beach
tref – town
tŵr – tower
tŷ/tai – house/s
uchaf – higher
wal – wall
ynys/oedd – island/s
Ynys Enlli – Bardsey Island, the island off the tip of Llŷn
Ynys Môn – Anglesey
Yr Eifl – a range of three hills in Llŷn
Yr Wyddfa – Mount Snowdon
ysgol – school

Glossary of Some Eisteddfod Related Words

Anerchiad – address made by the archdruid
A Oes Heddwch? – Is there peace? A question used as part of the ritual during the ceremonies
Archderwydd – archdruid
Bardd/Fardd – poet
Blodeuged/Flodeuged – flower display used in the ceremonies
Cadeirio – chairing ceremony
Cerrig yr Orsedd – the circle (cylch) of Gorsedd stones used in ceremonies
Corn gwlad – trumpet used in the ceremonies
Corn hirlas – horn of plenty, used in the ceremonies
Coroni – the crowning ceremony
Cyfansoddiadau a Beirniadau – Compositions and Judgements book released at the end of each National Eisteddfod, containing details of the competitors, winners and their works.
Ffugenw – false name
Gorsedd – society of Welsh language poets
Maen Llog – flat stone platform used in ceremonies
Prifardd – chief poet
Testunau – book with details of all competitions
Urdd Gobaith Cymru – national voluntary youth organisation
Y Fedal Ryddiaith – Prose Medal

Shops, Cafés and Other Small Businesses Mentioned in the Book
Most of these also have websites and Facebook pages

Becws Glanrhyd – Llanaelhaearn village, LL54 5AG
Becws Islyn bakery and café – Aberdaron, LL53 8BE
Becws Islyn bakery and café – The Beach, Nefyn LL53 6ED

Braf Café – Dinas Dinlle, Caernarfon LL54 5TW
Browsers Bookshop – 73 High St, Porthmadog LL49 9EU
Cadwaladers café and ice-cream shop – Castle Street, Cricieth, LL52 0DP
Caffi Largo – Embankment Road, Pwllheli LL53 5AB
Caffi Ni, Nefyn – Wern Caravan Park, Pistyll, Gwynedd, LL53 6LW
   Caffi Porthor
Caffi Tŷ Newydd – Tŷ Newydd Farm, Uwchmynydd, LL53 8BY
   Canolfan y Gwystl
Caffi Tŷ Winsh – Balaclava Road, Caernarfon, LL55 1SR
Castle Fish and Chip Shop – 5 Castle St, Cricieth LL52 0DP
Cei Llechi – Caernarfon, LL55 2PB
Crasu Coed – Coed y llan, Pwllheli LL53 8HL
Cwrw Llŷn brewery, shop and bar – 1 Parc Eithin, Ffordd Dewi Sant, Nefyn LL53 6EG
Cwt Gafr – Bryncroes, Pwllheli LL53 8EG
Cymdeithas Yr Iaith – Welsh Language Society – 01970624501
Driftwood Designs – 16 Pier St, Aberystwyth SY23 2LJ
Dwyfor Coffee – Parc Dwyfor, Nefyn, LL53 6EG
Dylan's Restaurant, Cricieth – Maes y Môr, Cricieth, LL52 0HU
Dysgwyr Dwyfor – Martyn Croydon – see Facebook page
Ecoamgueddfa – www.ecoamgueddfa.org
Farmer and his Wife – see Facebook page
Felin Uchaf – Rhoshirwaun, LL53 8HS
Galeri Caernarfon – Doc Victoria, Caernarfon, LL55 1SQ
Glasu icecream shop – 3-4 Mitre Terrace, Pwllheli, LL53 5HE
Gwalia bakery – 82 High Street, Pwllheli, LL53 5RR
Gwasg y Bwthyn, Caernarfon – Publishers
Hen Siop y Crydd – see Facebook page
HM Catering (pizza van) – order online – https://hmcatering.f4food.net/tableHunaniaith
Idris Bakery – 60 High St, Cricieth LL52 0HB
Janglerins – www.janglerins.co.uk/
La Parisienne Bakery – 105 Conway Rd, Colwyn Bay LL29 7LW
LleArt Carys Bryn – Hendre Bach, Rhos-fawr, Pwllheli LL53 6NF
Llen Llŷn book and music shop – 5-6 Mitre Terrace, Pwllheli, LL53 5HE
Llŷn Maritime Museum – Old St Mary's Church, Stryd y Llan, Nefyn, LL53 6LB
Maritime Museum, Porthmadog – The Harbour, Porthmadog LL49 9LU

Nant Gwrtheyrn National Welsh Language and Heritage Centre – Llithfaen, LL53 6NL
Neuadd Dwyfor library, cinema and theatre – 19 Penlan Street, Pwllheli, LL53 5DE
Oriel y Môr Tonnau art gallery shop – 21 Penlan Street, Pwllheli, LL53 5DE
Palas Print bookshop – 10 Stryd y Plas, Caernarfon, LL55 1RR
Pant Du Vineyard – County Rd, Penygroes, Caernarfon LL54 6HE
Plas Carmel with Caffi Siop Plas – Anelog, Pwllheli LL53 8LL
Plas Glyn y Weddw art gallery and café – Llanbedrog, LL53 7TT
Plas Heli – Glan Y Don Industrial Estate, Yr Hafan, Pwllheli LL53 5YT
Plas yn Rhiw – Rhiw, Pwllheli LL53 8AB
Popty Prysur (bakery), Canolfan y Gwystl – Ystâd Ddiwydiannol Y Ffôr, LL53 6UW
Portmeirion – Minffordd, Penrhyndeudraeth, Gwynedd, LL48 6ER
Posh Puds – see Pwllheli Market and Y Sied Llaeth
Pwllheli Market – Wednesdays and Sundays in the summer
R Gwynedd Evans and Son Ironmongers – 9 Stryd Moch, Pwllheli LL53 5RG
Saith Seren – 18 Chester St, Wrexham LL13 8BG
Sarn Pottery – Sarn Meyllteyrn, Pwllheli LL53 8DY
Saysomethingin.com – Online Welsh language courses – www.saysomethingin.com
Siop Iard – www.siopiard.com
Siop Shop – Welsh café in Manchester – 53 Tib Street, Manchester M4 1LS
SJW Graphics and Signs – see Sarah J Wray Facebook page
Spar – Pwllheli, LL53 5HA
Tafarn y Fic community pub – Llithfaen, LL53 6PA
Tir a Môr café – 1-3 Mona Terrace, Criccieth LL52 0HG
Tŷ Coch Inn – Porthdinllaen, Morfa Nefyn, Pwllheli LL53 6DB
Tyddyn Sachau garden centre and café – Y Ffôr, LL53 6UB
Tŷ Pawb – Market St, Wrexham LL13 8BB
Welsh Lady Preserves – Bryn, Y Ffôr, LL53 6RL (also available in many local shops)
Whitehall Hotel – Stryd Moch, Pwllheli LL53 5RG
Woodlands Hall Hotel – Lon Pwll Clai, Edern, Pwllheli LL53 6JB
Y Deli Newydd – 52 High St, Criccieth LL52 0EY
Yr Heliwr community pub – Y Groes, Nefyn, LL53 6HH
Ynys Enlli/Bardsey Island Boat Trips, Colin Evans – 07971 769 895

Yr Hen Lys/ The Old Courthouse – Castle Ditch, Caernarfon, LL55 2AY
Yr Ysgwrn – Unnamed Road, Blaenau Ffestiniog LL41 4UW
Y Sied Llaeth – see Facebook page – sheds in Pwllheli, Nefyn, Llanbedrog

Artists, Musicians and Writers Mentioned in the Book

Most of the current artists, musicians and authors can be found on Facebook or Twitter.

To purchase art work, books or music by any of the below, try shops Llên Llŷn in Pwllheli, Browsers Bookshop in Porthmadog or Palas Print in Caernarfon

(see addresses previously)

Alis Glyn – singer/musician
Al Lewis – singer/musician
Angharad Jenkins – singer/musician
Angharad Tomos – writer
Ani Glas – singer/musician
Anni Llŷn – singer/musician
Arlunwyr Sarn – group of local artists
Bethan Gwanas – writer
Bob Delyn a'r Ebillion – band
Bwncath –band
Calan –band
Carys Bryn – artist
Catrin O'Neill – singer/musician
Cerys Hafana – singer/musician
Cerys Matthews – singer/musician
Cian Parry Owen – artist
Côr Dre – mixed choir
Côr Meibion Carnguwch – all-male choir
Côr Yr Heli – all-female choir
Cricieth Creadigol – creative group in Cricieth
Cynan/ Sir Albert Evans-Jones – writer (1895 – 1970)
Cynefin/Owen Shiers – singer/musician
Dafydd Iwan – singer/musician and politician
Dafydd Llywelyn – writer
Darren Evans – Coastal Painters and Decorators – 07580 406928
Dewi "Pws" Morris – singer/musician and actor
Dylan Morris – singer/musician
Dylunio Swi Designs – artist – see Etsy Shop SiopSwi and Facebook page
Edwin Humphreys – instrumentalist

Einir Humphreys – singer
Elidyr Glyn – singer/musician
Elin Mair Roberts 1 – artist
Elin Mair Roberts 2 – silversmith
Emyr Lloyd Jones – singer (baritone)
Esther Stubbs – artist
Esyllt Maelor – writer
Eve Goodman – singer/musician
Fiona Colins – writer and storyteller
Ffion Meleri Gwyn – artist
Gareth Evans Jones – writer
Gerwyn Williams – writer
Glain Rhys – singer/musician
Gorllewinwynt – troupe of storytellers, folk musicians and artists
Guto Dafydd – writer
Gwenan Gibbard – singer/musician
Gwilym Bowen Rhys – singer/musician
Gwyneth Glyn – singer/musician and writer
Iestyn Tyne – singer/musician and writer
Ifor Ap Glyn – writer
Jackie Morris – writer and illustrator
John Meirion Morris – sculptor (1936 – 2020)
Kate Roberts – writer (1891 – 1985)
Lea Roberts – local musician
Lily Beau – singer/musician
Lowri Evans – singer/musician
Lleucu Gwawr – singer/musician
Lleuwen Steffan – singer/musician
Llyr Gwyn Lewis – writer
Manon Steffan Ros – writer and singer (with band Blodau Gwylltion)
Mared Williams – singer
Marian Brosschot – artist
Meic Llywellyn – writer and storyteller
Meinir Gwilym – singer/musician
Meinir Mathias – artist
Meinir Pierce Jones – writer
Mererid Hopwood – writer
Miriam Jones – woodturner – www.miriamjones.co.uk
Morwen Jones – artist and writer
Myrddin ap Dafydd – writer and publisher
N'famady Kouyate – singer/musician
Nicky Arscott – artist
Nikolaz Davalan – musician
Padraig Jack – singer/musician

Patrick Rimes – singer/musician (member of band Calan)
Pedair – band – collaboration between Gwyneth Glyn, Meinir Gwilym, Gwenan Gibbard and Siân James
Plu – band – collaboration between Gwilym Bowen Rhys and his sisters Elan and Marged
Pys Melyn –band
Rhiannon Ashley – singer (soprano)
Rhianwen Art – artist
Rhys Mwyn – singer/musician, writer and archaeologist
R. S. Thomas – writer (1913 – 2000)
R. William Parry – writer (1884 – 1956)
Russ Chester – artist
Sera – singer/musician
Siân James – singer/musician
Siân Northey – writer
Sinfonia Cymru – orchestra
Siôn Aled Owen – writer
Sioned Erin Hughes – writer
Steffan Hughes – singer and lead of Welsh of the Westend – musical theatre performers
Stephen Faherty – sculptor
Steve Eaves – singer/musician and writer
Super Furry Animals –band
Tacla – band
Tant – band
Tapestri –band – collaboration between Lowri Evans and Sera
Tess/Therese Urbanska – artist – see Etsy Shop "TeskaArt" and Facebook page "teska"
The Gentle Good/ Gareth Bonello – singer/musician
Trials of Cato – band
Tudur Owen – comedian and radio presenter
Tudur Phillips – clog dancer
Twm Morys – singer/musician and writer

Further Reading – in the English language unless otherwise stated

Bardsey Now and Then – Jean Napier – Gwasg Carreg Gwalch

Ciplŷn – Lleisiau Merched Llŷn/ Voices of the Women of Llŷn (bilingual) – Edited by Einir Young – Ecoamgueddfa

Geiriau Diflanedig (Welsh) – Robert Macfarlane, Jackie Morris and Mererid Hopwood Hamish Hamilton at Penguin

On Bonfires, Butlins and Being Welsh – Jos Simon – Y Lolfa

Real Gwynedd – Rhys Mwyn – Seren

Singing in Chains – Mererid Hopwood – Y Lolfa

The Cadfan Way – A Journey from Tywyn to Bardsey – Jean Napier – Gwasg Carreg Gwalch

The Lost Words: A Spell Book – Robert Macfarlane and Jackie Morris – Hamish Hamilton at Penguin

Walking the Llŷn Hills – Des Marshall – Gwasg Carreg Gwalch

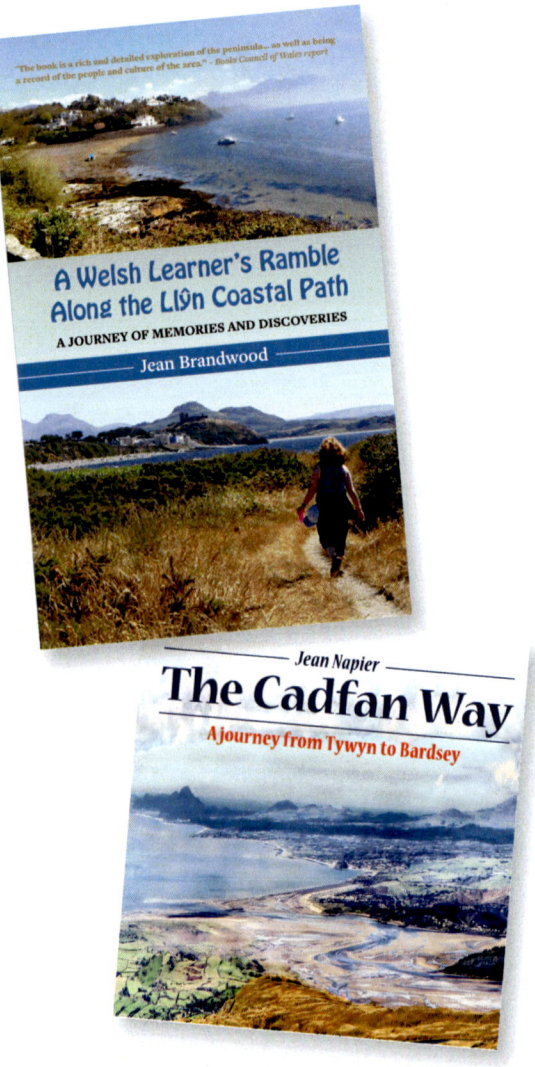